LEAD, FOLLOW OR GET OUT OF THE WAY

LEAD
OR GET OUT

The Story of
TED TURNER

by CHRISTIAN WILLIAMS

Times
BOOKS

FOLLOW
OF THE WAY

Published by TIMES BOOKS, a division
of Quadrangle/The New York Times Book Co., Inc.
Three Park Avenue, New York, N.Y. 10016

Published simultaneously in Canada by
Fitzhenry & Whiteside, Ltd., Toronto.

Library of Congress Cataloging in Publication Data

Williams, Christian.
    Lead, follow or get out of the way.

    Includes index.
1. Turner, Ted.   2. Businessmen—United States—
Biography.   3. Telecommunication—United States—
Biography.   4. Sports team owners—United States—
Biography.   5. Seamen—United States—Biography.
I. Title.

HC102.5.T86W54   1981   338'.04'0924   [B]   81-50095
ISBN 0-8129-0977-1   AACR2

Designed by Ed Kaplin

Manufactured in the United States of America

10 9 8 7 6 5 4 3 2

These poore people knew not how wel he could husband time: For he often repeated, that the skill to embrace occasions in the nicke, is the chiefest part of an absolute Captaine: And truely the diligence he used in all his exploits, is incredible; and the like was never heard of.

—MONTAIGNE
Observations Concerning the Meanes to Warre
After the Maner of Julius Caesar

LEAD, FOLLOW OR GET OUT OF THE WAY

Introduction

June 1, 1980. Time, 5:55 p.m. Altitude, 22,300 miles. It was very cold and still. Below, the earth lay under a ragged quilt of white clouds. Where the quilt was broken, vast oceans shone brilliant blue. There was neither up nor down, but there was a sky above, black and overrun with stars. Periodically a bright-red streak appeared as a meteor plunged toward the atmospheric wall below, its iron-and-nickel surface melting off like fat on a barbecue grille. Sometimes the cloud quilt parted to reveal a brown continent, cloven, if the sun angle was correct, by the glint of a mighty river. There was no sound at all. There were no cities to be seen, nor any sign of life, from 22,300 miles in space.

But the region was not entirely dead. The planet below had stretched up its hands to place there small, golden globes. The first had arrived in 1957, riding a tail of flame in a curving arc from a launching pad in Russia. It had circled the planet for several years, but then its orbit had grown old, and decayed, and it had spun back down into the atmosphere and vaporized.

Many more of the globes came thereafter, however, spreading their metal-and-silicon wings in stronger, higher, orbits. Now, over the continent of North America, there were nine of them. They were 800 miles apart, threaded like pearls on an invisible string over the equatorial band of the planet. These globes did not circle the earth, but remained ever in place over a fixed point on the blue oceans. In the great vacuum there, void of warmth or sound, the globes crackled and buzzed with messages. With billions of telephone calls, with football games, with military surveillance information, with the location of merchant ships at sea, with the words of the Pope in Rome and with the color of his vestments, and with the adventures of a redheaded inhabitant of the planet, a woman named Lucy, who time and again, in ritual fulfillment of some need on the part of her species, explored the limits of patience of the Cuban bandleader Ricky Ricardo.

The tiny satellites, holding on station 220,000 miles beneath the natural moon, chattered in their microwave language day and night, for all to hear. When a signal rose to them, beamed strongly and accurately from an upturned parabolic dish on the surface below, they caught it and threw it back. The signal they returned was much reduced in power. It was, in fact, only 4 watts—hardly enough to light the smallest bulb. But it covered a very wide area when it came down. It covered almost every part of the planet the satellite could see.

Among the chattering satellites was one which was silent. It had been launched a few weeks before Christmas 1979, but it had died before ever transmitting a message or a TV program, and without ever reporting the news, which was to be its mission. No one knew where it stood among the string of pearls. Perhaps it was in position, but damaged. Perhaps it was upside down, beaming Lucy and Ricky toward the unresponsive moon. Or perhaps, riding its rocket stages up from Cape Canaveral, it had just kept on going, away from the earth, toward nowhere. It was a pity that the new satellite, called Satcom III, had disappeared. This day was to have been its premiere, too.

June 1, 1980. 5:55 P.M., EDT. Atlanta, Georgia. It was very bright and hot, but a breeze from the west made the flags on Ted Turner's three new flagpoles stand out smartly. The Stars and Stripes flew at the center, and to the right, the flag of the state of Georgia, with its Confederate motif. At the left were the familiar blue colors of the United Nations.

Turner stood on a reviewing stand. Behind him, the four pillars of the new headquarters of the Turner Broadcasting System gleamed white. It had once been a country club, but now the bowels of the old club had been torn out, and in their place hummed the nation's newest and most sophisticated television studio, as yet untried. Turner fumbled with his microphone as three hundred invited guests squinted into the sun.

"I'd like to call our ceremonies to order," he said. "You'll notice that out in front of me we've raised three flags. One is of the state of Georgia, where we're located. In the center, the flag of the United States, which represents the nation this Cable News Network intends to serve. On the other side is the flag of the United Nations, because we hope with our greater depth, and our international coverage, to make possible a better understanding of how people from different nations can live and work, and so to bring together in brotherhood and kindness and peace the people of this nation and world. I'm now going to read a little poem that was written in dedication.

"To act on one's convictions while others wait
To create a positive force in a world where cynics abound
To provide information to people where it wasn't available before
To offer those who want it a choice
For the American people, whose thirst for understanding and a
    better life made this venture possible
For the cable industry, whose pioneering spirit caused this great
    step forward in communications
And for those employees of Turner Broadcasting whose total com-
    mitment to their company has brought us together today
I dedicate the News Channel for America, the Cable News Net-
    work. . . .

"Now if we can have the presentation of the colors and the national anthem. Everybody please stand."

The drums rolled and the bands played, and as Ted Turner stood with his hand over his heart, the television screens scattered about the grounds showed pictures of the reviewing stand, and the crowds, and the band, and of Turner. When the music stopped there was silence for a moment, and the cameras zoomed in on the row of six dish-shaped satellite antennas near the building, continuing the zoom until they filled the screen.

Somewhere in the untried electronic heart of Cable News Network a switch was thrown, and in that instant a team of news anchors—a man and a woman—opened their mouths to speak. As they did, their television image sped at the speed of light to the RCA satellite uplink facility nearby. The signal streaked upward, was caught by a satellite in geosynchronous orbit over the equator, and brought the nation's first all-news network to cable television systems from Hawaii to Boston. The cable system passed the picture on, through coaxial cables, until the news of the shooting of Vernon Jordan in Fort Wayne, Indiana, arrived in full color, simultaneously, in two million American homes.

Ted Turner had bet his entire fortune of $100 million that that signal would herald a revolution. He had staked everything on the satellites hanging in orbit far overhead, for he believed them to be the fault line of an inevitable economic and social earthquake. He believed that American life was about to change, and that he himself would change with it. In fact, Ted Turner had already come to be known as something of an economic and social earthquake himself. He was just forty-one, but he was being noticed by the people of the land. Their curiosity was pricked.

The faces in the crowd looked closely for signs of the brazen, wisecracking, giddy entrepreneur that many of them had known for years, the ambitious, difficult, brilliant, comic Turner of the yacht races and the sports pages and the business sheets. Was he still there? Or had another Turner, through a metamorphosis not yet made clear, taken his place?

The 300 invited guests were not the only ones wondering who or what now stood before them this June day in a faded blue yachting blazer, come of age and slouching toward Bethlehem.

The *Wall Street Journal,* in a lead article a week earlier, had begun its consideration of the new evidence with a question: "Is America ready for Ted Turner?"

"They'd better be," he had replied. " 'Cause I'm here."

1 A Dream Remembered

"Don't anybody move!"

The command startled, though there was but one listener to hear it in the middle of this grassy field at noon. But commands come naturally to Robert Edward Turner III, and leadership is necessary even in an army of two.

"I think they're coming closer."

Though the eye strained, there was no brigade of Redcoats, no pack of salivating wolves, no horde of scar-faced buccaneers advancing on this sunlit plantation, Ted Turner's personal retreat in the lowlands of South Carolina. In fact, the only living thing between Turner and the carefully fenced wildlife pond a hundred yards ahead was a seemingly dumbfounded herd of Canada geese, waddling and honking in confusion at the gates of their immaculate compound. The gate was open, but the geese did not come out. On the other hand, they did not go back in. They just pecked at the corn at their feet, and at each other.

It had been like that for an hour, but still Turner's face beamed bright with anticipation and confidence. He stood still, bent at the waist like a cement-sculpture stableboy at the entrance to a deserted estate. Instead of a bridle ring, he held a battered enamel saucepan filled with corn. Only his full head of prematurely gray hair, tousled by the pleasant breeze, defied the general immobilization. Turner looked at the geese and the geese looked at Turner.

A few hundred yards to his rear, on the side porch of a large white plantation house, an attractive blond woman stood with hands on hips. "Ted?" she called for the fifth or sixth time. The seventh time it was "Ted!"

"Just so you know that your lunch is absolutely cold," she added in exasperation, shaking her head and letting the screen door slam loudly as she reentered the house.

Lunch? The thought seemed hardly to enter Turner's mind. This was man against goose, and there could be no distraction. Skillfully, like a Coast Guardsman tossing a line to a lifeboat filled with grandmothers, Turner wafted more kernels of corn through the air, watching them fall at the feet of the untrusting geese. In the past hour he had carefully led them a few hundred feet from their pond, and they stood now—although without momentum—at the portal to the outside world.

"Isn't this a neat idea?" Turner said, speaking like a ventriloquist. "See, these geese would really like the grass out here if they only tried it. They already ate all the grass on their side of the fence, so I'm luring them out here where the grass is fresh."

The boldest goose took a few more steps toward freedom.

"This is it!" Turner cried, falling to his knees. "Here, goosie," he called. "Here, goosie goosie goosie goosie goosie." Corn kernels were landing like mortars among the geese. "Here, goosie goosie goosie. Here, goo goo goo goo goo goosie goosies! Come on, little geesie geesies! Goosie goosie goosie goosie geesie goslings! Dammit they're coming *out,* do you see that! Pretty goosie geesies!

The first goose, however, had stopped eating for a moment to listen. The natural Canada goose communication is a raucus honk, and the bird knew all its nuances; but this conversation was a new one. He gave Turner a hard sideways glance, the kind of glance Khrushchev gave Nixon in the Kitchen Debate.

"Goosie goosie goosie."

Suddenly, with a 180-degree waddle, the lead goose turned and headed back toward the gate, his flock following suit instantly, the momentum of the herd also gathering up a few greedy mallards and hen ducks so that soon there was a web-footed stampede back through the fence, down the bank and into the water.

"Noooooooo!" came a dying wail from the green field, as Ted Turner, hip-shooting millionaire businessman, world champion yachtsman, revolutionizer of television, professional sports magnate, billboard scion and simultaneous Father of the Year and *Playgirl*'s Sexiest Man, collapsed head-first into the turf.

"What went wrong?" he asked, tears welling up in an impossibly theatrical face. "How could it happen? They're my own geese, I bought them and I brought them here and I built a pond for them and I took the alligators out and made it safe. I did all that for them." Then one corner of the tragic mask broke into a cracked grin and he raised his arms to the brilliant South Carolina sky. "And they don't even like me!"

He pondered that development for an instant.

"But you know," Turner said, "that's all right. It's always like this with me. At first it's hard, at first it looks bad. People always say, 'Who is this guy?' But I just want these geese to come out where the grass is green. And they're going to come around. I mean, what's the sense of having geese in the world if they won't come out and play? They don't know what I'm really like, anyway. Hell, half of them just got here today, they've been living in cardboard boxes. But I'm going to show them. I'll show them that I'm a good guy, I'm not going to shoot them or anything like that. Wait till they get to know me. After they get to know me, they got to like me a little!"

Turner's normal pace, a breakneck stride which covers the mile in ten minutes flat, had already brought him across the broad meadow to the front porch of the mansion house. He bounded up the steps, two at a time, not looking back at the long double row of centuries-old live oak trees, or at the wheel-rutted path beneath them shaded by necklaces of hanging moss. The house echoed as Turner banged the screen door and strode through a wide hallway to the dining room, where two women waited, already seated, and an array of serving dishes brimmed with quail, biscuits, wild salads, jellies and sauces.

Turner was late, all right, but after fifteen years of marriage his wife was not expecting an apology. In truth, she was still not sure what to expect.

"Janie," Turner shouted, grabbing a plate and heaping it with quail that was by then conspicuously cool. "I've got the most wonderful news."

For a heartbeat there was silence, a silence in which Janie and the two houseguests could each conjure up a separate possible announcement: There would be another hike like that morning's, in which the merry band was led on an 8-mile forced march across the 5,232-acre plantation while the owner, swinging a machete, declaimed upon every living thing observed; or perhaps another breakneck car tour through the South Carolina lowlands, during which the driver declaimed upon every animate or inanimate object; or perhaps a new purchase was to be revealed. Turner had recently inspected a $900,000 ranch near Atlanta. Had he bought it?

"Yes, Ted?"

"Really, I've got just really super news, and I'm so happy."

"What is it, Ted?"

"Those new geese down at the pond, I came within this much of getting them to come outside the fence. And I can tell, I can tell already."

"You can tell—what?"

"Janie, those geese, they like me. They only hardly know me and they like me already. They're almost, they're almost eating out of my hand."

"Yes, Ted."

"Also—I got the plan for after lunch," he said, as eyes widened around him. "We'll all take a nap. Then we can have another hike and then do some deer hunting and we'll be back in time for dinner and then we can watch the Superstation for a while, I think the Braves are playing, and then I'll show you my box of plantation artifacts with the actual china doll leg in it."

Yawning, he stood up and moved to the dining-room door. "Ain't it great here? You know, when we left Atlanta yesterday I was burned out, the top of my head was about to blow off from the pressure. Now I've been here a little over a day and my batteries are almost all the way up again. I mean, I can feel the juice flowing back. When I get back to Atlanta"—he was talking from the bedroom now, leaving the three people at the dining table straining to hear—"it's going to be great." The voice seemed muffled. Apparently Turner was having trouble getting his sweater over his head. "I won in Congress and I won the Fastnet Race and the Hawks are turning into just a terrific basketball team and I'm going to start the world's first twenty-

four-hour-a-day television news program. I can see it all coming.
. . ." The voice had declined almost to the inaudible level. Almost.
"Janie! Aren't you coming to bed?"

"Sleep well," said Mrs. Turner, rolling her eyes in amused resignation. "It's always like this, you know."

Ted Turner, age forty-one, was asleep for the moment with his dreams. Unlike most people, he would remember them when he woke up, for they have changed little over the years. One by one he hunts them down, singling each out of the herd like a cowboy with a branding iron. As a boy, alone with himself at military school, he dreamed of leading dangerous missions into the unknown, fueling his imagination with the campaigns of Alexander the Great, Napoleon and General MacArthur. Now, when he wakes as a man, it is as their composite. And with each of his dreams as mission and purpose.

The purpose, as Turner had described expansively during that morning's fast-paced hike, was to be part of the long-overdue new awakening of America. And he aimed to make sure that for the three television networks, at least, it was a very rude awakening indeed.

"We don't have to get fat and lazy," he'd said, charging through the bush. "Let's not take things as they are, let's have fun again, let's stick up for ourselves. Look at me, I'm out to be the Fourth Network. We already are, in fact, with Channel 17 in Atlanta. I coined the word 'Superstation,' we got on the satellite first, we're in nine million American homes right now, where only the networks were before.

"And do you know why we're going to be such a big success and why I'm going to make a billion dollars? It's because people know things are screwed up, and they're looking for a change. It's not that I'm a genius, it's that television is lousy, and the three networks have it all to themselves and they want to keep it lousy. The networks are like the Mafia. The networks *are* the Mafia. Do you know they spent a quarter of a million dollars in Washington trying to stop my Superstation from showing movies and sports in people's houses? Well, their day is finished now. It's over. They've made unbelievable profits, and what have they brought us? Mr. Whipple squeezing the toilet paper. *The $1.98 Cheap Show. The Newlywed Game. Love Boat.* The networks are run by a greedy bunch of jerks that have hoodwinked the American public, and now I'm riding in on a white horse. I'm telling you, the networks are scared. But they can't stop me, because people are demanding—they're insisting—on alternatives."

Turner had not crushed the networks yet, but they were watching with interest as his satellite-borne Fourth Network, already reaching forty-eight states, grew at a rate of 300,000 viewers monthly.

The yacht clubs of the world might have sounded a warning. They had already learned that when Turner caught the scent of a trophy there was almost no way to throw him off the track. His ocean racer was aptly named *Tenacious,* and Turner was always at his best when in the role of underdog.

He was an underdog when he won the America's Cup, the most famous yachting trophy of them all, in *Courageous.* Since 1851, the New York Yacht Club has defended that ungainly silver mug against all foreign comers. The weapons are super-expensive, ultrasophisticated thoroughbred sailboats raced on the waters off Newport, Rhode Island. In 1974, Turner decided to join in the fray of the elimination trials to select the American defender—and was soon both frayed and eliminated.

A lot of people in Newport thought that had taught Turner a lesson, and in fact they were right. When he returned for the next America's Cup in 1977, he showed them what the underdog had learned by laying waste to the entire field of American contenders, and then defeating the Australian challenger 4-0. What's more, he delivered into the national lap a new kind of sailing hero—Captain Courageous, the red-blooded, fast-talking New Souther with a two-dollar railroad engineer's cap, a Hollywood grin and a train of cameramen that followed everywhere he went. "Colorful" was the word the newsmagazines used.

"Sure I was drunk as a skunk on national TV, and you would be too, right? I mean, we won! And we went through so much bull along the way you wouldn't believe it. But we'd been beaten in 1974, and when we came back we wanted it bad, the way underdogs always do. We could've quit after that, like Muhammad Ali did several times, but did we? Hell no. We went right back there the next time, in 1980, and we gave Dennis Conner his shot against us. Competition is what it's all about. You beat the hell out of somebody and then you say, OK, here's your chance to beat the hell out of me. And then you beat the hell out of him again—if you can."

Competition, he had explained on that morning's walk, was an important force of nature. It was the way things worked. It had the rightness of natural selection behind it, and it was therefore the joy and the vindication of winner and loser alike. In business and sport and even in his personal life, it was the fuel Turner's engine's burned. He was its proselyte.

"Lightning strokes, sneak attacks, hit them before they know what's happening, don't give them a chance to regroup," he said. "That's the only way it will work, that's the only way a little guy can beat a big guy. No holds barred. Don't stop just because you're little and you're afraid and it looks like you haven't got a chance. The rabbit can get away from the fox, but he better get on his hind legs and hop."

Turner, for one, had started hopping early. His father, a complex and demanding man, had shot himself in 1963, leaving the family billboard business in tatters and an only son who, at twenty-four, seemed utterly unprepared for responsibility. After a childhood in which he was shuttled from boarding school to relatives to interim jobs as his father's errand boy, he had gone off to Brown University. By the end of his first year he was undefeated on the college sailing team. By the time his class graduated he had been kicked out of school. The only things Turner could do well, it seemed, were talk, sail and chase girls. Those things, however, he did extremely well.

When his father's will was read in Charleston, South Carolina, the family billboards were finally ceded to Ted. The irony was that the business had already been sold, and the son's only remaining duty was to see that the deal went through. The way in which he saw that the deal did not go through, how he "stole back" his father's company, remains a legend of wheeling and dealing in the Southeast today.

The legend grew up also around the way he ran his sailboats, and his baseball team, and the way he attacked the networks, and the way he conducts a dinner conversation, and hires people, and fires people (including a midget with twenty-five years' seniority in baseball), and even the way he cuts his hair. In other words, colorfully—and against the advice of his friends. Friends, by their nature, do not advise the taking of risks.

Turner's friends know that, and Turner's Krugerrand reminds them when they forget. A Krugerrand is an ounce of gold, minted as a coin by the South African government and used as a handy unit of exchange for gold buyers. Turner keeps one in his pocket. He likes to flip it, which he does expertly with the fingernail of his right thumb. He is not quite as skillful at catching it, so the Krugerrand is nicked and dinged around the edge. Turner companions are forever diving under the restaurant table to retrieve the Krugerrand that Turner has dropped, and returning a quarter instead. Turner bought $2 million worth of gold at $270 an ounce, all in Krugerrands. He was advised against it.

His most trusted financial adviser, Will Sanders, took him aside. "Ted," Sanders said, "come on. Let's be serious. Gold has never been higher. We both know this is not the time to buy."

Months later Turner flipped his pocket Krugerrand to Sanders in the hallway of Channel 17 in Atlanta. "Seen the price of gold today, dummy?" he asked pleasantly. The price, of course, had nearly doubled.

Just about everyone had advised him not to try to get back the billboard company his father had sold, too. And later, when Turner decided to buy Channel 17, a failing UHF station in Atlanta, his own board of directors rose up against him. His accountant, announcing that disaster was finally at hand, resigned.

As a result of these and other experiences, it is very difficult to give Ted Turner any advice. Especially while he is flipping a Krugerrand.

"Business is full of lawyers and advisers, and you've got to remember, whatever you're doing, that these guys are trying to keep you from getting burned. That's their job. So if you get a new idea, don't expect everybody to say, 'Let's go.' You're the one who says that. I don't believe in marketing studies. Do you want to do it? Are you committed to making it work? Then it will, or at least it'll have the only chance it ever had. The reason nothing gets done in this country anymore is that there are so many committees. It just has to be you. Like McDonald's says, 'You—you're the one.' "

So when his Fourth Network was under way—financed by the profits of the revitalized Channel 17—he was the one who started a fifth. This time it was not Mr. Whipple but television news that became the bull's-eye of his target. The fact that Turner knew virtually nothing about news gathering or newsmen hardly fazed him. As usual, he was advised that a twenty-four-hour-a-day TV news service with a staff of three hundred could not possibly be put together in less than a year, and as usual he blew cigar smoke at the doubters.

"Television news just hasn't been doing its job," he said again and again. "This country is in trouble, and all you hear about is the surface stuff—rapes, murders, fires in abandoned buildings. I don't know much about it but I know it stinks. Every night we watch anchormen on the news who look like they know what's going on, and then the Arabs give us an oil crisis and it takes us by surprise. Everybody notices suddenly that American cars are pigs. How come they never told us that on the news? Then all of a sudden Chrysler needs to get bailed out, and we didn't even know they were in trouble. But we heard all about which plane crashed that day, and which rock star got his marijuana confiscated, and whether Gary Gilmore liked his last meal or not.

"You know why? It's because you've got three networks and they're really one monopoly. They only give the news twenty-two minutes a day, and whatever the news says about cars is just swallowed up, because the next thing you see is a commercial for a gas guzzler. It's just totally irresponsible. But I'm doing something about it. I'm going to prove there's room for competition in the country, even if I go broke doing it."

Turner was perhaps not altogether candid in saying he knew nothing about news. After all, he had been making it for years. And he was even among that select group of men who have heard their own obituary announced and lived to laugh about it.

Fifteen competitors died in the Fastnet Race of 1979, when a hurricane-strength storm sent two hundred of the world's sleekest ocean-racing sailboats scurrying for cover off the south coast of England. Turner, at first reported lost at sea, not only survived, but won first place in the fleet of 303. That accomplished, he took nearly as severe a lashing from the press as he had from the storm. It was a typical

Turner performance: no regret, no contrition, no apology. Fifteen of his fellows had died and he declined to look at the ground and tell sad stories.

Instead, he said, "The king is dead, long live the king. It had to happen sooner or later. We won because we had a good crew and a strong boat and a lot of experience, and the people who didn't have those went to the big regatta in the sky. I'm not going to say I'm sorry I won. I'm not going to say it."

It was 4:00 P.M. that day of retreat in South Carolina, and Turner was up and back to the business of branding his dreams with reality. He had his hiking boots on and a package of Beechnut chewing tobacco crammed into the pocket of his khakis. He was looking around for Janie and her friend.

"Are we ready for the next hike, ladies? It's a great afternoon, and we'll only go a couple of miles."

The women, however, seemed to have temporarily disappeared. "Just as well," Turner said. "They can't walk that fast anyhow."

The sun was still warm as Turner crossed the wide meadow, looking longingly at the geese paddling in their four-acre pond, where four cypress-wooded islands floated delicately on waters he had personally helped clear of a choking invasion of pigweed. His destination this afternoon was the old rice fields, once the economic reason for the claiming by man of this former swamp.

In 1978, Turner had plunked down a small fortune for Hope Plantation, and more than any other possession or trophy it was his personal symbol of attainment. The first surveying references went back to 1820, describing a 16-square-mile tract 40 miles south of Charleston, a lowland sanctuary bounded on either side by the quick-running rivers Ashepoo and Edisto. It is a land of ducks and dikes, a crosshatch of drainage canals that require constant clearing and dredging by the half-dozen men who watch over it in Turner's absence. Of open fields and upland there are 219 acres; of timberland, 1,581; of timbered lowland, 376; of duck and snipe fields, 1,833. More than 1,200 acres of Hope Plantation are given over to what the surveyor calls "idle marsh and ti-ti." The land, much of which is peat in bogs more than 12 feet deep, retains a prehistoric strangeness.

The prehistory is what Turner cherishes. It seems a link with the ancient heroes whom he so admires. More recent events he finds not so admirable, but equally fascinating in their strangeness. "We walk with the ghosts of five hundred slaves," he remarked quietly. "They worked the rice fields well into the nineteenth century. There were three plantation houses then, not just one. Not even a trace remains of the other two, nothing but the trees." He had stopped on a grassy knoll, and there, in the mosquito-buzzing forest, stood two perfectly aligned rows of live oaks—precisely like the lines of oaks that led to his own house two miles away. But these oaks, festooned in hanging moss, led nowhere. They stood as planted, obeying the old symmetry, but the house they had once shaded was utterly gone.

"You'd think nature was peaceful, but it's not," Turner said, picking up the pace again. "You'll see what I mean."

At the first brown canal he spat tobacco juice onto a lily pad, and a great commotion erupted. A 6-foot alligator had lunged for the water with the suddenness of a Doberman pinscher rushing a fence.

"Weren't expecting that, huh? It's like we tell the children. If a 'gator wanted you, boy, he'd get you. Hope Plantation seems like a sleepy place, but things aren't always what they seem. All around us you see the survival of the fittest going on. Every little animal competing for what's his. It's natural. You can learn a lot from it.

"Do you know why I got to where I am today? The reason is that most people trust me. Most little, medium people—not the bigwigs—but most regular, happy people are with me. They don't understand phoniness, they don't understand bull, they don't understand why they have to say 'mister' to some people. They'll do it, but they don't know why they have to.

"Same thing happens to me all the time, because I'm not a bigwig myself. That's what made me so different from some of the people at the America's Cup. They're riding around in their big cars and everything, and I've got a little Toyota with a stick shift. I fly tourist class on airplanes—always. I'm not a big shot. You could never accuse me of that."

As he spoke, Ted Turner was enjoying the sights of his own personal wilderness. His current holdings in the Turner Broadcasting System were valued at approximately $80 million. And he was returning to Atlanta the next day to resume his attempt to muscle still more power and capital from the hands of his fellows in the communications marketplace.

"And yet here I am on my plantation," Turner added. "It seems like a contradiction, doesn't it? Well, let me tell you something about my plantation house. It's probably the only one in South Carolina that isn't air-conditioned. I don't like air conditioning. I don't even use it in Atlanta half the time. I try not to use it in cars. My hired man, Johnny, sits in his house here with his air conditioning on, while I'm sitting in my house just a couple hundred yards away, sweating.

"You have to be strong, but you don't have to waste. That's why I can live here and still not be a bigwig. I like to fight, I fight all the time, and most of the fight is against bigwigs. I would prefer live and let live, but it's not nature's way. Not when there're alligators. The alligators ate the last six swans I put in my pond, and they drove the geese and the ducks away. So I put up the fence and kicked the alligators out."

Turner was laughing, for the walk was nearly over. It was the laugh of *Tyrannosaurus rex* striking its funny bone. "The poor little duckies and goosies," Turner repeated. "You know what the alligators do? They pull them down from under water. They swim up under the little guys while they're paddling around and then *vump!* Which would you rather be, a duck or an alligator? It's only us human beings who get to decide. . . ."

Turner had put in a few hours deer hunting, and the deer were again safe. The menu, in fact, had been blue-claw crabs all along, prepared by Turner's old sidekick Jimmy Brown, a local black man who had been Turner's own boyhood companion, counsel, retainer, sailing instructor and driver, and who now served similarly Turner's own five children. As often happens in midevening, Turner was falling asleep.

One ritual, however, remained. It was one he had performed for Janie when they first bought the plantation, and for *60 Minutes* when Harry Reasoner arrived with a camera crew, and for many visitors since. Turner pushed a few buttons on his Panasonic videotape machine and flopped into a chair, silent for the moment.

The screen flashed to life, and as the sound track fell into synch a familiar melody wafted through the big house, carried by an evening breeze which entered through the eight-foot French doors at the side porches. The movie, by far the most important property ever to pass through the studios of Metro-Goldwyn-Mayer, began with a scrolling introduction, one well known to generations of filmgoers. The slow-moving sentences begged to be read aloud, and immediately one of the guests took up the challenge, intoning . . .

"It was a land of cavaliers and cotton fields
Called the Old South. . . ."

Instantly, Turner's voice, louder and more Southern, overwhelmed it, as he himself picked up the poignant narrative.

". . . Here, in this pretty world
Gallantry took its last bow.
Here was the last ever to be seen
Of knights and their ladies fair,
Of master and of slave.
Look for it only in books,
For it is no more than a dream remembered . . .
A civilization
Gone with the wind."

There was a brief pause, as in a church just before the first chords of the Recessional. Turner sighed a deep, theatrical sigh.

"Not too shabby," he pronounced. "But it ain't all a dream, my friends. We're here, aren't we? And what's more, we'll be here tomorrow."

2   The Yearling

SINCE he became a man, an event which occurred on March 5, 1963, Ted Turner's life has resounded with drama of a Shakespearean intensity, proceeding scene by scene from one epic challenge to the next, through gigantic friendships and enormous enmities, grand voyages begun and bloody defeats endured, skirmishes fought for everything and for nothing, all in a plunging, helter-skelter charge through a contemporary landscape that still rings, to his ears, with the clanging swords of a great medieval battlefield.

The extemporizing playwright of this tragical-comical-historical-pastoral show is, of course, Ted Turner himself, but though he puts an antic disposition on, his ghost is as real as Hamlet's: It is the ghost of Robert Edward Turner, Jr., his father, who took his own life that March day in 1963 and is now an offstage voice that speaks forever in the son's ear.

Turner was twenty-four when his father, a complicated and demanding man, inexplicably shot himself. If Ed Turner was blunt throughout his life, so is Ted in remembering:

"My father could be absolutely charming or he could be a horse's ass. He could be the kindest, warmest, most wonderful person in the whole world, and then go into a bar, get drunk, and get into a fistfight with the whole place.

"He was a rugged individualist. It's an old phrase, but it describes him well, because he was in fact a throwback to the past. He didn't have a whole lot of fear, but sometimes he did have remorse—remorse for the things he had done. He had a bad habit, and it was that he would always say exactly what he thought, without being diplomatic at all. That got him in a lot of trouble, along with drinking too much.

"I've tried to learn from that. Maybe I tend to be outspoken myself, but he was so outspoken that I saw it cost him a lot of friends, and it cost him a lot of money, too. He would have gone a lot further if he hadn't been so controversial.

"I loved him, I know that. We loved each other, and yet we were so cruel. He was a hard man, and I tried to please him, although I didn't a lot of the time, and we had terrible, terrible fights. It was after one of those fights—we disagreed about how the business should be run—that he blew his brains out."

Ed Turner was hard, but it seemed from the beginning that he was tutoring his son for survival in a hard world, creating, as best he could, a descendant as tough and direct as he. He devised many tests for his son to pass along the way, although he was not always there to administer them personally, since he was busy, very busy, making his own fortune.

Ed Turner was a self-made man who had started a billboard advertising company from scratch in Cincinnati, before World War II. It was in that Ohio city that Ted Turner—later to become the cigar-chomping symbol of New South aggressiveness—was born, and first attended school. In those days the outdoor advertising business was hot, and Turner's father was determined to move wherever the money was. It meant, among other things, a peripatetic childhood for young Ted, and it also meant that he became a Southerner—and fast.

"When I was in the fifth grade my father put me into Georgia Military Academy, and it was pretty rough. I was from Ohio, I was a Northerner, and I didn't enroll until about six weeks after the regular term had begun, so I was coming in late. I was expecting trouble, I guess, because I was always getting beat on as a youth. Even in Cincinnati I got beaten up all the time, or at least I had to fight all the time. I don't know what it was. Yes, I do know what it was: the other kids thought I was a show-off and a smart-ass.

"I've always had a high opinion of myself, and you have to put up with that, and so when I got to Georgia I expected it to continue. And it did. There were four of us in a little room, and right away I got into a fight with the biggest guy in the room and knocked the hell out of him. I sensed that if I didn't come out swinging they were going to kill me. That night, I said to my roommates, 'Who's the boss in here?'

And I got the other three guys to go around saying I was the boss. But there was a hitch. There was actually a little bathroom joining two dorm rooms, which really made eight of us in this little cell. So the next day I went into the next room and said, 'OK, I intend to be the boss in here, too.'

"That was a big mistake, because all four of them jumped on me at once, and three of them held me down while the other one kicked me in the head until I could barely see. And then all seven of them ganged up on me and the whole dormitory joined in until they just about killed me. All kinds of things happened, like once a kid started a rumor that I had said Robert E. Lee was a bad guy. At Georgia Military Academy, nothing could have been worse. We wore Confederate gray uniforms, and I can remember about forty kids in gray running after me saying, 'Kill the Yankee bastard!' "

Young Turner may have had a chip on both shoulders, but there was a pastoral side too, a romantic fascination with the mysteries of the natural world—a world that, unlike that of the dorm, he could not hope to dominate. He was intrigued by animals, large and small, and one of his first hobbies was taxidermy. He could always retreat, when fighting lost its charm, to the world outside.

"It was fortunate for me that I got the exposure to the outdoors when I did, because it gave me something to fall back on. I moved around a lot, and wherever I went nature was always there, even if something else wasn't. My grandfather had a cotton farm, it was down in Sumner, Mississippi, a little town that became famous later on because that's where the civil-rights leader Emmett Till was murdered. I lived down there for a year or so. I used to catch turtles with a hunk of meat on a line. Then later on my father got himself a plantation, and we used to go there as well. It was a good thing I moved around, because I never got that sense of regionalism and sectionalism, which can be a problem. If you've never lived outside of New Jersey, you can easily think that New Jersey is the universe, but it isn't. So I never thought the North was better than the South, or the South the North, or one state was better than another."

When Turner was ten, his family was living in Savannah, where Ed Turner had bought another billboard company, and where Ted was coming to grips with something about himself that there was no way to avoid and no way to talk his way out of. He had learned, as the majority of boys do, the most terrible truth of pre-puberty: He was apparently not going to be very good at sports. He was competitive, fanatically competitive, but if there was a ball involved, no matter what the shape or size, he would drop it.

"I tried all the sports, football, basketball, baseball, even swimming, but I was no good. I tried and I tried, but I could see it wouldn't work. I was on all the teams, every one, but I couldn't make a contribution, and it hurt me a lot because I'm naturally a player, not a spectator. And that let me out of a lot of things, and I think it made me appreciate animals, who were naturally good at running and jumping. You know—the way a cat can run straight up a tree."

So while the other kids played organized sports, Turner slipped away to read books, his first taste of the literature of heroes that would sustain him through adolescence and far beyond. He read all the fables he could find, Aesop first, and moved quickly on to the never-ending tales of Greek and Roman gods and goddesses, trading the world of bats and balls for the Olympian challenges of Zeus versus the Titans, and the excitements of Ovid. It was a world where the sun did not merely rise, but was pulled across the sky behind fiery horses, and where a maiden too zealously pursued might turn herself into a tree in heartbreaking allegiance to chastity.

It was about then that Ed Turner bought himself a 40-foot schooner built of wood, and took up cruising. Sometimes he took his son along, when he was back from boarding school. Ed Turner was not an expert sailor, and he did not enter races. But he did become interested in the junior program at the yacht club in Savannah, and enrolled Ted, who was eleven. He could not help but notice that Ted seemed to like sailing.

Sailing! Here was a sport with no ball involved, a sport his own father had taken up, a sport in which individual skill was all-important and which, his first instructors informed him, could be learned. If you wanted to be good, you could be good.

In those days the kids in Savannah raced Penguin class dinghies, 11½-foot plywood boats with cotton sails that were responsive enough to provide adults with exciting "frostbite" racing in winter, and tractable enough for junior programs in the summer, too.

The Penguin is an excellent boat, but in the hands of two junior lightweights it is also easily overpowered when the breeze comes up. The scene was familiar to many children learning to sail in the 1950s: the wild-eyed scramble for balance as a puff of wind struck, heeling the open boat until its leeward rail submerged to admit a rush of warm water. Then the slow-motion capsize that sent the youthful crew splashing into the drink.

Today's dinghies are self-rescuing, and to tip over means only a moment's delay. But when an early Penguin swamped, it meant rescue by a committee boat, or what could be hours of exhausting bailing.

Turner quickly earned a reputation in Savannah as Turnover Ted the Capsize Kid, who pushed his boat to the limit, took crazy chances, and seldom won a trophy as a result. But at least he was competing, and it was exciting as hell. A Penguin's top speed is only about 7 miles an hour, but to blast along through the wavetops with spray flying and the boat at the edge of control—ah, it was almost like riding Phaeton's chariot across the sky. It was romantic, glamorous and scary—and there were spectators.

When summer ended, McCallie—the Chattanooga military school where Ed Turner placed his son for the next leg of his forced march toward manhood—began. At first it was predictably difficult, with Turner once more experiencing the Southern American equivalent of *Tom Brown's School Days*—starting off as the only seventh-grader in a dorm inhabited by eighth-graders. But it was at McCallie that Turner began to grow up, and even to flourish, so that he looks back now upon those high school years with both a bemused horror and a fierce pride.

Turner has five children, and the oldest of the three boys, Teddy, was enrolled at McCallie upon reaching the appropriate age. Now the next two boys, Rhett and Beauregard, are being announced as McCallie material too.

Janie Turner is not pleased. "I don't understand why they have to go off to school when they could have just as fine an education here in Atlanta," she told him in one of a series of debates on the issue.

"Why, to get them away from their mother, that's why," Turner replied. "Boys shouldn't be around their mother too long, it makes them into girls."

"That's the most ridiculous thing I ever heard, Ted."

"But it's true. Why Janie, don't you know? Old McCallie is a wonderful place. As a matter of fact, of the three men you've been in love with, two of them have been from McCallie." Turner's eyes lit up with amusement as he continued. "There was your first real love, Charlie Rutherford. And your last real love, me. And we both made it through there OK. The first one turned out to be a fine upstanding doctor, albeit a little fat and baldheaded. I say a little fat and baldheaded, although an outstanding doctor. And then there's me. So the place can't be too bad."

Wherever Rhett and Beau wind up, McCallie has changed since Turner's day. The uniforms and military program, if not the principles behind them, are gone. But in the father's day, McCallie offered an example of social order as fascinating to him as the workings of a clock in a glass case. At first, and as usual, he set out to be the monkey wrench in those works, but military schools have methods of dealing with such behavior. They are called punishment tours, to be marched off in direct proportion to the size of the crimes. Young Turner began to wear out his shoes.

"At first, I was just a terrible cadet. I did everything I could to rebel against the system, although I think I believed in it from the beginning. I was always having animals in my room and stuff like that, and getting into trouble one way or another, and then having to take the punishment like a man. But at least everybody was equal there, because that's what the military system does. I went through a lot, but it changed me, and after a while I shaped up. I wanted to be the best, and I saw that it could be done if you worked at it. By the time I got out I had accomplished something. I was the Tennessee state debating champion. I beat a girl in the finals. She broke down into tears because I challenged the basic premise being debated. I was named best-dressed cadet, and in my junior year I got to be an officer and an inspector—and then it was me who went around looking for dirt and giving other people demerits. But I always tried to be fair when I finally got into a leadership situation."

Years later, Turner's home in Atlanta was burglarized, and the thieves took a number of things from his virtually limitless collection of souvenirs. Turner was badly stung by the theft for two reasons: He could not believe that even the burglars of Atlanta would want to steal from him; and he lost his best-dressed medal from McCallie and his cadet officer's sword. "Dammit, why did they have to do that? The sword wasn't worth but $26 when I bought it, but it had my name on it. I had worked hard for it, and I deserved to get to keep it forever."

At McCallie, Turner kept on reading, though not necessarily his assignments. He was older and had passed from fables to history, and he became a frequent figure in the school library.

"I was interested in one thing, and that was in what you could accomplish if you really tried. So I looked around for guys who had tried. We had four hours of study hall every day, and I'd blast through the uninteresting part of my homework, particularly in the early years, and be content to get Cs. But there were always monitors coming up and down the halls, and since you had to be busy, I could read anything. I read about the sea because I had a little sailboat of my own. I read C. S. Forester's books, and Nordhoff and Hall about ten times—*Men Against the Sea, Mutiny on the Bounty* and *Pitcairn's Island.* I read about the War of 1812, and about the *Constitution*—you know, the ship. I remember reading the story of the Marines at Tripoli, and then I would go on to the dreadnaughts in World War I, and then when I'd gone through that, on to World War II. My interest was always in why people did the things they did, and what caused some people to rise to glorious heights, like the Macedonians did under Alexander the Great. Alexander decided to go farther than anyone had ever tried to go; there were no limits to his imagination."

So Turner, giving plane geometry the once-over, filled his head instead with the story of another sixteen-year-old, one who commanded his own army. A worthy competitor, a useful instructor and a most dangerous companion.

Alexander was born in 356 B.C., the son of King Philip of Macedonia, a vigorous general who turned the boy over to Aristotle for his early education. Alexander was good in every sport, a brilliant hunter, horseman, fencer, runner, a dashing natural leader who sought out hard work and danger. He was a man of action and of influence, careful of his diet so as to remain youthful, and vain enough to shave his face with a knife each day. Men followed him for decades in the field, where he was often the first to leap into hand-to-hand combat, and more than once the first terribly wounded. He tried to be fair to those he conquered, but he was also capable of Homeric cruelty, once ordering a defeated general pierced through the feet and dragged by chariot around his own city precisely as dead Hector was dragged around Troy. He persevered through famine, mutiny and constant harassing attacks to drive deep into Persia and win her for Greece. No man ever questioned his courage, his loyalty or the vastness of his imagination. Alexander the Great, even the schoolboy texts would add, accomplished all of that without ever completing his education, for there wasn't time.

He was a brilliant debater, though capable, we are told, of quickly making a fool of himself when talk turned from war. He could administer armies, but he could not control his own outrageous temper. He was wise in the ways of men, yet an easy victim of flatterers. His ambition was overwhelming and uncontrollable. In 323 B.C., in a camp in Babylon, he won a drinking match with his officers by draining a goblet containing six quarts of wine. Within days his army of 10,000 was filing through his tent, in a last goodbye to their fevered, dying commander.

"Well, that stuff just knocked me cold," Turner says. "I used to cry over those stories. Alexander the Great was far from perfect, and yet he accomplished all that because he wanted to, and worked at it all the time. And his men loved him, even though they mutinied after about fifteen years on the hike. It was so exciting, going to new lands all the time. They had trophies, and I always loved trophies, I still do. You got gold and silver when you won a battle—something tangible."

When Turner finally graduated from McCallie, having not only survived but flourished in the end, his father made sure there was a trophy. He got Ted a Lightning class sailboat, a three-man racing boat that could be campaigned on the regatta circuit, where competition was stiff. Lest there be any suggestion that Ed Turner was spoiling his son, Ted was expected to come up with half the purchase price.

His father knew he had the money, because his father had been his employer for the previous five summers. In fact, Turner had spent much of his childhood working on Turner billboard gangs sent out to tend properties, change posters or erect new signs. It was hard labor, and the rawboned boy with the fast-talking mouth was expected to bang his share of nails without favor. Young Turner enjoyed it, though, for it was his first chance to see how hard he could work, and he knew that the harder he worked, the better his father would like it. His father paid him a salary, but most of it went directly into the bank, or was otherwise used to keep score in the game of growing up. One summer, for example, Ed Turner decided that it was time Ted started paying rent, and announced that the bill thereafter for living plushly at home would be $25 a week. The son was scandalized, and let his father know it, arguing that it was unusual to have to pay room and board as a teenage son, and that anyway the rent asked was unreasonably high. Ed Turner's advice was to look around. If he could find someplace cheaper, he could move out.

So Ted Turner came up with half the purchase price of the Lightning. It was all the money he had saved from five summers' work on the billboards. His father sailed with him only a few times, but there was no doubt that he was watching carefully from the yacht club ashore.

In the matter of payment to sons, as in so many other matters, Turner learned his father's lesson well. Instead of an allowance, his own boys receive payment in accordance with work done. The oldest, Teddy, working as a deck hand on the family ocean racer, receives $44 weekly subsistence. The younger boys receive $1 an hour for general farm labor and $2 an hour for pigweed. One recent summer day an accounting was held.

"You boys been paid yet?"

"No, sir," said Rhett, fourteen, owed $45.

"No, sir," said Beau, thirteen, owed $64.

"All right, it's payday then. Remind me to have Miss Woods draw up your checks when she does the corporate payroll at the end of the week. If you bank half, you can spend the other half."

"Yes, sir."

"Yes, sir."

"You almost don't have to get paid for pulling pigweed," Turner concluded, relishing his family's many hand-to-hand battles, waist deep in the canals of his plantation, with the ubiquitous, choking waterweed. "It's so much fun working up a sweat pulling it out by the roots."

Ted Turner's summers of boyhood ended in 1956. He had graduated from McCallie and learned to admire the military; he had his own Lightning and was in love with sailing, ships and the sea. The choice of a college seemed obvious: He would apply to the United States Naval Academy at Annapolis. No, his father said, you must enter the Ivy League. So Ted went off to Brown—having been turned down by Harvard.

Turner's college career was a replay, in many respects, of his previous school experiences. Things happened rapidly. In his first year at Brown he was undefeated in intercollegiate sailboat racing. In his second year he was suspended from school for causing a disturbance at a nearby women's college. That episode also cost him $5,000—the reward his hard-drinking father had offered for staying on the wagon until age twenty-one. By his fourth year, Turner had been kicked out for good, having violated a rule about women in dormitory rooms. In Savannah, the strict Southern family he measured himself against was struggling with tragedy and breakup. His mother and father were finally divorced. His sister Mary Jane, stricken years before with lupus, a progressively degenerative disease, was at home, nearing death. And the war with his father continued, and became public.

Edward Turner intended Ted Turner to pick the brains of New England and bring them home to the billboard business, where they could be of some use. But Turner's fascination was with man, not economics, and he was studying classics. So Ted received a letter in the mail:

My dear son,
I am appalled, even horrified, that you have adopted Classics as a major. As a matter of fact, I almost puked on the way home today. I suppose that I am old-fashioned enough to believe that the purpose of an education is to enable one to develop a community of interest with his fellow men, to learn to know them, and to learn

how to get along with them. In order to do this, of course, he must learn what motivates them, and how to impel them to be pleased with his objectives and desires.

I am a practical man, and for the life of me I cannot possibly understand why you should wish to speak Greek. With whom will you communicate in Greek? I have read, in recent years, the deliberations of Plato and Aristotle, and was interested to learn that the old bastards had minds which worked very similarly to the way our minds work today. I was amazed that they had so much time for deliberating and thinking, and was interested in the kind of civilization that would permit such useless deliberation. Then I got to thinking that it wasn't so amazing after all they thought like we did, because my Hereford cows today are very similar to those ten or twenty generations ago. I am amazed that you would adopt Plato and Aristotle as a vocation for several months when it might make pleasant and enjoyable reading to you in your leisure time as relaxation at a later date. For the life of me I cannot understand why you should be vitally interested in informing yourself about the influence of the classics on English literature. It is not necessary for you to know how to make a gun in order to know how to use it. It would seem to me that it would be enough to learn English literature without going into what influence this or that ancient mythology might have upon it. As for Greek literature, the history of Roman and Greek churches, and the art of those eras, it would seem to me that you would be much better off by learning something of contemporary literature and writings, and things that might have some meaning to you with the people with whom you are to associate.

These subjects might give you a community of interest with an isolated few impractical dreamers, and a select group of college professors. God forbid!

It would seem to me that what you wish to do is to establish a community of interest with as many people as you possibly can. With people who are moving, who are doing things, and who have an interesting, not a decadent, outlook.

I suppose everybody has to be a snob of some sort, and I suppose you will feel you are distinguishing yourself from the herd by becoming a Classical snob. I can see you drifting into a bar, belting down a few, turning around to the guy on the stool next to you—a contemporary billboard baron from Podunk, Iowa—and saying,

"Well, what do you think about old Leonidas?" Your friend, the billboard baron, will turn to you and say, "Leonidas who?" You will turn to him and say, "Why, Leonidas, the prominent Greek of the twelfth century." He will, in turn, say to you, "Well, who in the hell was he?" You will say, "Oh, you don't know about Leonidas?" and dismiss him, and not discuss anything else with him the rest of the evening. He will feel that you are a stupid snob and a flop; and you will feel that he is a clodhopper from Podunk, Iowa. I suppose this will make you both happy, and as a result of it, you will wind up buying his billboard plant.

There is no question but this type of useless information will distinguish you, set you apart from the doers of the world. If I leave you enough money, you can retire to an ivory tower, and contemplate for the rest of your days the influence that the hieroglyphics of prehistoric man had upon the writings of William Faulkner. Incidentally, he was a contemporary of mine in Mississippi. We speak the same language—whores, sluts, strong words and strong deeds.

It isn't really important what I think. It's important what you wish to do with your life. I just wish I could feel that the influence of those oddball professors and the ivory towers were developing you into the kind of a man we can both be proud of. I am quite sure that we both will be pleased and delighted when I introduce you to some friend of mine and say, "This is my son. He speaks Greek."

I had dinner during the Christmas holidays with an efficiency expert, an economic adviser to the nation of India, on the Board of Directors of Regents at Harvard University, who owns some 80,000 acres of valuable timber land down here, among his other assets. His son and his family were visiting him. He introduced me to his son, and then apologetically said, "He is a theoretical mathematician. I don't even know what he is talking about. He lives in a different world." After a little while I got talking to his son, and the only thing he would talk to me about was his work. I didn't know what he was talking about either, so I left early.

If you are going to stay on at Brown, and be a professor of Classics, the courses you have adopted will suit you for a lifetime association with Gale Noyes. Perhaps he will even teach you to make jelly. In my opinion, it won't do much to help you learn to get along with the people in this world. I think you are rapidly becoming a jackass, and the sooner you get out of that filthy atmosphere, the better it will suit me.

Oh, I know that everybody says that a college education is a must. Well, I console myself by saying that everybody said the world was square, except Columbus. You go ahead and go with the world, and I'll go it alone. . . .

I hope I am right. You are in the hands of the Philistines, and dammit, I sent you there. I am sorry.

Devotedly,
Dad

Ted's response was elegant and harsh. He had the letter printed in its entirety in the campus newspaper. Each Turner, it seemed, had found a worthy adversary.

Ted and Brown, in fact, had made short work of each other. Colleges, especially New England colleges, exist as much for the amusement of their students as for their edification, and the preparation for the world to come pays off most often in useful persons met rather than useful facts learned. A young man may indulge himself in silly costumes and absurd intellectual posturings, and box the saturnalian compass, as long as he eventually hits the books too. The day-by-day discipline of the military school is replaced by the natural discipline of romance languages, reading lists and fast-moving freshmen survey courses. The discipline is subtle simply because the brightest of the budding humanists contend to study least, and a great humiliation can take the form of discovery in a hidden study hall, books open, pen scribbling notes. Turner, the swashbuckler who burned down his own fraternity's homecoming display, who kept an alligator in his room, whose study of female mysteries had already earned him an advanced degree on the topic, was seldom so humiliated. Besides, scholarship was a lonely occupation. Turner, smart as a whip, hated even then to be alone.

He was often kept from that fate by a young man named Peter Dames. Dames was from New York City, paid no attention at all to the sailing team at Brown, and was not in any of Turner's classes. They became boon companions.

"Basically, we both liked to get drunk and chase women, but we had a couple of things in common that were important," Dames recalls. "We had both come to Brown fresh out of five years in military school, me at Manlius in New York State and Turner in Chattanooga, and we had had parallel careers. We had both been the worst possible cadets at first, figured out the system, and gone on to run the places. So the metamorphoses were the same.

"This also meant we were both totally unprepared for Brown's social life. Everybody else had gone to Choate or Lawrenceville or some other fancy prep school, and they were all presidents of their class or captains on the football team. I mean, nobody was an average guy. So Turner and I had to look around for something to excel at, and we settled on drinking and lechering. We really worked hard at it, too, and we excelled. We became legends in our own time. If he got some money or I did, we would immediately invest it in improving our reputations. You have to understand that for the other guys this was nothing new, they had done it all at Choate and Lawrenceville. But for us, suddenly there was no lights out at ten o'clock, no bed checks, no inspection. You could drink and screw all you wanted. And we wanted. If Turner got thrown in jail, I would bail him out. One time I tried to bail him out and they locked me up too."

Dames is cheerfully unapologetic as he raises the glass of reminiscence to debaucheries of old, and for good reason. He is now a partner in the Turner billboard business, a millionaire in his own right, with the prettiest of secretaries, the largest of Cadillacs, and continued opportunities to excel.

Turner looks back more warily. "I was happier at military school," he says. "I really didn't like it when there were no rules, and there was a lot of bull at Brown. It mattered who your father was, how much money you had, what your clothes looked like. I was used to a certain directness, and there was very little of that. I never did graduate, but I learned a lot and I accomplished some things. I was the captain of the sailing team, and also the coach—we had student coaches then. I spent all my time at the Brown yacht club, working on the boats and traveling to college regattas instead of studying. But you never know. If I'd gone to Annapolis I would have done great, and I'd be an admiral by now. But no one would have heard of me."

After his first suspension from Brown, Turner had joined the Coast Guard. After his final expulsion, he and Dames set out for Florida—

then the candy-coated wonderland to which college-boy Pinocchios detoured in the winter cold. Turner and Dames, however, as their donkey ears and tails began to sprout, couldn't even find the candy. "We were there for two months," says Turner. "We were just living like bums, really. We set ourselves up in this poor Cuban neighborhood, and we didn't have a dime between us. We used to drink water out of paper cups that we washed out so we could use them again, and we ate peanut butter, and for toilet paper we used the Florida telephone directory. We tried to find jobs as short-order cooks, but we failed, because it was right after the semester and the state was absolutely flooded with college dropouts. It was cold as hell and we were miserable, to tell the truth. We used to sleep under the overcoats that we'd worn down from Brown. I said to myself, 'Look, I'm basically a happy person, and if I'm unhappy, why don't I go home?' No! I was an independent man, I could find work somehow down there in the advertising business, or I could just paint signs, I had learned to do that already. I was determined not to go back to my father, and yet I knew being a bum wasn't for me. Then along came the Coast Guard. I had already been in, but I think I still owed them some time, and they said why not serve it now."

Dames still marvels at the Turner luck in action.

"Here we were, starving to death in Miami living with the Cubans, and Ted's father forwards a letter saying the Coast Guard is after him. So we report to the Coast Guard office, and I'm expecting trouble. Eventually they find Turner's records and they say, 'You have a cruise coming up, Mr. Turner. Where would you like to go?' And I'm standing in a corner, scratching my head, while they outline for him which dream cruise he can go on. He finally says, yeah, all right, he'll accept the cruise to Yucatán. I just shook my head. And went back to New York."

So Turner found himself back in the military, which was all right with him but required a certain period of adjustment on the part of his officers and mates. He reported to the U.S.S. *Travis* in Fort Lauderdale, a vintage vessel with an unclear role in the Coast Guard of the 1960s.

The Yucatán cruise was not a dream.

"My job was chipping paint, and I determined to be the best

paint-chipper on the boat. I chipped paint during the day and I chipped paint at night, and by the time I left I had the whole damned boat cheered up, I really did. At first, though, they hated me.

"They gave me the worst job every time. I would do it, and then run back to the second-class petty officer and say, 'I've finished that job, sir, have you got something else for me to do?' They always got mad. See, the whole deal was that you stayed there at the job you had all day long, and stretched it out, because they really didn't have enough jobs to do for all the people on the ship. It was just a game, you did as little as you possibly could. That was the deal—but it wasn't any fun. The days took forever.

"So they'd give me the latrine to clean up. Other guys who got the latrine, it took them half a day. There were eight heads, for about eighty people on the boat. You took a brush and cleaned the crap out of the toilet, and picked the hair out of the shower drains, and scoured the wash bowls and stuff. And I, who would one day affect the destiny of the nation, was down there cleaning crap up. And you know what? Whistling while I did it. One thing they sure teach you in military school is how to clean up. I could finish the latrine in an hour flat. So naturally, they got on me. Nobody could clean up that place in an hour, they told me.

" 'Well, I have, sir,' I said.

" 'Don't call me "sir"—I'm a petty officer.'

"So of course I said, 'Well, I'm accustomed to calling all officers sir, petty or not. I was raised that way.'

"The guy went down on the floor behind a toilet and he found a speck of dirt. One speck of dirt. So the next day it was the same deal, only this time he couldn't find the speck of dirt. And again I had done it in an hour. I'd cleaned it so good the first day it was easy the second day.

"What they did was punish me for doing such a good job, or maybe for being so proud of it. They put me in the bilge. Ha. This was really an old, beat-up ship, it looked like one of those gunboats from the Yangtze River. It was built about 1920, and was given to the Coast Guard as unfit for any duty at all in about 1940, and this was more than twenty years after that. On one of these same ships they chipped so much paint off the bottom that they chipped right through the hull and the damn thing sank. Ours was worse than the Caine in *The Caine Mutiny*.

"They put me down in the bilge, between the double hulls. It was, aggh. Cleaning out grunge that was six inches thick. No one had ever been down there before. It took me four or five days to do the job, and I almost died from claustrophobia. I had to crawl from stem to stern and scrape the whole way. It wasn't a question of making it spic and span. There were rats down there, and dead, rotted rat bodies, and scum and muck and armies of silverfish. This was no sailboat bilge. This was a 140-foot boat with a nearly flat bottom, and the square footage was just astounding. For some reason nobody understood, it was just about covered with sour milk, which must've dribbled down from the galley.

"When I came out at five o'clock each day, everybody on the boat felt sorry for me. I would always come out trying to smile, because I had been cheerful through all the rest. But now I was covered from head to foot in muck and scum; you couldn't even see my eyes.

"But I did like I did when Bowie Kuhn suspended me from baseball. I just said these guys aren't going to get me down. I'm going to be cheerful, and I'm going to do my work whatever it is. And finally, one day, the chief petty officer said, 'OK, now go do the latrine,' and I was off and thirty-five minutes later I had it clean.

" 'Sir, the latrine is done.'

"And he said, 'Turner, I can't take it anymore. Please. Will you please just go down to the living quarters and read your book? Just lie there and read your book. Turner, there is no more work remaining on this boat.'

"I had done it all. The bilge was the last. The captain of the ship came to me later and he said, 'You've got to make a career of the Coast Guard. I want to recommend you to the Academy.'

"I said, 'No, sir, I'm going back home. That is where my father is. You're supposed to love and emulate your father.' "

So Turner went back to Savannah, and work, duty and loyalty. His father was almost relieved that the experiments in formal education were over and the polishing of Ted's business skills could begin in earnest. Ed Turner, by all appearances, had done well for himself. He owned two plantations on the coast, where he entertained clients and friends with elegant gusto; he had his schooner, his lady friends, and a string of billboard companies that grew longer and more knotted every year. There was plenty for the boy to do.

Dick McGinnis, now vice president of Turner Advertising in Atlanta, is a few years Ted Turner's senior, and watched from that vantage point his leap into the billboard world. It was mostly with amusement—at first. McGinnis, a proper foil for his colleague Peter Dames, is a professed homebody and "goody-goody." Together they have presided over the uninterrupted good fortunes of the company, and earned Turner's highest compliment: He leaves them alone. Unlike Dames, who looms stormy even while leaning peaceably against a bar, McGinnis's manner is one of bemused wonderment. His voice, softened by the accents of the South, rises periodically toward question marks that never appear.

"When I met him he was Turner-from-Savannah. That's what he called himself and you had to ask, 'What was your name again?' It was 1959 or 1960, at an outdoor advertising conference in Atlanta. I was working for a company there at the time. Well, he looked me up again the next day. He said he heard what a good salesman I was and all that good stuff, and he said, 'You're going to work for me someday.' 'What was your name again?' 'Turner. Turner-from-Savannah.' And I said, 'Sure, Turner, see you around sometime.'

"About three years passed, and on a September afternoon he and his daddy walked in the back door of our company. Ed Turner had on a brown tweed suit and some Johnson & Murphy light tan shoes with square toes, and he was smoking a cigarette. Turner-from-Savannah was flying along behind him in a jacket too small and pants he'd grown about four inches out of.

"The first thing Turner says when they come in is, 'Where's McGinnis's office?' And in he comes, without knocking, and he says, 'See? I told you. We bought this company. You work for me now.'

"The guy never forgets anything. I been working for him ever since."

It quickly became known in Atlanta that Ed Turner had a very talkative, somewhat gangling and probably ambitious son, but the father was very much center stage.

"I knew him some, although we weren't close by any means," says

Tench C. Coxe, a courtly, Yale-educated Atlanta attorney whom Ted Turner later came to admire enormously. "Ted's father was a man with a great deal of authority and personal style. He had a lot of women around him, and I think that was very important. Ed Turner told me that loyalty and honesty were the most highly regarded of attributes. He was the kind of man who set up criteria for everything, and then compared you to them. During the time I knew him, I don't think he ever mentioned Ted even once."

Ed Turner was an extremely demanding employer who made equal demands upon himself. He had once thrown a fellow guest into the pool at a ritzy party in Savannah, and the same violent energy found expression again and again in other ways. It baffled and frightened his friends, and it increased the number of his enemies.

"When Ed Turner took over our firm in Atlanta, he wanted to change everything around right away," McGinnis says. "He had me out running up and down the main drag looking for great big antebellum homes so we could get one of them as a business headquarters. We had to move fast, because he wanted a high-class operation right away. We finally compromised on a place on West Peachtree Street downtown."

McGinnis knew that his boss was driving himself very hard, and seemed consumed by work and the need to dominate every business and social situation in which he found himself. But McGinnis, at the time, did not sense the foreboding in the air.

"Ted's father was a changing person, and people who'd known him for years maybe never knew the whole man. I noticed that he was losing his sense of humor about things, and that he was tightening up a lot. Actually, he was acting irrationally in many areas of my contact with him. One day he would tell you to do something, and then when you did it, he wouldn't remember the order.

"He didn't think my personal car was so great for a salesman to have. I didn't make much money, and I couldn't help but agree with him. So he said, 'Go out and get yourself a real car and I'll pay you so much a month to operate it and that will help you pay for it.'

"So I took him at his word. I was inclined to respond quickly around him because he was a strong leader. So bang, I went running out and bought this Impala Chevrolet, and just a few days later I showed him the new car and brought up the proposition. He didn't even remember it. He got real mad and flew off the handle and started shouting at me.

"I said, 'Jeez, Ed, you told me to get the car, I got the car, and here it is.' But he just walked away."

Those who had known Ed Turner longer were more concerned. They had seen the pressure building within the billboard empire. An observer at close range was his accountant, Irwin Mazo of Savannah.

"I knew him for the last seven or eight years of his life," Mazo says. We were great friends. Several of us were well aware of what was going on—Tom Adams, his attorney, and Dr. Victor Irving, who was also very close. Ed was a great guy if he liked you, and if he didn't you had to watch out. Even so, he had more humility than Ted. But there is no question Ed Turner was a great businessman.

"He was also a great drinker. He would go off on a binge for a week and then come back good as new, ready to go again. He smoked all the time. When he married for the second time, to Jane Dillard, her father was president of the Central Georgia Railroad. That gave Ed a certain social status he hadn't had before, and he went off to the Silver Hill Foundation in Connecticut, where the rich ones go to dry out. After that he didn't drink for several years.

"When he bought the Atlanta company, it was a very big transaction," Mazo said, "and he was uptight. Dr. Irving treated him for depression. He wanted to hospitalize him, but Ed wouldn't go along.

"One day Ed came to me and said, 'I made a big mistake with the Atlanta company. I want to get out.' I was astounded. 'Why?' I said. 'There's no problem. Everything is going fine.' But he insisted. He wanted his money back. His wife came to me and said, 'Don't let him sell, this is what he's dreamed of.' But Ed, well, he was really scared."

Ted Turner speculates that his father had made the mistake of giving himself too limited a goal: He had once told his mother in Mississippi he would make a million dollars, and when it came true he was suddenly a man without a future. In fact, the billboard company was doing adequately, and the complications that seemed gigantic to Ed Turner did not impress others as unusual. What Ed Turner had done was to buy the billboard enterprises in Atlanta, Norfolk, Richmond and Roanoak for about $4 million. The purchase was financed by the sellers, and Turner had put up his other holdings to borrow the down payment of $750,000—so in effect, the entire scheme floated on other people's money. In the meantime, he also owned outdoor advertising operations in Columbus and in Macon, Georgia.

Ed Turner had a tiger by the tail with each hand, and he felt his grip slipping. It was not a boom period for billboards. The postwar buying spree was waning as Americans began to question the need for a new car every two years, and small recessions ebbed and flowed through the economy. Advertising was becoming more sophisticated as television taught new, more subliminal methods of pushing soap, tobacco and ways of life. The newspapers, always an enemy, stepped up their campaigns against "billboard blight," offering their own ad space as a happy, if not circumstantial, alternative. Ed Turner, uncharacteristically, seemed overwhelmed.

His son, who now knew the business intimately and was waiting impatiently for his chance to prove it, was not. He accused his father of lack of courage. He invoked his father's favorite word, "tenacity," which had previously been almost a mantra for Turner men.

"We argued bitterly," Turner recalls, chilled by the memory. But Ed Turner's course was already set. He had persuaded a close business associate, Robert Naegele of Minneapolis, to buy him out of the Atlanta deal and clear his slate of debts. He put his other affairs in order and updated his will. He then retired to his plantation in South Carolina, a man who, from his accountant's point of view, "was really very well off."

Ed Turner shot himself to death with a pistol in his bedroom on the morning of March 5, 1963.

When the will was read it was revealed that the business had been left to Ted, and also that the business had been sold. The irony was sharp.

"The night of the funeral in Savannah, Ted and I went to a restaurant. He was very agitated," Mazo says. "He looked me in the eye and he said he didn't want to go through with the sale. 'I want to run the business my father left me.'

" 'Come on, Ted,' I said, 'forget it. Why don't you go sailing? That's your first love anyhow.'

" 'No,' Turner said, 'my father wasn't in his right mind. I have to do this.'

" 'But you don't have the line of credit your father had. You're only twenty-four, and the banks don't know you. Besides, we've got estate-tax problems, plus certain stipulations made by General Outdoor Advertising, which is buying. Even the things that were easy for your father wouldn't be available to you.'

" 'I still want to do it,' Turner said."

Mazo told him he didn't think he could.

Meanwhile, the Naegele group went ahead with the buy-out plan. They sent inspectors to Atlanta, who arrived on the day of the funeral in Savannah to begin the process of takeover. McGinnis drove them around town in his car, answering questions from them and wondering what was going to happen next.

It does not seem to have occurred to anyone that Ted Turner might have an effect on their futures. He had been trouble as a kid, dropped out of college, and been sent down to manage the Macon billboards by his father upon his return. In Atlanta, he was ever in his father's shadow. It was natural to dismiss him, underestimate him, wait for him to go away. It was a mistake that has been made many times since.

Ted Turner had learned the rules, and was most ready to play the game. Even the Capsize Kid was gone: Turner, a year or so before, had won his first national sailboat championship, and his thirst for victory had only begun. Today, wrapped in the smoke of a Cuban cigar and tapping the toe of his $150 Italian loafer, Turner marvels at what he did then.

"I was sad, pissed and determined," he remembers. "I had to get that company back. I knew Mr. Naegele was my father's best friend, and I thought I'd just call him up and it would be fixed. But it was still cold in Minneapolis, so Naegele was out in Palm Springs. I jumped on a plane and went out there.

" 'Just tear up the purchase agreement and let me keep my father's company,' I said. 'You won't be sorry.' I appealed to his friendship. 'You don't really want to do this anyhow,' I said. But no, he was going to go through with it, he wanted to close the deal." So Turner got on the phone back to Atlanta and started some balls rolling.

"I was actually on my way back to Atlanta when I grabbed a phone in the airport and scheduled a meeting of our lease department. That's the department that has all the contracts for the leases on billboard locations, which in that business is the most important asset you really have. The meeting was set for that night, and when I got back I just hired the whole department, and put them on the Macon payroll. The same people, but a different payroll. See, the deal with Naegele was we were just supposed to operate the Atlanta company temporarily until they took it over, but because all they'd signed was a purchase letter there was no actual noncompete agreement.

"So the next morning my new employees and I went out and started transferring the Atlanta leases to the Macon company. Just a little paperwork, we'd say if anybody asked. I delayed as much as I could with Mr. Naegele, so that when they finally came down with the closing documents two weeks later I presented them with a *fait accompli.*

"I told them I'd already hired the entire lease department of the company they're supposed to be buying, and I've already jumped the leases—that's when you go out and get a new lease, for another company. It's sabotage. If you ever want to steal a franchise, that's how you do it. 'Furthermore,' I said, 'I can delay another two weeks, and then I'm going to burn all the records. You're going to have nothing but a disaster.' Boy, did they get back on the telephone to Minneapolis."

Turner told McGinnis what he was planning to do. "He said it was war," McGinnis remembered. "He would start another company from scratch in Atlanta just to hurt them, he would build billboards in front of theirs, he would play as dirty as it takes. 'My father wasn't in his own element when he sold out, but I'm in mine,' Ted said. He was willing to lose everything to defeat them. He would destroy them both, and bank on the fact that he was young enough to start over."

Even if Turner's saber-rattling was received as little more than a distant tinkle in wintry Minneapolis, there was indeed a counteroffer the next day.

"The big cheeses out there had an idea," Turner chortles. "They said they would give me $200,000—and this was fifteen years ago—if

I'd give them all the leases back and be a nice boy. Or, they said, if I'd give them $200,000, then they'd release me from the contract. They said I had thirty seconds to decide, but I didn't even take the thirty seconds, I said, 'That's a fair deal. I'll give you the $200,000.'

"Well, they all fell over backwards. There were actually three guys involved in the deal, and all three of them were in the 90 percent tax bracket. They only owned the thing for a couple of weeks, so it was a real short-term deal, and all the $200,000 would have been ordinary income. They could see it all going to Uncle Sam, and they didn't know what to do. They had given me thirty seconds, but when I said yeah, they ran away to think some more."

According to Mazo, the Naegele group, after a few weeks, agreed to accept the $200,000. But if Ted defaulted on the payment, they would get the company. "How long have I got?" Turner asked them. "Ninety days," came the reply.

Mazo was no better prepared for this chain of events than the Minneapolis investors.

"At that time, we had a total of maybe $25,000 on hand. In fact, I had to personally loan Ted $30,000 once to make a payroll. So Ted says to me, 'By the way, Irwin, where are we going to get the $200,-000?'

" 'I wish you'd asked me that before,' I said. "But we knew they didn't want this cash as ordinary income. Somewhere along the line, we were convinced, they would want to change the deal. The next time we met them it was out there. One of the investors involved was Curt Carlson, a really big hitter, and he had founded Gold Bond trading stamps. So Carlson picks Ted up in a solid gold Cadillac—all of his execs had gold Cadillacs at the time. We met, and they said, 'Here's an idea, let's give the money to the children, we'll set it up for our kids, not us.' 'Oh no you don't!' we said. 'No shelter deals. We're dealing with you gentlemen directly.' "

Turner grins broadly at the recollection. "I wound up convincing them that they should take stock in the company, so later on they would get a long-term gain. In the end we didn't even have to pay the $200,000. But boy, I had plenty of other debts. There was a $600,000 payment coming up in six months to the First National Bank of Chicago. I was only a kid, but I learned how to hustle. I went out and convinced the employees of the company to buy stock in it, I sold off all the real estate that I possibly could, I sold my father's plantation, I borrowed against our accounts receivable, and I squeezed the juice out of everything."

"It was a day-by-day crisis," says Mazo, "but we finally got over the hump. Of course, as soon as we did, Ted immediately became restless as hell."

McGinnis says that period offers the key to understanding Turner. "When Ted was twenty-four and he went out to Palm Springs to see Mr. Naegele, it was a pivotal point. All the cards seemed stacked against him. But he played his to the hilt and won the game, and don't think he's forgotten it."

Jim Roddy, whose fate it was to later teach Turner a lesson about themselves neither would ever forget, agrees: "Despite all his other remarkable accomplishments, his salvaging of that company, with real big sharks biting at his heels, was the first proof of the pudding. He rallied his people and he worked like hell, and it may have been his finest hour."

3 Starting at 90 Miles an Hour

THE OMENS were not good as Ted Turner, age twenty-seven, headed out of the protected harbor at St. George's, Bermuda, toward the starting line of his first transatlantic race. The crew of six, looking forward—if that is the phrase—to several weeks on the North Atlantic in a 38-foot sailboat, felt more than the normal prerace queasiness in their stomachs. The ocean was welcoming them with a gale, and they were already hanging on for their lives as the small sloop pitched, yawed, plunged and rolled in the steep chop that stumbled against the island's flank. Turner shouted orders this way and that, keyed up as always by the ritual of finding the starting line, eluding the sharp bows of his fellow contestants, and keeping track of the progression of signals that would set the fleet on its way. The wind howled at 40 knots, gusting to 50, and the flying spray quickly washed away memories of the pretty island now roaring by to starboard, where just the day before tiny automobiles had shuttled sailors from party to party amid the wild philodendrons and lime trees. Now the time of combat had returned, and even the largest yachts had stripped for action with sails reefed and hatches dogged tightly against the storm. Aboard *Vamp X,* Turner's first ocean racer, each man tried to imagine what the next weeks would be like.

None was greatly experienced offshore, but *Vamp* (named to honor Hard-Hearted Hannah, the Vamp of Savannah) had been an instantly successful boat. Turner had surprised the yachting world the previous winter by coming out overall winner in the Southern Ocean Racing Circuit off Florida, the world series of blue-water sailboat racing. In the 650-mile race from Newport, Rhode Island, that had brought *Vamp* to Bermuda, Turner had placed a respectable ninth overall. The fast-talking dinghy sailor was already holding his own against the big boys—and now he was out to prove he could do it for 3,600 nautical miles.

"I was still learning," Turner recalls. "And I sure learned fast on that one. I had Jimmy Brown along, who's only got one good arm to start with. The navigator was old John Tuzo, a ship's captain who had a club foot. A lot went wrong. We ran out of everything."

Vamp X took off across the line heeled over on her ear, and within hours the crew was soaking wet, as were their quarters below. Gales are to be expected in the North Atlantic, but it is not particularly cheering to have one blowing at the start. Once wet, never dry, the saying goes.

Skip Ryder, now a partner in Gulfstream Yachts of Miami, was on the first watch. His father and uncle had founded Ryder Trucking, but he and Turner had met on the dinghy racing circuit. It had been at a regatta in which he placed first and Turner last, with the result that Turner bought his boat—cash, on the spot.

"The sea in the Bermuda channel was really in a rage," Ryder says. "We were afraid the whole race would be extremely rough. The first night I had just left the helm and gone up on the rail when a gigantic wave broke on us, submerging the whole boat about 3 feet. I was washed right all the way back to the cockpit, and for a minute we thought we were sunk. Everybody's eyes got real wide, including Turner's."

The race was to end in Copenhagen, so the fleet headed north on the Great Circle route, just skirting the iceberg lanes. It began to be cooler, and with a change in wind, the powerful spinnaker, an intractable, parachute-shaped sail, was set. Ryder's recollection of the spinnaker run tends to be hazy.

"Well, we had to jibe the thing, which means you change the pole that holds it up from one side of the boat to the other, and just as we were doing that a squall line came through. As the pole was released it came forward and conked me pretty good on the head. One of the other guys ran up on the foredeck and grabbed me or I would've been overboard for sure. I finished what I was doing. Then I went into convulsions. We contacted a ship by radio, and they were going to come evacuate me. Turner told the ship, 'Don't bother, we're just going to bury him at sea.' But I was OK after a few days."

Jimmy Brown's duties on the boat were officially cooking and maintenance, but as always he was able to fill in wherever needed. "After he got hit, Skip couldn't really work anymore, and it started to get real cold," Brown says. "There was ice forming everywhere, and we had to chip it off. It was real chilly down below, because a fiberglass boat doesn't hold any heat. Everything got real hectic—know what I'm talkin' about? Mr. Ted kept having to go up the mast all the time to fix things. We had this conference in the cockpit and there was quite a debate about who would go up. Everybody said not me, not me."

"So we hauled Ted to the top of the mast—several times," Ryder says. "It was blowing pretty hard and the waves were big. Once I was steering, just trying to keep the boat steady for Turner while he was working up there, and when he finished we lowered him down. Just then I lost control and we broached right around. Lucky for me we got him down first. We were going so fast there was a rooster tail in our wake half the time, just like a motorboat's."

By midpoint in the race, radio reports had *Vamp X* leading the entire fleet. Turner, elated, was pushing even harder. "We broke the tiller off too, and Jimmy and I tried to get the spare one on but it wouldn't fit. So we were steering with a tiller held on by a whole bunch of C-clamps. And we started running out of water."

This gave Jimmy Brown, as designated cook, something of a problem. "Well, Mr. Ted didn't want to carry a lot of canned stuff on board on account of the weight, so mostly what we had was this dehydrated food. You had to mix it with water. But after it looked like we would have a lot of wind all through the race, he ordered everybody to take a shower to lighten the boat. Then the wind died and we only had a gallon of water left. I had to mix the dehydrated food with seawater—know what I'm talkin' about? It tasted horrible. Mr. Ted made everybody eat it, but it just made you thirstier still."

The main boom broke and had to be jury-rigged, and the constant chafe of the long voyage kept Jimmy Brown busy repairing sails and gear. With Ryder weakened by his concussion, the navigator busy with his charts and other members of the crew laid low by seasickness, Turner had plenty to occupy his time. He stood many watches alone. He was repeatedly hauled to the masthead to re-reeve broken halyards. He clambered forward himself to change headsails, rather than risk losing a moment's advantage to his rivals, unseen over the horizon. There were a dozen good reasons to slow down, shorten sail, take it easier, but he ignored all of them for twenty days. "Mr. Ted likes to win," explains Jimmy Brown. "No way he likes being a loser."

When *Vamp*'s crew finally arrived in Copenhagen, numb with exhaustion and salty as anchovies in brine, it was as winner of their class. Skip Ryder's X-rays showed his concussion was healing well. And it was forty-eight hours before *Vamp*'s nearest competitor crossed the finish line.

"I was really whizzing along in those days," Turner says. "At home, I just went out and started buying more and more billboard companies. It was great, it really was. I started out at ninety miles an hour. I was doing more sailing than anybody else, and two years after I took over the company I won the Flying Dutchman class North American Championships in Montreal. A year later I chartered my first ocean racer for the Florida races, and a year later I bought *Vamp X* and won. Then we raced to Bermuda, then transatlantic, and I owned a 5.5-meter boat too, so I stayed in Denmark for the world championships in 5.5s. I owned three or four boats at the same time and I traveled all over the world looking for the best competition I could find. I was learning all the time. I mean, nobody could stop me."

Stop him? Few could keep up, and even following was difficult. As one medium-close observer said of those days, "The way Turner was zigging and zagging, it would have broken a snake's back to follow his wake."

The 90-mile-an-hour pace had already cost him his first marriage. It had been a marriage made on the water. Ted Turner had met Judy Nye at a college sailing regatta, where they were both competing in dinghies. She was the daughter of Harry Nye, one of the founders of Murphy & Nye Sailmakers, then as familiar a name in yachting as fiberglass is now. They were married when Turner was still in Savannah, and she went with him to his post in Macon and the billboard holdings there. Their children—Laura Lee and Teddy, who is Robert Edward Turner IV—are teenagers now.

"We were just a couple of kids when we got married," Turner says. "We didn't really know each other at all, and it sometimes happens that people aren't compatible. We just weren't. It was a joke a lot of the time. But there were some good times, as there always are. Judy is an excellent sailor, and together we won the Y-Flyer national championship. I thought that was really a great deal, to win as a husband-and-wife team. Because I was really nuts over sailing then, even nutsier than now. But we got divorced. About six months after I married Janie, Laura Lee and Teddy came to live with us."

Shortly after his father's death, Turner, finding himself a bachelor again, had moved with characteristic speed to remedy the situation. He appeared without warning in the life of Jane Smith of Birmingham, Alabama, a proper young lady of the South who had graduated from the University of Alabama with a degree in home economics and was stationed in Atlanta as a Delta Airlines stewardess. Miss Smith was quite unprepared for what happened next.

"We met at a party. It was Peter Dames who introduced us," Janie recalls. Her diminutive nickname has stuck, though it contradicts the formality of bearing that instantly identifies Jane Smith Turner on a yacht club dock, on the sidelines of a school playing field, or in the sprawling grandstands of Fulton County Stadium in Atlanta. Mrs. Turner is not now, nor has she ever been, an imitation of her husband. At first she wished mightily that he would settle for some imitation.

"I really didn't know what to expect at first," Janie says. "My impulse was to run as fast as I could the other way. In the first place, he was a divorced man, and I had been taught never to date a divorced man. I couldn't for the life of me see why he was interested anyhow, we were so different. And he came on so strong. He used to telephone me every day. He had this Ferrari car he drove, and every night he came to take me to dinner in the Ferrari.

"I thought, oh boy, this isn't for me. I thought he was crazy, you know? But there was no getting away, even though once I let the telephone ring all day long without taking it off the hook. I thought I'd never be able to make another phone call. He was really skinny then and boyish-looking, he didn't have the mustache yet. I thought he was, well, cute, but he already had two children and he was kind of ferocious. Always bragging about this and that, which I had been taught wasn't right. But my father liked him, and he never liked the other boys much. He said to me, 'Ted's the most amazing young man I've ever met.' "

Turner was very persistent. "He finally wore me down," Janie says, almost with a sigh. After the marriage, on June 2, 1964, Janie settled down in Atlanta with Laura Lee and Teddy. Jimmy Brown and Ted did not.

"When Ted was courting me, he was very bored with the office. He had the billboard companies going real well, and he used to sleep until ten-thirty or eleven o'clock in the morning. Sailing became everything. He would race every single weekend, and I always stayed on the shore and watched. I never sailed with him at all, and of course I didn't want to. My own babies came along one after another and I was left alone.

"I was miserable a lot of the time. Every chance I got I would load up the car with cribs and diapers and stuff and drive home to Birmingham. Three times Ted was away from home sailing over Christmas. One Christmas I was so pregnant I couldn't even go home and my parents couldn't come to Atlanta for some reason, and so I just stayed in Atlanta. I cried and cried.

"And I was always on call. After that first transatlantic race he telephoned from Denmark and I flew over to meet him. I had to wait for the phone to ring, because we never knew how long a race would take, or where they might end up. Rhett was just a tiny baby, so I left him with my mother and took off. We didn't even come right home. Ted had arranged to be in another regatta in Copenhagen, and we stayed for that. King Constantine of Greece was sailing—I remember his high boots and the wonderful jackets that he wore. Prince Juan Carlos of Spain was there for the races too, and King Olaf of Norway, who's a wonderful man. I guess you could say it was exciting."

It was from such transatlantic adventuring that Turner returned to the loosened-tie, don't-forget-your-friends world of the billboard business. He was a young man in search of romantic challenges in the strident commerce of outdoor advertising.

Billboarding has changed little in the ensuing years. Although neon is out of vogue, large highway signs are still either pasted up one strip at a time or hand-painted by artists trained to render graceful a 2-foot-long human nose or a 35-foot mustard-covered hot dog. Although Turner seldom visits the plant today, Turner Outdoor Advertising—an entity separate from the high-profile Turner Broadcasting System—still clatters along with the legendary robustness of American enterprise. Dames and McGinnis, who got on the train early, now have well-appointed offices with Jackson Pollock abstract art works on the walls. Secretaries are much in abundance in a busy visitors' lounge, where copies of *Business Week* and *Time* lie for perusal by businessmen waiting to contract for their names in lights. In the adjoining shop, however, the clang of channel iron is incessant as workers weld and bolt the standing structures for 24-by-48-foot boards requiring $60,000 in steel—before the sign itself is put on. Molds pop out smaller, plastic messages, to be backlit by electric bulbs for use on storefronts, service stations and pizza parlors. Elsewhere in the din, teams of painters, brushes in hand, oversee the Alice-like expansion of commercial images to ten and twenty times actual size.

While men move about steadily from station to station against the background screech of heavy machinery, pictorial artist Ed Gaines, brush in hand, is midway through the creation of a 30-foot-wide smile. His subject smiles brightly from a glossy color photograph 8 inches wide, stopped absurdly in the act of placing a piece of broccoli in her mouth. The observer witnessing her aggrandizement cannot but think of broccoli in a larger context.

"That's the idea, I guess," says Gaines.

Billboards still take root on remnants of land not useful for other purposes, such as odd slices left by freeways or divided otherwise by some right-of-way. Turner Outdoor Advertising is not actively in the real estate business, but may buy if a property seems likely to appreciate, and can bear a sign in the meantime. Contracts for the boards run from one month to three years, and new posters are pasted up monthly. The big painted boards, Ed Gaines's personal works of superscale art, are sold only by the year. Since superscale art has of late been much admired by the Warholian hordes of big-city art galleries, it may be that billboards now make an artistic statement not heretofore understood.

"Yeah?" says Dames, puffing his cigar. "Yeah," he adds.

In fact, on the wall near the painters' bench is another Jackson Pollock. Like the similar work hanging on Dames's office wall, it is an excellent example of the New York abstract expressionist school that flourished in the 1950s. This canvas, in the seemingly random drips and splotches of pigment that present themselves upon its surface, creates a color field which wonderfully illuminates the essential dread—yet capacity for love and hope—of twentieth-century man. An Australian museum paid $2 million for a similar Pollock not long ago.

"Lots more where that came from," Dames says. "It's the splash cloth from under the paint cans, and whenever we get a real pretty one we get it framed up."

Well-run billboard businesses still turn a smart profit today, helped along by a traditional tax depreciation advantage. If you buy an outdoor advertising company for $1 million, for example, its value can be depreciated over ten years at $100,000 a year free and clear. There may not be an abundance of glamour, but business is good, and there was actually a boom when cigarette ads were banned from television.

Billboards may be far in the background of the Turner empire now, but there was a time when he lived their every image, for it was through billboards that Turner himself first intended to become ten or twenty times larger than life. He did not, however, plan to devote all his time to that marketplace. On the contrary, he had a thousand ideas buzzing in his head, and to let them free he needed help. He was ready, as chairman of the board, to delegate some authority. He took on a president.

The president's name was Jim Roddy, and he and Roddy disagree by only an adjective about the outcome of this noble executive experiment.

"It was a complete disaster," says Roddy.

"It was total disaster," says Turner.

Roddy was president of the Media Group of the Rollins Company when Turner hired him away to be president of Turner Communications Corporation. At Rollins, Roddy had been in charge of outdoor advertising, radio, TV and cable TV, and his group had grossed $45 million the year he left. He was charming, he had the competitive streak necessary to foment corporate action, and he was known as a brilliant administrator. He and Turner remain friends today. In fact, when his employees made a satirical film in honor of Turner's fortieth birthday, it was Roddy who played the lead—as The Brat Who Ate Atlanta.

"The first thing I learned about Ted," Roddy says, "was that he was very, very bright in addition to being completely wacko. I'm more conservative. I like to have the bills paid, money in the bank, and the planning done for next year. But Ted can't stand a nest egg; he's been a plunger from the beginning. We're both competitive guys, with strong personalities, I guess, and right away we began competing. He used to introduce me, wherever we went, as his 'first and last president.' He did it for years. Ted as an idea man is one of the most innovative people alive. But he's not an administrator at all, he's a free-thinker with extraordinary business judgment. But off we went, anyhow."

By the time Roddy signed on, Turner Outdoor Advertising was out of its desperate period and its owner was looking with interest at a new medium, where the billboard talked. Radio!

"Hell, after about four years in the outdoor business, during which time I was racing my boats most of the time, I could have retired," Turner says. "We had a lot of fun, getting up at five o'clock in the morning to go out and put up a new sign before traffic got too bad. We were like Michelangelo painting the Sistine Chapel, except you could stand up—you didn't have to lie on your back. One night we were painting this 48-foot billboard of the Coppertone girl, and the guys forgot to put on her bikini. It was a work of art—the chest and the crotch were perfect. I always regretted making them put the bikini back on before she hit the street. But after a while I felt the billboard industry had matured, and you always have to move ahead."

When Turner heard that a radio station in Chattanooga was up for sale, he gathered Roddy and McGinnis and off they went in a car. McGinnis shakes his head at what happened next.

"This station was kind of down and out, but that made it cheap, and besides, it was in the town where Ted had gone to school, and he really wanted it. It was going to be his first radio station. So we looked it over with the owners and we played it cagey, like we weren't that interested, and said we'd make them an offer the next day. On the way home in the car, we figured we had it for sure. But before we were thirty minutes down the road another buyer came in, made them an offer, and they accepted.

"When Turner heard, he was furious. He really likes to get his own way, and he'll do a lot to get it. So he called up the new owner and insisted on buying it from him. We wound up having to come up with another $300,000, and keep some people on the payroll, and there was a stock deal too. It really cost us two or three extra ways. Ted learned a lesson from that. Now he just decides on the spot."

This was not exactly the way Jim Roddy was used to doing business. He did not mind being in the fast current, but he kept seeing signs that said "Waterfall Ahead."

"The radio station we bought in Chattanooga was the worst radio station in America," Roddy says. "I believe it was last in its market in every way. We had to change everything. In radio, if the public is confused about you or if you stink, you just change the call letters and reappear as a brand-new station. The phenomenon is that radio is known by call letters, whereas people always remember TV by channel number. But nobody remembered this station at all. The idea in radio is to program your station on the basis of what isn't being done by somebody else, or isn't being done well. If there is no disco station, or good music station, there you go. If all the spots are filled, then you program against whoever has the weakest signal or who does the poorest job.

"When we got Chattanooga, it had no format whatsoever. Zero format. I mean, breakfast time there were these two people who said good morning to each other and then there was nothing else to say. Really. After that came a preacher who opened envelopes from listeners and you could hear the coins dropping out on the table. That show had live music—a bass, a piano and a bugle right there in the studio the whole time. Then these two weird guys who were inseparable at all times, so much so that you got them both for the same contract, played albums until six o'clock. That was followed, and I'm not kidding, by a teenager with a nasal condition who played rock albums from his own collection at home.

"The station was really something. The manager loved golf. You ever hear of a radio station covering golf? This station, I mean they covered golf. Live. On radio.

"So we changed right away to a Top 40 format, and brought in young announcers with good voices, and it was all right," Roddy says, relief still evident in his voice after many years.

To Turner, of course, the adventure made perfect sense. Once he has figured something out, the rest is easy.

"One reason I wanted the station in Chattanooga so much was that I also owned the billboards there. See, I could take my vacant signs and promote my radio station. One of the things that was wrong with the billboard business was that although we had a 25 percent profit, we would also have 25 percent of our signs not being used. It seemed like an awful waste to have any unsold signs, because you have to do the upkeep on them anyway. It's not like a newspaper, where if you don't get ads you can cut the number of pages. So I would put up my own radio ads on the open billboards, and use them that way. It doesn't sound too brilliant, but it worked. I got the idea from an oil refinery. It had an open flame on top. That heat was being lost uselessly, and I wondered why they didn't put it under the cooker and make oil with it. It's fire, right? At least put it under a coffee pot. That bothered the hell out of me, believe it or not, that little wasted flame. You really have to be dumb to waste your resources, because you've only got so much."

Once Turner figured that out, there was hardly a billboard or a radio station in the South that could rest easy. By the time he was thirty he had bought or merged five broadcast companies: two in Charleston, one in Jacksonville, and two in Chattanooga. He also owned outdoor advertising firms—each an effective monopoly in its market—in Atlanta, Charleston, Chattanooga, Covington (Kentucky), Norfolk and Richmond.

Turner had come to put great faith in the value of momentum. He noticed that in sailboat racing, the early leader often built up an insurmountable margin; that a second billboard company was easier to acquire than the first; that four radio stations begged a fifth; that a pretty girl on each arm begat one more to open the door of the taxicab. There was magic in movement; it made an airstream that sucked everything with it. The danger was inertia, the force that kept his opponents rooted to the earth as he sped by.

As long as he kept moving, he was safe.

Dick McGinnis was amazed at how Turner kept up the pace, caroming off the walls as he did. He would react to many challenges by firing the first shot, then declaring war. "You know, you expect to hear a little skirmishing before all the troops are committed," McGinnis says. "But with Turner it's boom all at once. Business can be a pretty conservative card game at the levels he plays, but Ted's a damn maverick, and that's what they can't figure."

Once a billboard baron from Greenville, North Carolina, apparently assuming that Turner was so consumed with sailboats as to lose interest in his Charleston signs, made an incursion into Turner's turf there.

"Oh boy, was Ted mad," says McGinnis. "But the way he saw it, if the other guy was trying to cut into the action in Charleston, he must not be busy enough in his home town. Because if he was busy, see, he wouldn't be fooling around in Charleston. So we sent some guys to keep him busy. Actually, we sent an armada of Turner people and trucks to Greenville, and we built a whole bunch of billboards overnight. It was a lightning attack, and it brought the guy to his knees. Bang, he went down. We ended up selling him, at a premium price, all the boards we built in Greenville, and got from him everything he'd put up in Charleston."

Turner seemed always willing to press to the limit. He would change the premise being debated, he would strike without warning, he would lay secret, fatal traps for the unwary or the weak at heart.

It was not easy being his lawyer, but Tench Coxe still enjoys it. "A lot of times back then, we sort of went to the edge," he says, "but Ted never wanted to be involved in anything that wasn't fair game. Once we were going to buy an outdoor plant in Knoxville that was in bankruptcy, so you had to submit sealed bids. You put in for, say, $100,000, then waited to see if you got it. I got a call from our representative there, who said, 'I think they will tell us the other bids. Should I try?' So we had to decide whether to play along. Maybe someone was just $5,000 over us and it would help to know that. We felt we had to transmit this information to Ted, and so I did. He just said, 'Let it lie.' You know, Ted is very concerned with having a long-lasting influence. He will risk a lot, but not his reputation."

Drawing the line is not easy for Turner, who occasionally feels helpless when confronted by himself. "Yeah," he says, "I always tend to overdo things. Like I buy too much land all at once, or too many radio stations, and too many sailboats, until even I can't keep track. There's not much I can do about it. I manage to exercise just enough good judgment that I don't totally bury myself. But by normal people's standards I would be, what do you call it?"

An overachiever.

"Yeah, that's it, one of those guys who overachieves to the point where you wonder if it's good sense."

At an advertising conference in Richmond, in the 1960s, Dick McGinnis told Turner he had been a high school sprinter. Within moments they were standing in the middle of Broad Street right in front of the Holiday Inn, coats off, ready to find out who was faster.

"He did to me what he does to a lot of people," McGinnis says. "He proved he was a better salesman. And I'm pretty good. I said, 'Let's race to the corner, for $10.' He said, 'Nah, that's too close, let's continue on to the drugstore.' Well, I beat him to the corner, but by the time we hit the drugstore he was ahead, and he took my 10 bucks. That's a simple little story, but let me tell you, that story's been told in some boardrooms. Because people know that Turner has won a lot of races by sticking people into a higher-stakes game than they wanted to play."

Sometimes the greatest challenge of the people around Turner has been talking down the stakes a little so no one would get hurt—Turner included.

It came to pass that Turner was sailing in Florida one winter and called the office between races to receive some shocking news: Coca-Cola, a wellspring of economic life in Atlanta, had unveiled a new marketing strategy, and it all but excluded billboard advertising. Turner immediately got on the phone and was told that Coca-Cola had found outdoor advertising not as effective as it once was. Despite an impassioned long-distance argument, Turner lost. It was a big account to lose.

"Now at this same time," a Turner executive recalls, "there was also a rumor that Coca-Cola was moving out. They were going to pull out of Atlanta and go to New York, and the papers were making a big deal out of it, and Coke was being kind of mum on the issue. About a day went by and Ted called back again. He had been thinking about it all, and he had an idea. He ordered us to make up a hundred billboard posters right away to read, 'Goodbye, Coca-Cola, We'll Miss You,' and he wanted them put up within forty-eight hours. 'All the stockholders and the public will see them,' Turner told me, 'and their phones will ring off the hook. Then they'll know people read billboards.' "

Dick McGinnis, hearing of this plan in a late-night phone call, immediately called Tench Coxe at the law firm, who had visions of a lawsuit to end all lawsuits. The one hundred posters were half made up when Turner called back and said forget it.

"It came even closer during the 1974 oil embargo," McGinnis says. "Ted was so mad he made me print up a hundred posters which said, 'Arab Oil—Buy It, Or Take It.' We came within two hours of putting them up that time."

Such will-he-do-it episodes were part of the fabric of everyday life for Turner's employees and friends, who came to accept their antic leader as a man who needed them every bit as much as he said he did. He was in many ways a spectacular contradiction of likelihoods. The merger plans and purchase agreements he conceived were brilliant, often expanding his holdings without any actual cash outlay at all. But he signed contracts without reading them. His vanity was substantial, yet his personal wardrobe—random neckties, ill-fitting jackets and high-water slacks—often gave the appearance of an orphan on the first day of school. He was disconcertingly young-old, the bright-eyed leer capped with a head of hair that had been yielding to gray since his teenage years. He cultivated people skillfully, but often felt obliged to add—in all honesty—that in some other respects his listener was a "dummy," a "numbnuts," or worse. The stupefaction factor was high. People walked away waiting for Alan Funt to interrupt and say, "Smile, you're on *Candid Camera.*" But there was never any Funt.

"Ted is extremely open with people, and it goes both ways," one old friend mused. "He will tell you anything about himself, and that vulnerability is his charm. But nobody has figured out to this day whether Ted really trusts him or not. When somebody lets him down, it really wounds him, and he's been burned more than once by people. He seems to accuse all his friends equally when that happens, it hurts him so much."

"We had a guy one time abused a credit card," McGinnis says. "Bought himself a boat and hid the purchase in the company, and got caught. Turner loved this guy, and it broke his heart. Another Trojan horse came down the road later, and this horse took him too. He set up his own business while on our payroll, and channeled business to himself. That was real bad. A guy up in Virginia did almost the same thing. All in all, a half-dozen bad characters have come in and taken advantage of Ted. He's basically an extremely honest guy, and when someone else isn't, he can be a sucker and a mark."

These offenses against him were not lost on Turner, and years later—after hearing about the increased use of lie detectors by corporations from a seatmate on a plane—a memo circulated at Turner Corporation. It assigned each employee a time at which to appear at a designated office, and when they appeared, they found a man with a polygraph. One employee who followed the instructions was R. T. Williams, a 6-foot-3-inch television producer who would later play a key role in Turner's bid for TV network status. Williams was a card-carrying member of Turner's "creative team," as opposed to his more buttoned-up corporate players, and his emotional reaction time was as short then as it is now.

"When I saw what it was I was really pissed," Williams said. "Jesus Christ, Ted and I were friends and I had to take the lie-detector test too. We all did. You sat facing the wall. The polygraph operator sat down behind me so I couldn't see him. He asked me my name, and where I worked and so on, and then a bunch of questions. One of them was, 'Did you ever misuse company funds?' Well, this was right after I had gone on vacation and done some work for another company. So when the session was over the operator goes back to the question. He says, 'Hey, when I asked you if you ever misused company funds, the machine went up.' So I really blew. I started shouting and everything.

"The next day Turner called me in, and I figured he was going to apologize because I was so mad. I had phoned his secretary right after the test and threatened to quit and yelled a lot.

"So I get in Turner's office and he says, 'Hey, R.T., how come the lie detector went off when they asked if you misused company funds?' I was just about crazy. At first I wanted to strangle him, and then all I could do was shrug. I didn't feel like screaming anymore. We had been through so much together and here he was making me take the lie detector."

Some of the greatest strains imposed by Turner on his associates, however, came not in the office but on the water. It was on the water—pond, lake, river or sea—that the Turner competitiveness was set free to soar to its own height, and at first he took the fellows from the office along. That does not happen so much anymore. Ted Turner has always yelled a bit on his boats. He also yells a bit in the office. The twain have learned not to meet very often.

Jim Roddy used to crew occasionally on the Y-Flyer. One day he and Turner were in a light-air race on Lake Altoona in Atlanta, with the summer sun burning down and the wind shifting unpredictably in 50-degree increments. "We were both totally frustrated," Roddy says. "He was mad and I was ready to kill somebody, and a Y-Flyer is a pretty small boat. So we finally win the race, and as we cross the finish line Turner stands up, and I stand up. I thought, Jesus, we're finally going to slug it out. Ted just stuck out his hand and said, 'Nice race.' But sailing with Ted did not make working with him any easier."

Sailing and business not only met but actually merged when Turner met a young man from Texas named Andy Green. They were both at Sebring, the automobile track in Florida. Turner was considering an all-out plunge into racing sports cars, and Green, a veteran of the aircraft industry, was building Chaparral race cars and sailboats on the side. Turner decided to combine business and pleasure.

By stock mergers he obtained a controlling interest in PlasTrend, Green's boat works in Fort Worth.

Both men had their eye on entering the Olympics in the Flying Dutchman class. The FD is an extraordinarily demanding 21-foot dinghy, traditionally the weapon chosen by the world's most skillful small-boat sailors. Turner and Green, by manufacturing their own boats for fun and profit, figured to have an edge.

"Between the two of us we came up with an entirely new kind of boat," Green says. "It had a hull made out of aluminum only 12 mils thick, over a balsa-wood core. The aluminum was so thin you could cut it with a pair of scissors. We built only one boat that way—for Ted and me. It wasn't too practical, because in salt water aluminum doesn't last very long, and if we left it in the water it would corrode right through. But we didn't care."

Green and Turner won the North American championships together, but when they went to the pre-Olympic trials in Acapulco it was a different story. Green remembers fouling out of four of the seven races in the series. "We did everything bad you could—we hit other boats, we hit a mark, we screwed up the start. But Ted loved to compete, and he was actually a better loser than a winner. He'd congratulate everybody when he lost, but if we killed them he really rubbed their noses in it. On the other hand, he would do anything. When I met him he was already rich, and I had always campaigned in an old station wagon. He said, 'If you can do it, I can,' and off we went on a thirty-hour ride from Fort Worth to some regatta."

PlasTrend built racing sailboats from 14 to 32 feet long, and although it showed little profit, the company had an excellent record for workmanship and innovation. But eventually even Turner grew tired of the technological side of the struggle.

"Oh God, it just got to be ridiculous," he says. "Britton Chance—a naval architect who I was friendly with at the time—convinced me that we had to drill about a hundred tiny holes in the front of one of our boats. Then we could attach a little spaghetti tube to each one and pump this stuff called polymers into the water. It was supposed to make you go faster. We would sort of ooze our way to victory on a carpet of polymers. So we actually put all this garbage in a 5.5-meter named *Nemesis,* along with a hydraulic pump to ooze the stuff out of the tubes. I was disgusted. It was a completely asinine plan. Totally idiotic. We never even used it once. Right after that they passed a racing rule that said, 'You shall not eject polymers.' The year after that Chance came back with a plan using a bunch of wires and stuff to move the mast sideways while racing, and I vetoed him right away."

Turner did not want to ooze polymers, he wanted to become the world's most famous sailboat racer. He sold *Vamp X* and ordered a new ocean racer built. When the new one was not completed in time for the winter races in Florida that year, he chartered a famous yacht named *Bolero,* got together a crew, and appeared in Oyster Bay, New York, in December expecting to sail south. It was 4 degrees, and the harbor was frozen in 10 inches of ice. Turner was in a hurry, so he chartered an oceangoing tug to break a path to open water. The night before they were to leave, *Bolero* sank at the dock. The crew pumped her out and they left anyway.

"Well, there was still a lot I didn't know. Everybody said it was very dangerous to go out in the Atlantic in December, but how else could we make the races? I was on board because I couldn't get anybody else to sail it. We had a hard time getting insurance, and finally wound up with Lloyd's of London. I assumed the boat was in good condition when I chartered it, and that was my big mistake. I didn't check it out personally. And I paid for that the hard way."

The first thing the crew learned was that this enormous yacht, much larger than anyone on board had ever sailed, leaked. The next thing they learned was that the bilge pumps did not work. This lesson came as a winter gale struck them off Cape Hatteras, the legendary North Carolina shoal that has claimed hundreds of ships and lives. It was so cold that ice formed on the foul-weather gear of the on-deck watch. The men formed bucket brigades. The mainsail blew out. The engine, switched on as the breaking seas of the cape appeared on the horizon to leeward, would run for a few seconds, then die. Diagnosis: debris in the fuel tanks. Solution: none. Turner radioed an SOS to the Coast Guard at Morehead City. A tanker was diverted to their position, and stood by, waiting.

Jimmy Brown was on board, as always. "This big old tanker came over and got up next to us and let down a cargo net over the side—

you know what I'm talking about? We were supposed to save ourselves anyhow we could. We had a couple of greenies on board, and they were sick. A couple of men had been washed overboard, only they were caught by their safety harnesses. We got about 300 yards from the breakers at one point, but the wind was blowing diagonally and Mr. Ted said, 'Hang on, we'll make it.' We never got any closer than that."

When the gale subsided, *Bolero* was towed into Morehead City. Turner announced that one day would be allowed for drying out and general recovery. Teams were assigned to repair damage and clean up the yacht. The next day they were off again, in time to make the first race of the Southern Ocean Racing Circuit of 1968.

If the yachting establishment thought it was crazy to sail the ocean in winter, they also thought it was crazy to go anywhere offshore in a 12-meter—the class in which the America's Cup battle is fought over mere 25-mile courses. (The 12-meter designation is not a simple indication of the length of the boat but is based on an elaborate formula that includes a number of other factors as well; most 12-meter boats are at least 60 feet long.) But Turner's next boat was a 12-meter, all right: *American Eagle.* He sailed her south too, leaving New Bedford in January of the next year—no problem. He raced in the SORC, and broke the mast off. The year after that *Eagle* won first place overall.

But by that time the days when Jimmy Brown would be dispatched to outdrink other crew members and extract yachting secrets ("Mr. Ted! Mr. Ted! They use a thing called a boom vang to hold down the sail!") were over. His pickup crews, previously "inadequate" by his own description, were replaced by loyal, self-sorted veterans. He had learned racing by taking chances and making mistakes. The mistakes became fewer and fewer, and by 1970 he had been named Yachtsman of the Year.

Meanwhile, back in Atlanta, a job opening seemed to have developed. Wanted: Dashing, high-energy executive to direct day-to-day operations of six billboard companies and five radio stations. Jim Roddy thought he'd been brought in to do it, but had learned that wasn't Turner's way. "No, he has to do it himself. He was always off sailing in Acapulco or someplace, and then coming back and complaining how hot and miserable it had been there. He would launch a whole bunch of new projects and then disappear, and when he'd return he'd start yelling that things weren't being done right. He may be a genius, but he's also the least sensitive person I've ever known."

Turner was at a dangerously restless point in his business life in the late 1960s. His string of billboard companies was generating an excellent cash flow, and he had the chips to play any sailing game he chose. Yet he admitted to friends that radio just didn't excite him. And in fact, none of the stations he had acquired was a rousing success. PlasTrend, the boat company, was losing $100,000 a year. Several of his smaller projects—a commercial silkscreening company, a direct-marketing enterprise—had flopped. But in general, the empire was beset with success and the attendant glorification of the status quo. Worse still, Turner's business associates began to look upon him as a young man who had already made his millions and was settling down to a life of leisure and absentee ownership.

Ted Turner was thirty years old, and he had become the billboard baron who knew who Leonidas was. The trouble was, as his father had predicted, that the other guys at the bar had never heard of Leonidas.

His wife Janie and his friends and partners could see the dark clouds forming. They knew that the calm is never Turner's time. Bring on the howling gale. It was a lesson not lost upon Dennis Conner, a former Turner shipmate and rival in the America's Cup trials of 1980.

"Ted's strong point is neither innate ability nor attention to detail and preparation—it is his enthusiastic competitiveness and leadership ability," Conner said in *No Excuse to Lose,* an autobiography written with John Rousmaniere. "He drives himself and his crew as hard as men can be pushed. This combativeness can be good some of the time and bad some of the time. Ted has a tendency to think only of the battle and not of the war. This may mean grinding down one opponent on a corner of the course while he forgets about the rest of the fleet. It may also mean steering for a dozen hours straight until he collapses from exhaustion. His kind of aggressive leadership works well when times are tough, but it can be counterproductive when things are going well."

Turner figured if he was going to fight anyway, he might as well start a more interesting war. He was bored with radio, but he wanted to become a public corporation and go big time. Big time, it occurred to him, would be television. In television he would again be an underdog, because he knew absolutely nothing about it. It would be fun to risk everything he had built, scare the hell out of everybody, and get back in the front seat of the roller coaster.

"As soon as I heard that a television station in Atlanta was for sale I got interested right away," Turner says. "Somebody told me it was an underground UHF station, but I didn't know what that meant. I had never watched the station because I couldn't even get it on my set. I never watched any television in those days. I had no idea what UHF stood for. But the owner had taken a billboard, and I read it on the board."

The TV station was WJRJ, Channel 17. There were five television stations in Atlanta at the time, and Channel 17 was dead last, a weak-signaled ultra-high-frequency enterprise with an undistinguished past and a less promising future. Most TV sets in those days were only capable of receiving Channels 2 through 13 anyway. UHF, in general, was considered to be on its way to the same graveyard in which the World Football League is now buried, and had even stimulated a bitter joke derived from its deleterious effect on a specific class of unlucky investors. UHF, they said, was a plot perpetrated by the Federal Communications Commission to bankrupt Jewish doctors.

Turner's stockholders had had about enough, too. They had been with him scheme after scheme, trying to keep up the pace, but now they were slowing to a walk and shaking their heads. Mazo, his father's friend and the son's chief economic adviser, saw disaster ahead.

"When Ted looked at Channel 17 it was owned by Rice Broadcasting. God almighty, the station was within thirty days of going off the air. Ted got the idea that he wanted to buy it. Well, I had been through one big crisis when he took back the billboard company from Bob Naegele, and I said I just couldn't take it another time. Jim Roddy was with me. He said, 'Why are we doing this?' It was just an atrocious business proposition.

"Tench Coxe, his lawyer, went to Turner with me at one point and we tried to make it clear that—yes—this thing might work, but if it doesn't everything will collapse. Everything you've got will be gone. We don't want to put it all on the line, because the result can't possibly be worth the risk. It wasn't just us, either. Everybody told him not to do it."

Turner was attracted to the risk, not repelled by it. He had conceived a plan whereby his company would merge with Rice Broadcasting, and be absorbed briefly by it. But since the absorption would then give Turner's people a majority vote in Rice, which was a publicly held corporation, they would immediately change the company name back to Turner Communications. Little or no cash would be required—for the no-down-payment plan was already the linchpin of Turner's theory and practice of acquisition. The value of the stock exchanged would be about $2 million or $3 million, whereas any other similar TV property would go for five times that amount.

There was one little hitch. Channel 17 was losing $600,000 a year. Unless its new owner could completely reverse this worsening trend, Ted Turner would lose everything—and his backers with him.

The day of the stockholders meeting brought a dozen tense businessmen together for a vote none of them could predict.

"It came right down to the wire," Tench Coxe recalls. "Nobody knew which way it would go, and Ted was lobbying hard, but he didn't know either. One of the directors who was skeptical of Channel 17 was Charles E. Smith from Charleston. The day we were to meet on this, Smith sent a wire, which was to be his proxy vote on the issue. The trouble was, the wire was garbled so badly that I couldn't read it. I tried to figure it out, but there was no way I could make out the sense. We attempted to get hold of Smith, but for some reason we couldn't. I think he may have been hospitalized at the time. So it got late, and we were all there, and I decided not to vote Smith at all.

"What the wire said, it turned out, was no. Don't buy Channel 17. If we'd known, it would have been enough to stop the whole thing right there."

"That's right," Turner says. "But it went through, and the first year I owned 17 we lost $900,000. Wow! But at the same time I found another station that I could get cheap, a UHF in Charlotte, North

Carolina, and I told the board of directors I wanted that too. They said, 'You got to be kidding.' So I said, 'OK, I'll buy it myself.' And I did, with my own money. That station was even more messed up than the one in Atlanta.

"After that Irwin Mazo resigned, and it's pretty tough when your own accountant quits because he thinks you're doomed. He had been a friend of my father's, but he just didn't think I was going to make it. In fact, he tried to organize a deal to get me thrown out as president. But I had 48 percent of the stock. I was down to that because of mergers. Later on I got back up to 87 percent.

"Irwin and the others thought I was crazy, and in all fairness it looked pretty dark there for a while. I had to actually go on the air in Charlotte and solicit loans from the viewers. I said it's a telethon—a telethon for me, because I need money to get the wolf away from the door. The wolf was breathing all over me. The telethon took in $35,000, just as gifts to us. But you know what? I paid all those people back within three years. If I ever need money in the future I know how to get it. I'll just go on TV and say, 'I'm Ted Turner and please send me some money. I promise to pay it back with interest.'"

The wolf, indeed, almost mauled him that year. "I had kind of overestimated the profits of the billboard companies, and they were making money just a little bit slower than the TV station was eating it. So I started selling stuff. I sold the smaller outdoor advertising companies, Macon and Charleston and Columbus and Richmond too, all the ones I had worked hard to get or keep. I ended up putting everything I could into television, to develop it and pay off the debts we'd inherited. It was a period when I came back from the storm off Cape Hatteras, and I had just as big a storm going on at home."

About this time a new vice president for finance signed on. His name was William S. Sanders, and he had done some sailing and had known Ted as a young man in Savannah, where his family was also in the outdoor advertising business. Sanders's vertically striped suits and businesslike gaze suggested a fellow who knew what end of the pencil was sharp, and the quality of sharpness has always been beloved by Turner. Though their styles were different, both men enjoyed the various games of skill that could be played with the score kept in dollars; but if Turner preferred poker, Sanders's game was contract bridge. They had much to offer each other, for while Turner was flamboyantly persuasive, Sanders was persuasively precise. And if the fire in Turner's eyes scared bankers to death, Sanders looked like a man you could reason with.

Will Sanders saw what Turner was up to. "Ted had seen that television was garnering a larger and larger share of the advertising-dollar pie. It was a powerful medium, it had a lot of appeal to the advertising community and the agencies. It was making inroads against newspaper advertising and it seemed to be the fastest-growing medium available. Channel 17 may have been a real loser when he bought it—and it did almost sink us—but the license itself would be very valuable if it could be made to work. In the meantime, the billboard company would just barely keep us afloat."

Sanders and Turner were to remain a high-powered investment team for nine years, but back then the new financial man had some straightening out to do in Turner's portfolio. One of the first things to go was PlasTrend, the boat company. "I said, 'Look, Ted, perhaps hobbies are getting in the way of business. This is a small-scale operation a thousand miles away in Fort Worth, and it will never be a major part of this company's future.' He didn't want to let go, but eventually the losses convinced him, and we arranged for a transfer of paper to get us out. One week before the signing the whole plant burned down, which added $400,000 to the loss. When we finally swapped paper I heaved a great sigh of relief."

The streamlining, and the hard-lining, continued. R.T. Williams, who was then producing commercials for Turner's new station, had a project for which he needed $212.50.

"Turner said, 'For what?' I said, 'For a roll of videotape, what do you care?'

" 'We're going broke, I can't afford it,' Turner said.

"I said, 'How can I make money without videotape to make commercials with?'

" 'Well, how about that stuff in the cellar that came with the station when we bought it?' The stuff in the cellar was piles and piles of old *Divorce Court* programs that Channel 17 had been showing, and Turner made me erase them and do our commercials on that horrible old brown used videotape."

Turner knew better than any of the others how close they were to drowning in the corporate sea. That winter he went hunting on the Eastern Shore of Maryland, a cold, gray and nearly deserted land of ducks, geese and Chesapeake estuaries. His host was an old friend, the owner of the Arnold C. Gay Yacht Yard in nearby Annapolis.

"We were out hunting and talking about various things," Gay says, "and suddenly Ted said, 'Uncle Arnie, will you give me a job?'

"I said, 'Sure Ted. You can always come to work in my yard.' He asked me if it would pay enough to support his wife and his children, and I said I guessed so. He thanked me. He said I'd restored his faith in himself. I guess he was having a rough time down there at home."

Atlanta had two, not one, UHF television stations that were in trouble at the time, and the staff of Channel 17 was as surprised as anyone when their rival went belly-up one day. Everybody said it was an enormous stroke of luck, but Turner announced that it was a great victory. He proclaimed that the other station had yielded to superior strength and prowess in battle. He even ordered up a "thank you, Atlanta" party on Channel 17, filling the studio with balloons, hiring a band and congratulating his viewers for their choice regarding which station was to survive. R.T. Williams produced the show, which was two hours long. After an hour and fifty minutes of aiming cameras at balloons, he walked out.

"We had nothing to put on. Nothing. Zip. Zero. I just put my audio man in command and took off. It was really embarrassing. Here another station had gone out of business, and Ted goes on the air to thank Atlanta. You got to have brass when you do that."

Channel 17 turned its first profit eighteen months after Turner bought it, setting what remains as a record for total reversal of fortunes in television. Channel 36 in Charlotte followed along a few years later, and was eventually purchased back from Turner by his own stockholders. Andy Green no longer builds boats. He has a new plant in Fort Worth, where he is president of Composite Technology, Inc., successful manufacturers of structures for use in highly corrosive industrial atmospheres. Irwin Mazo, Ed Turner's friend, is still living in Savannah. "You know how they say there's a genius behind every successful man?" he says. "Well, the only genius behind Ted is Ted." Jim Roddy is in the outdoor advertising business in Pittsburgh. He is a millionaire.

"You know," Roddy says, "Ted has actually asked me several times about returning to work for him again, and I would genuinely enjoy several of his current projects. But I'm not at all sure I could adapt. The last time he called I said, 'All right: What exactly would you have me doing? You want me maybe to run the baseball team?'

" 'Nah,' he says, 'that's . . . I keep an eye on that myself.'

" 'Well then, the basketball team?'

" 'Nah, I like to . . .'

" 'How about my taking on the TV station?'

" 'No, I want to keep my finger in that myself. . . .'

" 'All right, then should I run this new twenty-four-hour-a-day television news network you're starting?'

" 'Ah, that's an idea, but of course you understand I'll have to be deeply involved in that myself because it was my idea and . . .'

"The point is," Roddy says, "Ted has to be able to make his own mistakes. He doesn't need anybody else there to make them for him. He's like a center fielder who always goes in the wrong direction the first step, then sees where the ball really is and makes a spectacular catch. If anybody else tries to chase the same ball, there's going to be an awful collision."

4 Superstation Superman

HERE IS the Red Baron over New York. He has a firm grip on the controls, goggles down, silk scarf waving in the slipstream. On the well-patched fuselage a new marking has been added, dwarfing the row of victory silhouettes already there: THE SUPERSTATION. He drops one wing for a better look at the citadel glittering below, checks over his shoulder to confirm that his wing man is in place, and puts her into a dive toward Madison Avenue. From below, a solid wall of flak rises to meet him, seemingly impregnable. . . .

It is 7:45 A.M. and Ted Turner is striding down Central Park South to a breakfast appointment at the Essex House hotel. A dig-we-muster puts up his air hammer a moment to call, "How 'bout those Atlanta Braves!" Turner gives him the OK sign and does a little jig. He is semi-nattily attired in the same blue-checked sports coat and blue slacks of the day before, when he delivered, in the main dining room of a four hundred-room New Hampshire spa called Went-worth-by-the-Sea, the most colorful call to arms the gaping, delighted members of the New England Cable Television Association had ever heard. The blue clothes are while-you-wait replacements for his entire suit bag, left behind on some now-untraceable airplane. But Turner doesn't care about clothes; he is ebullient.

The mood is somewhat different in the King's Wharf restaurant at the Essex, where a dozen newly shaven businessmen are munching croissants and reading about the fall of Skylab and the imminence of recession. The only sound is the leafy rustle of *New York Times* pages being turned, until Turner appears in the window outside. Suddenly three loud reports startle the room, and every head turns toward the glass facing Central Park, upon which Turner is pounding gaily with his fist. What the hay! Let's start the day!

Turner wolfs down a quick breakfast, insisting as always that his credit card be taken simultaneously with the order so as to permit a quick departure. In a moment he spies Bill Ganley coming through the door, and heads him off there.

"You've already eaten."

"Uh, yeah, Ted, I already ate," Ganley says.

Ganley, a tall, studious advertising account executive, heads up the Superstation national sales office in the Gulf & Western Building at Columbia Plaza. He is himself an ace in the big-city ad agency budget wars, and will be Turner's wing man today. The first meeting has been set up for 9:00, with a "real important guy."

As a Checker cab bounds from pothole to pothole, he briefs his commander. "Now this guy is kind of set up against the superstation concept," Ganley says. "And he's a great zinger. He loves to throw the zinger at people. Now they already warned me—"

"I think I know this guy already," Turner says. "Sure I do, I already met him and we get along great."

"Well, they told me, they already let us know, that they don't want to be, uh, badgered today."

"Aw," Turner says, "I always have laughs with these agency guys. They really enjoy having me stop by." But Ganley is determined that Turner be briefed, and he keeps talking about just where the advertisers find fault with Superstation rates, about national penetration, about their misunderstanding of this new medium Turner has adopted and named, about how some people still don't know how the satellite works or how to sell soap and cereal and cars effectively with it. Ganley's soft yet confident delivery is all but lost, for Turner is simultaneously unloading on him a barrage of advice, correction, orders, questions and arguments. Ganley doesn't stop, because he knows: Turner is listening even while Turner is talking.

The important man is not yet at his office when Turner and Ganley arrive, disgorged by a crowded elevator to cool their heels in a modish eleventh-floor reception area.

Turner paces, Ganley sits.

"You got a phone here I could use?" Turner asks the receptionist.

"Not really," she says, filing her nails.

Ganley seems to be saying a silent prayer. God let him not have to wait, God let him not have to wait. Turner lights a cigar, the first of the day. He paces for two minutes. He looks at an array of magazines, not seeing them. In his head he is turning over powerful arguments, all of them clear proofs of why large national advertisers should expend significant portions of their budgets on his satellite-borne Atlanta television station, formerly, it is true, a sardine among mackerels but now the Medium of the Future. He believes these arguments with all his heart. And since there is as yet no one else to convince this morning, Turner, for the ten thousandth time, reconvinces himself.

"Boy!" he blurts out. "I just know we're going to make it, you know that? But where the hell is everybody? Damn! I shouldn't even make these calls. We ought to make them come to us." The receptionist, whose nasal membranes are in the path of the cigar smoke, wrinkles her nose.

Fifteen minutes later Turner and Ganley are ushered into the office of their appointed vice president, whose train from Long Island was late. His corner office has several deep brown velour sofa-chairs, TV trade magazines on the coffee table, pictures of his children on the wall, and a large desk with no papers on it. The vice president is about thirty-five, probably makes about $200,000 a year, and has the look of a man whose train has put him a half-hour behind schedule all day. He has barely gotten the lid off a Styrofoam coffee cup when Turner launches into his voice-over. The Superstation is the bright new future for advertisers, can't this agency see that? Don't they want to get in on the ground floor? Don't they care about innovation? Don't they see that ABC, CBS and NBC are dry husks of a dead age? Any questions?

"Ted . . ."

Turner grabs a Nielsen rating book off a shelf and pours forth a withering blast of numbers, showering the room with HUTS, shares, ratings, CUMs, CPMs, touching on HBO and SSS and ESPN, promising to deliver MEN 18-24, or if needed WOM 25-54 as well as any indie or net, and on Saturday morning he's got CHD 2-11 and fewer commercials. Fewer commercials! Turner's cigar glows red on the end, he is talking so fast. The jargon of television demographics and audience-delivery numbers continues, with the vice president, who has spilled coffee on his pants, missing none of it. He does appear to want to say something, however.

After fifteen minutes: "Ted, you said it wouldn't be a harangue this time."

After twenty minutes: "Ted, is this the harangue part coming up?" Ganley, who has been in this office many times, cannot get a word in either.

After twenty-five minutes, the media vice president, having had his presumed misconceptions about the Superstation corrected less and less gently as Turner's momentum increased, sees what is coming next. Deadpan, he observes:

"And now comes the part where you call me a dumb cluck."

For a split second the clock on the wall stops dead. Each of the players leans forward over his own knees. "Aw," Turner says, relaxing back into his chair and restarting the clock with his voice. "Come on, tell me the truth. You guys really like me. You got to like me a little, right?"

The vice president now talks, asking specific questions, precisely numbering the flaws in Turner's presentation as he sees them, calmly relating the hurdles the Superstation must clear for acceptance by the New York agencies. Turner's mouth springs open again, but before it can speak the vice president stands up.

"However," he says peremptorily. "However, Ted, you have sold me. You've got some wrinkles to work out, but all right, basically I'm sold." And to Ganley: "Now get him out of here."

Turner hits the street in a gallop, and is into a cab almost before the last member of his party is through the revolving door. The next agency is known to be more friendly, and in fact about to recommend that a major client, Crisco, buy time on the Superstation. One of Ganley's salesmen has about clinched the deal, it is thought. So this is a "setup" call. A laying on of hands. A bit of the old bedside manner.

The agency rep, Turner seems surprised to find, is a woman, blond and well informed, who has a corner office, too. She says she is thrilled to meet him. She has never met anyone this famous before.

Ahem. Turner allows as how winning the America's Cup was the achievement of a boyhood dream, how it is very stimulating to do battle with the networks, which are profit-crazed, whereas his Superstation does not intend to be enslaved by the ratings game. "I hear you're with us, and let me tell you, you're doing the right thing. You're going to make us happy and your people happy, and you're going to be known as foresighted, probably even brilliant, because of it. I mean, we're having so much success, it's a surprise almost to me." Any questions?

Well, yes. Is it true that the Superstation steals all its programming, and as a result cannot buy any more, and will therefore go down the toilet, so to speak, in the long run? Isn't he having a lot of trouble with program suppliers?

A stillness falls in the room. Turner seems to be ignoring the question. He sorts and scrabbles in his briefcase, looking for something, muttering incomprehensively. Ah! Here it is. A Kodak photograph.

"There!" he says triumphantly. "I'll bet you know who that is."

The woman takes the picture, raising her eyebrows in puzzlement, and scans it. "Um, yes. It looks like Norman Lear. And that's you, with him."

"It's down at my plantation," Turner explains. "It's right after he testified in front of Congress about whether my station was going to ruin *All in the Family*. Look at his face there, he's smiling, right? Doesn't he look like he's having a good time?"

Trouble with program suppliers? Here is photographic proof that Lear and Turner are pals. "Norman's top lawyer came to see me too, and they both like me fine."

Case closed. One other thing. This agency, with its Crisco ad on the Superstation, is a pioneer. Heads nod. "You're going to be glad, because I stand for something good. More diversity in programming for the American people, with less junk. For example, I can't stand things like Mr. Whipple squeezing the Charmin. Now, there is an offensive ad, insulting to me personally and to my family. They run it over and over again. We've just cut commercial time on our Superstation because too many commercials, let's face it, aren't good."

Turner has made all his points, touched the flesh, and things have gone well. But the blond account executive is going to say something else before he leaves. Ganley, closing his briefcase on his lap, already knows what it is.

"You know," she says in a tone devoid of clues, "Mr. Whipple was created by this agency. We made that ad campaign. Right here."

Next stop, the New York Yacht Club. Turner and Ganley breeze in through the door at exactly noon, since Turner has two meetings here, one with an adman whom he may hire, the other with Bill Donnelly, the vice president for electronic media of Young & Rubicam, perhaps the most powerful of all the agencies. This is the club that has borne the burden of the America's Cup for 129 years, and for the past few years of Ted Turner too. It is the Club He Would Never Be Able to Join and the Trophy He Would Never Have the Chance to Win. But he throws open the West 44th Street portal as if it were the screen door to the porch of his plantation. "There's the Cup over there," he says, cutting left into the Model Room, where his job applicant—whose boss at ABC thinks he's having lunch at Nedick's—waits nervously.

The Cup itself sits on a pedestal set on a vaulted landing carpeted in thick blue. It is a garish thing, a rococo sterling vessel three feet tall, but its presence fills the room. On sconces at the four quadrants close at hand, lesser trophies hover like courtiers about the queen. The trophy is inscribed:

100 Guinea Cup

Won

August 22, 1851, at Cowes

England

By Yacht America

at the

Royal Yacht Squadron Regatta

"Open to all Nations"

In smaller legend are listed by name and displacement the seven cutters and six schooners defeated in that race. As the years passed, however, the cup ran short of surface area, so that the contest of 1977, Ted Turner's contest, appears far at the base. Only the yachts are named, not their helmsmen. The trophy remains forever in this room, or at least until it is won by a foreign challenger—a day which the New York Yacht Club intends shall never come. If it does, it is said that the vacancy on the pedestal will be filled with the defeated skipper's head.

The model room is a brighter space, strewn with scale replicas of famous yachts, including fully rigged man-high reproductions of every defender from the original rough-and-ready schooner through the dinosaurlike J-boats, with their 160-foot masts and 2,000-pound mainsails, to the million-dollar 12-meter yachts of modern days. The oak floors creak as Turner's prospective account executive slips back to his network job, leaving Turner and Ganley to stroll chatting to the dining room one level below.

"You said he was a super jock, but he looks kind of small to me," Turner remarks.

"Twelve-letter man at Villanova," Ganley says.

"I like him, though. Turns out his family had a Cal 40, and they sailed it pretty good."

There are seven for luncheon, and the wizened serving personnel make a great, if understated, show of recognition for the Member. Heads nod to him from adjacent tables. It is never a difficult recognition: the thick head of silvery hair, rare on a man of forty; the Errol Flynn mustache; the slight gap that separates the well-formed incisors; the perfect dimple centered in the chin; the aggressive, probing glances this way and that. If there is any doubt, the voice removes it—a barely controlled shout, half-Southern in accent and slightly higher than expected. He is joined by Donnelly of Young & Rubicam, clearly a man to listen to.

When Turner decides to listen, he is a wonder to behold. The mouth seems clamped shut by sheer force of will, and the rugged profile bows slightly, as if in appreciation of his own sacrifice. He diddles with a fork, a cigar, he shifts in his seat. He murmurs to a seatmate, then shushes his reply. Turner has decided to let Donnelly talk, for he considers Donnelly a guru of Madison Avenue, and Y&R his ashram. Donnelly, a youngish fellow who seems to have developed his worldly air by practicing before a mirror, takes the opportunity for a long, chain-smoking discourse on the future of the Superstation. Along the way he tries to sell Turner on a medical program which Turner does not want. Finally, Turner says, "Look, I just don't want it. Period. I don't want it, I know all about it, now forget it. Don't mention it again." But he does not call Donnelly any outrageous names and he lets Donnelly keep on talking, smoking and theorizing before his mirror.

A few days later Maurine Christopher's column in *Advertising Age* began this way:

"If the country's largest and hottest ad agency has decided that WTCG, the Atlanta Superstation, makes marketing sense as a national media buy, will this be Ted Turner's breakthrough? Will other major agencies follow suit and buy the Turner notion of paying for widely scattered cable homes reached by satellite throughout America? We shall find out soon, apparently. Several Young & Rubicam–handled advertisers are due to run schedules on the pioneer RCA Satcom-distributed superstation."

Christopher, who went on to describe Donnelly as "the most cable-experienced agency exec in the U.S.," called Y&R's new willingness to do business with Turner "an intriguing bit of news." She was not quite able to fathom it, however: "Mr. Donnelly was secretive about who the purchases were for and how he got rid of his reservations about buying WTCG's satellite concept."

But there's nothing like lunch at the New York Yacht Club, especially if nobody calls you a dumb cluck.

Ted Turner's Channel 17 was the first Superstation, and he has copyrighted the name. His Superstation is a product of the technological revolution in communications, and although Turner has little understanding of the nuts-and-bolts world of space flight, he wrote the shop manual on drama and conflict. The Superstation promised both.

By the 1970s, satellites had begun to rise into the sky with businesslike predictability, riding atop rocket ships that roared and flamed and were gone in thirty seconds, arching off through the evening sky toward a downrange orbital window. Few were seen on national television, though the terse countdown and fiery lift-off made fine entertainment for Western Union or RCA guests invited to the traditional blast-off cocktail parties. Commerce often has a staying power that entertainment does not. The manned space program instituted by President Kennedy was a glamorous diversion until Americans actually got a look at the surface of the moon, declared it a bad buy in real estate and walked away. The businessmen stood their ground.

By the middle of the decade, the equatorial orbit adjacent to the United States was filled to capacity with communications satellites, small well-crafted spheres bristling with solar collectors and esoteric antennas. They hovered in space 22,300 miles high, occupying the only nine positions that could provide practical coverage of North America. Three of the "birds," as they were sometimes called, belonged to Canada; two were AT&T property, put there for telephone use. The two each that Western Union and RCA owned were intended for broadcasting.

These domestic satellites, fixed in stationary orbit in the frozen silence of outer space, had the effect of reinventing the communications wheel. They have turned out to be not a spin-off of the aerospace industry, but the industry itself.

Just one of them, RCA's Satcom I, makes Turner's Superstation possible. Satcom hovers over a point seldom visited by man—a bit of utterly vacant Pacific ocean 2,700 miles west of the Galapagos Islands, halfway along the equator to Christmas Island. It is from that lonely piece of sky that Turner's Superstation rains down, showering thirty-year-old movies, reruns of *All in the Family* and Atlanta's Braves in a microwave "footprint" that encompasses Honolulu, Juneau, Mexico City, Bangor and St. Croix in the Virgin Islands.

Before Satcom, the broadcast range of Channel 17 had been 45 miles on a good day. It could go farther only if relayed by another earthbound tower every 25 miles, or by expensive telephone landlines.

The satellite gave Channel 17 instant coverage of well over 10 million square miles. It is capable of doing the same for twenty-three other television or radio stations simultaneously.

The magic of satellite communication is its simplicity. Traditional television stations transmit signals to homes by microwaves, which are received by the rabbit ears atop the set or a larger antenna on the roof. If it rains, or a mountain or city building happens to be in the way, the transmission is washed out or doesn't get there at all. Such reception problems, in fact, led to the rise of cable television, known at first as CATV for Community Antenna Television. A big antenna would be built by investors in an area of poor reception, and a clear TV picture delivered to homes by coaxial cable. By building a series of relay towers, systems operators could coax a microwave 500 miles. But a lightning storm at the head of the string meant bad reception down the line, maintenance of the relay stations was high, and programming was in any case limited to broadcast sources.

The satellite is literally above all that. A TV signal beamed at it has escaped earthly interference even before it zips past the Concorde en route from France. The program is sent up by a powerful transmitter, captured by the satellite, and returned weakly to earth. But since it returns almost vertically through the atmosphere, there is little or no breakdown of the microwave, and the signal is easily collected by dish-shaped earth stations. There is no dispute as to its remarkable clarity.

Turner liked the sound of that. He could beam his signal up from Atlanta, and cover the nation. Cable television system operators were looking for new programming, and Channel 17 would be just that. The more Turner thought about it, the more he thought it could make a billion dollars. He had some company in optimism. Home Box Office, the first enterprise to offer movies at home by subscription, had beaten him to the satellite by a year, and was also relying on cable systems for delivery. HBO was charging its subscribers for the privilege, but Turner didn't think that would be necessary. Why not give Channel 17 away free?

Turner's motivation wasn't altruism, but hardball savvy. He wanted to be the Fourth Network. He wanted to take on the big fellows at their own game, one nobody else had so far been able to play because the ante was too high. He saw the networks as a Maginot

Line, impregnable to frontal assault, but vulnerable to attack from above. All he had to do was leapfrog the entire extant commercial communication system of America—ATT, the networks, and the six hundred broadcast stations that were the primary suppliers of TV programming to 75 million homes. He intended to do it with a $750,-000 earth-to-satellite transmitter and a $1 million contract for the use of RCA's Satcom.

ABC, NBC and CBS, the joint architects of the American video landscape, had long ago cast their lot with another delivery system— one which guaranteed control of American living rooms. Because of the 50-mile limitations of standard through-the-air TV signals, they had engaged the telephone company to install a huge land network of wires through which programming could be sent long distances to local broadcast stations, which would then make the final delivery to rooftop antennas. Of the seven hundred TV stations in the country, six hundred of them were "affiliated" with a network, promising to broadcast that network's programming in exchange for a piece of the large advertising revenues network shows could bring in.

It was a difficult game for anyone else to play, for the land-line rates were expensive: about 75 cents per mile per hour. The networks received a 90 percent discount, however, as a reward for their special status as heavy users. To compete with the networks on their own terms, a newcomer would have to ask the phone company to install approximately $15 million worth of equipment. The phone company would be glad to do it, if the fledgling network could promise a $50 million return in three years or so. But there wouldn't be many broadcast stations available as affiliates, and the chances of seducing the allies of lucrative CBS, NBC or ABC would be nil.

By the decade of the '70s the financial power of the Big Three was staggering. The United States had become a nation in which the seating arrangement of the living quarters of its citizens was dictated by the placement of the TV set. In the evening, Americans sat down and turned it on. By 7:30, during the winter viewing season, at least 70 million people would be watching on any given night. By 9:00, 100 million would be tuned in. At 11:00 P.M., despite protestations that "there's nothing on TV worth watching," 60 million people remained in thrall.

Into the lap of this seated nation the networks dump their advertisers' wares, paid at rates of up to hundreds of thousands of dollar per minute for the attention of the viewers. There is no competing with the networks. Public television is lucky to get 5 percent of the national audience, and independent stations are restricted by the local range of their signal.

The networks, in fact, have learned to do what they do exceedingly well. Television is only a wasteland for those who are left unsatisfied by heroical renderings of professional sports events, bouncy situation comedies, action-filled police melodramas, zany games, semi-existential talk shows and dramatic newscasts punctuated with colorful actuality footage voiced over by handsome announcers. Network executives do not see a wasteland when they look at the Nielsen ratings, they see a garden of profits. They understand that it is television itself that is the entertainment, not their programming; that no matter what is on during prime time, one-third of the American population will be watching. If the fare is objectionable, then the one-third will watch the least objectionable program. The great danger for networks is not in failing the public, but in failing to keep up with the competition. The object is to stay close, to be No More Objectionable. A pie cut in three slices can mean a big portion of dessert for all. And for the affiliates, each with a network to call its own, even the crumbs are rich.

A Superstation, however, has no affiliates. It has no protective web of land lines to protect it against upstart rivals. It exists in a fourth dimension, a twilight zone of power. To succeed, it must offer not Least Objectionable Programming, but Best Alternative Programming. It cannot march into the fray in red tunics, as the network armies do against each other, but must fight instead like the Minutemen of Concord, popping up from behind a wall to deliver a diversionary fusillade. A superstation has to be different, it has to be an alternative, for a simple reason. In place of the loyal affiliate of a network, it has a most fickle distributor: a local cable system. A superstation starts with the knowledge that it will eventually, if not immediately, have as many as thirty cable-fed competitors; and that the cable system owes its allegiance to none of them, only to its subscribers. To duplicate, therefore, is to die.

The battle lines between cable operators and broadcasters had been drawn years before. But Ted Turner, like Coriolanus, the Roman general who changed sides and led a foreign army against Rome, was the first broadcaster to turn mercilessly upon his old allies:

"What we've got here is a case of suppression of competition," he says, warming to a favorite subject. "The three networks are exactly alike; you couldn't tell them apart with a magnifying glass. The audiences know that, but after complaining bitterly about the garbage that's on, what can they do?

"Nobody admits it, but TV is really important in people's lives. For most people it used to be God, but television screwed that up. We went looking for God up there above the clouds and guess what—we didn't find him. What do you think we were looking for on the moon? Moon rocks? Hell no, we were looking for God, and we found out he wasn't there, the place is just a lifeless dried-out hunk of zip. But we did see something up there, and you know what it was? A television camera. Sure. Television loves me, this I know, for the TV tells me so.

"I'm not a religious man, at least I don't go to church much, but let me tell you the networks haven't worked out too good when it comes to being gods. When everybody sat down to listen, the networks preached to them with *Gilligan's Island* and Froot Loops. And they get converts at the age of six. By that time you know you have to get the King Kong doll from Mattel, and you learn your first song—a beer commercial. Instead of taking the opportunity to enlighten us, the networks decided instead to wring every dollar from us they could. What they found was that you could make the most money by getting as many viewers as possible and then selling them to the advertisers at a cost per thousand. People don't realize that it's viewers who are sold, not products. Talk about trading your birthright for a bowl of porridge . . . the networks sold humanity down the road for *The Gong Show.*

"So we've got *The Newlywed Game* and *Love Boat,* shows that are so terrible they intentionally give them names like that. These are unshows, like uncola—deliberately worse than the garbage they imitate. And it's hard to be worse than those other shows, so the unshows are a big success. They're a great accomplishment."

Turner happened to be driving his Toyota through the suburbs of Atlanta while delivering this analysis, and it was a good thing there was little traffic, because his attention to the road was inversely proportional to his attention to network failures. The car careered into the gravel shoulder and back out again.

"The whole lineup on ABC tonight is so bad I couldn't believe it. I saw the ads. They're presenting a two-hour show in which a school bus is attacked by truck drivers who have gone crazy, and somehow or other there are girls wearing bikinis all over the place. They are probably going to get a significant rating with that show, because there's not going to be anything any different on CBS and NBC. It's a conscious decision on the part of the network honchos, it's not some kind of accident. If you have a chance at half the audience you take it, and if you don't the stockholders will fire you and get somebody who will.

"The network system offers a great chance for leadership, and don't think we're not being led, and by the nose. Fred Silverman, the president of NBC, is a very successful leader. Sixty percent of the American people, the ones who are easily led, are following his course. They say Freddie Silverman really watches that stuff, and he probably thinks it's quality programming. But you got to remember that Hitler thought he was offering quality programming too; so did Napoleon. Believe me, an imperial wizard in the Ku Klux Klan really thinks he's performing a service to mankind."

Well, if the president of ABC is Napoleon, who is Turner?

"I'd like to be Charlemagne. I'd like to ride in on a white horse and save the world from the forces of evil."

But how is the programming on the Superstation, Channel 17 from Atlanta, that different? It's mostly just old movies and reruns of *Leave It to Beaver* and *I Love Lucy* and baseball games and basketball and soccer and preseason football. The news programs were for years literally a joke, a newscaster in a gorilla suit reading a story about a guerrilla attack. How can Channel 17 ever be a white horse?

"You missed the whole point, dummy! It's that I give them a choice. I break the monopoly. I give people a way out of the school bus attacked by truck drivers wearing bikinis. It ain't that hard, either, because you give people a choice between watching garbage or maybe a fine, classic movie and many people will watch the movie. At least *Leave It to Beaver* shows positive values in the family. With the Superstation, and the other cable channels you can get with the satellite, everybody can watch different things if they want. Free choice! That scares the networks to death, let me tell you. When we get that, ABC will shrink down to a puddle like the witch in *The Wizard of Oz*. They'll have to start serving the viewers again, and not just the people who sell soap."

Turner guided the car up the switchback grade to his house in the Georgia Hills, cruised into the garage and shut off his headlights. He sat in the dark for a second, savoring the image of mighty ABC dissolving and hearing the cheers as the network spell was lifted from the land. But the silence seemed to startle him.

"C'mon," Turner said, bounding to his door. "Let's grab a drink and watch the Flames game." His house, vintage 1972, is large and neat without being ostentatious. There are many like it in this subdivision of Marietta, about 20 miles from downtown Atlanta. Turner volunteers its value: $130,000. He got the house as part of a resettlement deal with a former employee, and some of the furniture in it came to him with his purchase of the Atlanta Braves.

"Janie honey!" he yelled, striding through the kitchen. "How's dinner going?"

"You're in a good mood," Janie said, looking up from a pan of seafood croquettes.

"That's because we're going to win. I'm sure of it!"

Janie nodded, not quite sure whether the victory was to be in baseball, the Southern Ocean Racing Circuit, the TV business or over the Organization of Petroleum Exporting Countries. Nor was she about to ask.

Turner greeted his younger sons, Rhett and Beau, who popped to attention as he approached. Had they been reading their books?

"Yes, sir."

"Yes, sir."

Daughter Jennie, soon to be ten, attacked from the rear, getting a good grip on his overcoat and spouting ideas for birthday presents as Turner's momentum carried both of them across the hallway floor. He entered a tiny den at the front of the house. It was suffused with the glow of three hundred sterling-silver sailing trophies reflecting the multicolor images of a geriatric console-model television set, turned on and blaring sound. The wrong sound, as it happened. The set was on Channel 50. The Superstation is Channel 17.

"Arrrgh!" Turner cried, his powerful voice filling the room. "It's not on 17. How come when I get home it's never on 17? How'm I going to get the entire nation to watch my Superstation if I can't even get my own family to watch it!" he thundered back into the now-empty hallway.

With a theatrical flourish, Turner himself changed the dial to Channel 17. As soon as the air was clear again Janie served supper in front of the set, and many of the serving vessels were yachting trophies. The house was littered with them, and since they have to be polished, she had decided they might as well be used. White wine was sipped from sterling goblets inscribed "Y-Flyer National Champion." When dinner was completed, Turner remained on the couch, his stocking feet tucked under him in an uncharacteristically vulnerable, almost feminine state of repose. By 9:20 P.M., as the Flames madly chased the puck back and forth across the screen, he had gone to bed.

Turner, despite his nonstop reputation, turns in early whenever he can. On his boats, he likes the off watch to get in their bunks and snore. "It's just basic," he says, "because you never know when you're going to have to stay awake for two days. You can work eighteen hours a day all you want, and screw around in your free time, but don't get worn down. Exhaustion you can see, and you can combat it with pride and toughness and whatever it takes. But there's also mental exhaustion, and that's harder to cope with. You can get it just from the pressure, the daily grind. I meet about a hundred new people in the course of every day, and that alone wears you down. I've learned to go to bed, it's that simple. Maybe you don't sleep, maybe you just lie there thinking. But it's preparation. If you're going out where there's storms, better get prepared."

There were plenty of storms in the first years of Turner's learning experience with television. His two nearly bankrupt stations had not got that way by accident, and there was plenty of work to do. The satellite revolution was still six years away.

One thing Turner knew was in his favor was that he was a one-man committee. So he made a one-man study of television. Experienced TV ad salesmen marveled at the grasp of ratings books—the data-crammed bibles which reveal what kinds of audiences watch what shows at what times—he acquired after one year. He could argue that *Leave It to Beaver,* a proven performer at his low price, was a better buy than the expensive newcomer sitcoms on Atlanta's network affiliates. And he could make it stick. He used the same line then as now: Look at me and what do you see—a winner, right? Turn your umbrellas upside down, fellas, and stand here next to me, this is where the gold's gonna fall.

He found counterprogramming a delightful game, and he wasn't afraid to play. His competitors felt obliged to run news coverage, but he did not. A Channel 17 slogan was "No news is good news." He offered only the minimum required by the Federal Communications Commission, putting the lightest entertainment he could find up against the unpleasant accounts of Vietnam, Watergate and oil embargos of the early 1970s. In those days he didn't like news anyway. It was too negative. It excluded the good things from its alleged mirror of daily reality. When men he respected said he was making a mistake, he wised off as usual. "When you're the last-place TV station in town, you can't make a mistake. They've already been made."

He played with little Channel 17 as if it were a 10-cent yo-yo with a new string, and he made it do new tricks. Observing that other stations ran religious programming Sunday mornings, he devised a movie showcase for that time period. It was called *Academy Award Theater,* and the host was R. E. Turner III.

R.T. Williams put together the production end. "It was kind of a joke, but Ted took it quite seriously, and he was pretty good. He'd just walk out through these spotlights with a book under his arm or something, and say a few words to introduce the movie. There was an armchair too, I recall. When it was over, he'd walk back through the spotlights. The whole time he was doing it he never knew I got the spotlights from Jimmy Durante, the "Goodnight, Mrs. Calabash, wherever you are" routine. Eventually somebody tipped him off about the Durante spotlights, and he was mad as hell at me. Thought

I was making fun." But counterprogramming the religious shows, which had always nauseated Turner, was a ratings hit—and *Academy Awards Theater* remains on the Superstation today.

There was very little Turner would not try if he sniffed an advantage, and his nose was good. He brought in professional wrestling, and the flamboyant behemoths found an instant following; he plunged headlong into the movie-collecting business, building a library of classic films which now numbers over three thousand. Turner would rather watch *Citizen Kane* than virtually anything else contemporary TV has to offer, and he assumed he had plenty of company.

"I programmed the whole station myself in those days. I sold ads, I signed all the payroll checks, I went to parties, I met people, I asked a million stupid questions and I educated myself. I would wander around in a daze all day, thinking, What am I gonna put on at four-thirty? No committees, no studies, no bull. I would ask Janie what she thought of a certain movie, or one of my friends, or the girls at the office. Not too scientific, huh? Well, I still program my own movies, and I still do it the same way, and it still works."

By 1973 he was out of the woods. His company had succeeded in obtaining a five-year contract to broadcast Atlanta Braves baseball games on Channel 17—luring the team from the city's number-one station—and had picked up some pro basketball too. In Charlotte, Channel 36 (WRET) was not quite so chipper, and in fact was still running a horror-movie host named Dead Ernest, whose success as a ghoul was somewhat undercut by his thick Georgia accent. But Arnie Gay no longer had to worry about his friend Ted coming to work at the boatyard in Annapolis.

The Ted Turner of 1973, to judge by the portrait in Turner Communications Corporation's annual report of that year, was a distinguished young man with shaggy sideburns and a cheering message.

To Our Stockholders:
Your company has just completed its most successful year in terms of both earnings and enhancing its prospects for continued growth. Net income of $1,645,000 ($1.11 per share) in 1972 represents a 78 percent increase over 1971. Income before extraordinary

items in 1972 was $669,000 ($.45 a share), an increase of 139 percent over 1971. The television station's revenues in 1972 were up $1,783,000, or 177 percent, over 1971.

The message ended with Turner's pronouncement that Channel 17 was now "firmly established as the leading independent television station in the Southeast."

Or as he told his comrades: "From shit to Shinola in two short years, that's pretty damn strong."

Turner, people started to say, was getting less crazy and more smart.

"I don't know if Ted was ever really crazy," R. T. Williams mused, actually pondering the question. "All I know is we were real proud of our TV tower, 1,093 feet high and the tallest freestanding tower in the country. One night we came back to the station drunk as skunks and decided to climb the thing. Turner says, 'Aw right! You go on ahead, R. T., and I'll be right behind.' So I climbed the tower, all the way to the top, but of course Turner just went home. I sure felt like a fool when the sun came up on me. Took me nine hours to climb back down."

To Tench Coxe, Turner's attorney and friend, the success of 1973 was most revealing. "Ted quickly got Channel 17 in shape, and WRET followed along afterward, and he really was set. Those two properties alone could have carried him for the rest of his life. He had won big, but he couldn't leave it alone. He kept seeing something else out there."

It's a pity that Ted Turner has not met William S. Paley, for they might find a fascinating common ground. Paley is the man who built the Columbia Broadcasting System media juggernaut. As a twenty-seven-year-old in 1928, he plunged all his chips into a shaky corporation called the CBS Radio Network, despite warnings that he would never dislodge NBC from its then-dominant position, and that radio itself might be only a passing fad. Paley had started out not in billboards, but in a perhaps equally unglamorous marketplace—his father's cigar company in Philadelphia. As David Halberstam writes in *The Powers That Be,* his study of the communications power structure, Paley showed early that he was "a very good salesman, particularly gifted at making other people believe that what he wanted was what they wanted too." He was up against formidable odds, for NBC at that time owned broadcast contracts for the biggest concert stars, and CBS was the poor sister, with only a handful of affiliates, little or no profits, and panache amounting to zero. But Paley was young, handsome and crafty, a compulsive who left no detail unstudied. And he was used to opening his own doors. If Turner has always been aware of his Southern, billboard-baron roots, so was Paley of his Russian-Jewish heritage. Paley developed exquisite taste, Turner a disarming candor, but the blackball has been felt by each.

Both men, however, could see a vast potential audience for their services, and both had the gift of imagination. Paley observed that NBC charged its affiliates for its network programming, so he offered CBS free of charge. He asked in return that the affiliates run the national advertising that he obtained. He could then go to sponsors and sell them a nationwide listening audience. In his first year at CBS, gross earnings went from $1.4 million to $4.7 million. The number of stations reached 114 in the first decade.

Paley kept up his momentum by craft. "If in the early days CBS was attacked by some critics for broadcasting too many laxative commercials," Halberstam writes, "then typically, in 1935, Bill Paley announced rather grandly that his network would stop using commercials for laxatives and other products of questionable taste. He was much applauded for his statesmanship, and nobody paid much attention to the small print in his announcement which said that the new policy would not apply to existing CBS contracts. Since in those days the laxative people stopped advertising in the slow summer months and signed new contracts in the fall, this simply meant that CBS could tighten the screws on the laxative people and keep them from taking a summer vacation. That year it broadcast more laxative commercials than ever before."

William S. Paley's CBS, after dominating television for decades, eventually became a target of Ted Turner's Superstation. When the networks began to take the satellite threat more seriously, their first move was to attack Channel 17 before Congress as a merchandise mart of schlock no less greedy than they.

Turner reacted by calling a press conference. It was the morning after he had been profiled by Harry Reasoner on CBS's top-rated *60 Minutes* program. Having filled a room with a hundred curious reporters at the Madison Hotel ("Washington's Correct Address"), he announced that he was immediately instituting a plan to "improve the quality of TV." Turner compared himself to Robin Hood and his adversaries to the Mafia, and dared the networks to follow his lead:

—An immediate reduction in overall commercials on his Superstation to 21 percent below National Association of Broadcasters standards.

—An hour each weekday of commercial-free children's programming.

—A commitment to prime-time adult programming of "outstanding quality" nightly, with a commercial load reduced further still.

—A substantial increase in public service announcements on "issues of significance."

Stories of Turner's challenge to "improve the quality of TV" immediately went out over the wires to newspapers all over the country. Few writers took the time to note that the reduction in commercials was virtually automatic, since nobody was buying anyhow; and that public service announcements pay for themselves in good will, but only when there's no more lucrative ad to run. His quality programming, however—*Civilisation, Upstairs, Downstairs, The Six Wives of Henry VIII* and more from the BBC—had indeed proved itself. Every single show had already been seen on nationwide public television, without any commercials at all.

Neither CBS, NBC nor ABC rose to the challenge, needless to say.

"This Paley guy sounds kind of interesting," Turner mused in his Atlanta office, puffing on a Cuban cigar. "Maybe we ought to have lunch sometime. But it can't be right away, because I'm busy as hell."

"The satellite really intrigued Ted," says Terry McGuirk, who was born in 1949, the year television became available to the general public. "Ted loves to step into the unknown, and when he went off on the Superstation tangent, I don't even think anybody in his company really knew what he was up to. Once he said to me, 'If they gave me all the McDonald franchises in the country I wouldn't take it. It would be too easy.' He would make a lot of money, but it would be a no-brainer. He'd die of boredom in a minute."

McGuirk, a former Middlebury tight end whom Turner has been sending out on long pass patterns of late, is an affable bachelor with a contagious grin and a philosophical air. The philosophy is a sort of theological hedonism. "Well, I went to Catholic schools, but I like to have a good time," he says, gunning his BMW automobile toward his tennis club for one of the various athletic contests that punctuate his schedule.

"Terry is rather young to be a vice president, but he's bright and he's good at what he does," says a colleague. "The only trouble with his job is that he has to listen to Turner talk all the time."

McGuirk's father was the station manager of the CBS affiliate in Atlanta, and he first met Ted Turner in his own living room. "My dad was having a cocktail party, and I guess I was home from college. I said, 'Who's that guy?' and my father introduced me to Ted."

After working for Turner during his summer vacations, McGuirk came on full time in 1973, and being new, volunteered to help out with the TV project in North Carolina. "I wondered why Ted couldn't get anyone else to go down there," he says. "The place was being run by religious fanatics, they had a prayer meeting in the station every morning at ten o'clock. It was a boiling caldron, and after six months I'd had it. I just quit and went to California for a year and drove around in a sports car, and wound up in Boston teaching sailing. Then Turner lured me down to crew for him on the Chesapeake, and said since I was still out of work I could be his paid hand. All I had to do was put on a suit and report to Atlanta Monday morning at eight-thirty. But of course it was one of those Turner traps. Fifteen minutes after I showed up, he made me vice president in charge of special projects."

The special project was the Superstation, yet unnamed. But Turner had been reading about the potential of cable TV, and assertions that direct transmission of programs by satellite was no longer theoretical, but an actuality waiting to be exploited. The problem was that an opaque cloud of regulatory gobbledegook enshrouded the entire issue, making capital investment extremely risky. For one thing, the Federal Communications Commission had more or less halted the expansion of cable television systems between 1968 and 1972, since cable companies had been declining to pay copyright fees on programming they relayed. But when cable operators acceded to that liability, the FCC relaxed its rules, permitting cable TV to bring in as many as three "distant signal" stations selected from the twenty-five cities nearest them. Even though through-the-air TV signals had to be relayed from town to town, and the signal deteriorated as it traveled, the "nearest twenty-five top markets" rules gave at least a regional franchise.

Turner's Channel 17 was already being received by cable outside its 40-mile range, in nearby cities such as Columbus and Macon, Georgia, and was being relayed as far as Tallahassee. If a satellite got into the act, a vast new market might open up.

Meanwhile, FCC Chairman Richard Wiley was calling for diversity of programming, and the Congress had learned the appeal of catchwords such as "decentralization." President Nixon, beset by nattering nabobs, saw to it that even public television moved toward more "grass roots" origination of programming, and away from the distracting influences of unfriendly, citified commentators.

The climate was right, but the weather was unpredictable. Predictably, Turner rushed to set all his sails at once. He wanted to get on a satellite, so he decided to build an earth station to send his programs up. He wanted to be able to guarantee sports to his viewers, so he bought a baseball team. It did not seem to matter that there was no immediate way for cable systems to get his signal down, or that it was not clear whether he was allowed to operate an earth station as well as a TV station. He plunged.

"I had been sitting in my office in Washington, telling anyone who would listen that this guy Turner probably had a better idea than even he knew," says Don Andersson, a cable research expert who talks as fast as Turner, though in a New England accent. "The next thing I knew I was hired, and we were out stumping from one cable system to the next, telling them what was in store."

McGuirk was also put to work. "Ted said to me, 'All right, we'll build an earth station ourselves.' Next thing I know I'm off for six months looking at land in Atlanta, with a microwave interference pattern overlap in one hand and a real estate guy in the other. It was unbelievably complicated, and nobody really knew what was going on."

"I wanted to be first," Turner says. "Damn right. You have to commit yourself. So I formed my own common carrier. I named it Southern Satellite Systems, and I got a contract with RCA to use their satellite. I figured that millions of dollars were going to be made just on SSS alone.

"I banked on sports. I didn't think a superstation would work just with old movies and reruns, and I had a five-year contract to televise the Braves. But what about after that? The better the team did, the easier it would be to sell advertising—but then the TV rights would become really expensive. Plus, I had this horrible recurring nightmare in which I picked up a newspaper and the headline said, 'Braves Move to Toronto.' Toronto was really looking at them at the time, and there went my baseball.

"It was the end of the season of '75, and I was out at the ball park rooting like always, and there were maybe two hundred people in Fulton County Stadium. The team really stank, ugh. They were in last place, and Henry Aaron had been traded to Milwaukee, and the fans were really down on the team. The team was just, you know, jogging around out there, 'cause why bother when nobody's looking? Wonderful. And I was putting them on TV and they were going to be hugely important in the future to us.

"I went up to see Dan Donahue, who was the team's president, and I caught him peeking out of the glass in the owner's box. I'd had a couple of beers, and I was really worrying about selling ads for the team the next season, so I said, 'Hey, Dan, what are we going to do to get these Braves going?'

"He said, 'I don't know what you're going to do, but we're bailing.'

" 'Oh my God,' I said, and I almost had a heart attack. 'Who're you going to sell it to? I got a five-year contract and this is only year two.'

" 'To you,' he says.

" 'To me? For how much?'

" 'Oh, about $10 million.'

" 'Yeah, well, how much is it losing this year?'

" 'Oh, about a million bucks this year.'

" 'What? I'm going to pay you that much so I can lose a million a year too?' But then I had the nightmare again right before my eyes. 'Braves Move to Toronto.' What the hell, I went back and told them I'd give them a million down, and the rest over seven or eight years. I knew the owners, eight or ten guys from Chicago, and they were real nice guys.

"I had no idea how I could afford it, but it turned out that the Braves actually had $1 million in their own organization. So I bought it using its own money, which was quite a trick. This was the first time a team had been financed like that, and the league was very concerned, cause they're real afraid of flaky owners. But the original owners agreed to stay close, saying that in the event that I busted my humper, they would step back in. Anyhow, I didn't have to worry about TV rights."

The plunge continued. Turner wanted RCA to build the earth station, a $500,000 item, but RCA wasn't quite ready. So Turner got hold of Sidney Topol, the hard-charging president of Scientific-Atlanta, a Georgia company that had cast its lot with satellite communications as a provider of sophisticated hardware. Turner and Topol are friends. Visiting the firm recently, he delighted in reenacting old times.

"I helped put this place on the map," Turner said, charging into the sprawling S-A plant on the roof of which three gleaming microwave receiving dishes are aimed dramatically toward the sky. In the crowded lobby, he thrust his face close to that of a pretty receptionist and waited till her eyes met his.

"Yes?"

"I want to see Topol, right now."

"Mr. Topol, our president?"

"Yeah."

"Um, sir, do you have an appointment? Some of these other men have been waiting for . . ." It took only that long to register: the wolfish stare, the Cuban cigar, the mustache, the dimple, the deafening voice. Ooops! It's Ted Turner.

"I'll interrupt his meeting, Mr. Turner. Please go right in."

"Yeah," Turner shouted. "Tell him I'm coming!" The fifteen well-dressed businessmen in the lobby looked up incredulously. "I ought to be able to see him," he shouted back over his shoulder. "He's so grateful to me he could cry!"

Topol's office was barely vacated as Turner stormed in—there were blurs in the exits as other executives cleared out of the way. President Topol rose to his feet.

"Sid, tell the truth, didn't I make you a millionaire?"

"Ted, sit down, how are you—"

"Topol, come on—didn't I make you rich?"

"Yes, Ted, you did."

"I wanted an earth station, and I called up and I said, 'You got one in stock?' You weren't selling nothin' then, and I didn't even quibble about the price. I just said give me a fair price, don't take advantage of me."

"Uh huh, Ted."

"And the next day, I sent you a check for my earth station and it didn't bounce, and then I went off and became a folk hero in cable TV and forced the whole cable industry to buy your equipment so they could receive my station and that's exactly how you got rich. Right?"

"All right, Ted. Fine. Is there anything you want?" Topol, unfazed, looked over his desk for some token of his appreciation. "How about a cigar?"

"Already got one, thanks."

Five minutes later Turner was back outside. "That guy loves me," he said. "I'm the best thing that ever happened to him."

Turner likes nothing better than to see the evidence of his Midas touch, and he doesn't expect the other party to golden opportunity to forget, either. In fact, if he pets a dog, the dog is likely to be later reminded that he owes his fur to Ted Turner.

The game is called touch-and-go, and Edward Taylor is one who felt the touch.

As it happened, the earth station that Turner bought from Sidney Topol would have made Turner, a broadcast licensee, a common carrier, too—and that, even in the regulatory smog, seemed in Washington a clear and present danger to the Republic. Turner was informed by his own lawyers that Southern Satellite Systems, to which he had just given birth, would have to go. "I hated to give it up, I really did," Turner says, "because of course I knew that I was making someone else an instant millionaire. But at least Ed had the smarts to jump in, even though back then a lot of people thought I was nuts."

Ed Taylor is an intense, bright-eyed fellow a few years older than Turner. He had had his eye on satellites for years, and when Turner met him Taylor was, at forty-two, the youngest corporate vice president of Western Union. He found Western Union a stodgy organization, however, and felt out of place "surrounded by fifty-five-year-old guys in Wall Street business suits who seemed more interested in getting out on the yachts every weekend than anything else." He does not dispute that he owes his fur to Turner.

"Yeah, Ted did spend a mad weekend in Atlanta convincing my wife and me that we should be so foolish as to pay him one dollar for this company called SSS, which he found he could not continue with himself. He said, 'Here—take 10 cents per subscriber as your fee. I'm going to have a lot of subscribers, and you'll make a million dollars off my station alone within a year."

So Taylor bought himself a paper corporation called SSS, a new enterprise that would exist solely to send programming by satellite from one point to many points. It was a new kind of electronic delivery system. As the telephone had supplanted the postman, SSS could supplant ATT.

"I was one of the first people who knew Ted's idea made sense, but the real reason I knew that the Superstation wasn't just a wild idea goes way back to 1967, when I headed the ATT task force studying the future of satellites. The guys on that team were so much smarter than I was it was belittling. They were the men who had invented Telstar, they were the brains of Bell Labs. But we actually wrote a business plan together that extended all the way to 1990.

"ATT had its own satellite already, and we analyzed what might happen to television communications, and new networks for voice and data. What we realized was that satellites were so competitive to ATT's terrestial monopoly that when we finished the business plan we went straight to Washington. We immediately started lobbying *against* satellites, and the lobbyists ATT had were so good that it was 1972 before any satellite systems were up in the sky. We literally delayed it five years in order to help protect ATT's existing technology."

Charmed by the notion of giant ATT's fearing for the life of its monopoly, Taylor and Turner set out to give them some competition —at no money down.

"It's true, we put hardly anything down," Taylor said. "The guys who really financed me were RCA. They owned the satellite, and Ted had a contract with them to buy time on it, and he was going to build the earth station needed to send his television programs up.

"Instead of Ted building the earth station, RCA agreed to take my name on the new corporation, even though we had no assets. All we had was financial commitments from some people in New York, about $20,000 each from twelve guys. We went $750,000 in the hole building the uplink, and then RCA bought the installation from us and we rented it back from them."

The result of this complicated deal was fairly simple. When little Channel 17 became the first Superstation, on December 17, 1976, SSS was the common carrier. Turner no longer owned any part of SSS, since he had thrown his lot with Channel 17. And he was right about what the decision had cost him.

The original 12 investors in SSS made back their capital outlay within thirty months, and wound up sharing 30 percent of the stock in a company now valued at more than $15 million. Taylor wound up with 70 percent of Southern Satellite Systems.

"What Ted says is true," Taylor concedes with a grin. "When I started with SSS I bought a Volkswagen. When my wife and I cele-brated our twenty-fifth wedding anniversary recently, I went out and bought her a silver Eldorado."

The switch that first sent Channel 17 to RCA's Satcom satellite was thrown on the very day that the Federal Communications Commission approved Taylor's application as a common carrier. The FCC also issued another finding that December 17: one that reduced the required size of a receiving dish—the key piece of equipment re-quired to bring Taylor's transmission of Channel 17 back to the ground—from 30 feet to 15 feet.

"That was a big thing," Don Andersson says, "and it couldn't have come at a better time. The price of an earth receiving station had been

$125,000, and it plunged immediately to $50,000, and then all the way to $10,000 or less." Sidney Topol at Scientific-Atlanta found himself deluged with orders.

The FCC had intentionally unleashed an unknown force, and was sitting back waiting to see what happened. Turner grabbed Andersson and a twenty-minute demonstration tape of his station in action, and took off to badger cable operators into hooking up to his satellite shooting star.

Soon the FCC could tell something was going on just by opening its mail. During the Bicentennial year the agency approved twenty earth stations; the next year eighty. By the end of 1978 there were 181 ground receiving stations in place, and applications on hand for more than 200 more. Incredibly, there were more than 1,900 operating by autumn of 1979. Three other superstations quickly emerged, following Turner's lead, and the satellite also dispensed three twenty-four-hour-a-day religious networks (offering the PTL Club and 700 Club, among other shows); the pay-cable services Home Box Office, Showtime and what later became USA Network; occasional news programming; some foreign language entertainment; and all of public television.

Cable system operators got most of it automatically, whether they transmitted it to their subscribers or not. And they got it in addition to the network programming that had been their stock in trade before the satellites era. The thirty channels were filling up. It seemed that a new open market in communications had been created, and though no one knew yet what the market would bear, Turner had been there first.

"For a while, even Ted wondered what he'd gotten into," says Terry McGuirk. "It was so impossibly complicated. We had committed millions of dollars not knowing what the FCC would do, we'd had to separate from SSS, we'd hired people on at big salaries. A lot of times nobody understood what was happening except Ted, and people would say to me, 'I hope he knows what he's doing, because nobody else does.' I was still new at the time, but one day about eight-thirty in the morning I got a call from Ted at his office in the Stadium Club, and he said, 'Come right over.' When I got there he was really down. 'Am I crazy?' he said. 'Am I absolutely out of my mind? Is this whole thing going to collapse around me?' I spent about three hours sitting in his office listening, and then he just walked out and started abusing people in the halls. I waited for a while and then I got up and went back to my own office. I don't think he even knew I was there that morning."

"Of course I did," Turner snaps when asked if he'd ever had second thoughts during his rush to the satellite. "I'm not an idiot, I know the risks. But I had to move fast, without a lot of people knowing what was up. I had to buy the Braves, and I also bought the Hawks for basketball, because if the leagues realized what I was doing—broadcasting my sports far, far beyond Atlanta, where the franchise supposedly was—they would've stopped me cold. I later picked up broadcast rights to the hockey team, too, and I helped a friend of mine get the Chiefs, which is the Atlanta soccer team. By the time the leagues found out what I was doing, the horse was out of the barn." The image cheers him considerably. "Yeah, the ketchup was out of the bottle, the plane was out of the hangar, the toothpaste was out of the tuuuuuuuube. . . ."

The headquarters of this grand scheme was, of course, Atlanta, Georgia, where Superstation central pulsated at 1018 West Peachtree Street, N.W., an address redolent of blossoms and savvy, a likely-sounding focus of the New South. Far-flung audiences imagined a modernistic complex of modular structures within which clean-cut young people tended glowing electronic consoles of this *Starship Enterprise* of the space age. Turner acted rather like Captain James Kirk anyhow, strutting about the country and addressing wayward TV executives as if they were representatives of some backward alien culture. R. T. Williams contributed to this impression by "classing up" Channel 17 at satellite time, redesigning logotypes, streamlining the station breaks and whipping up a new style of promotion spots for the station's old movies.

But in fact, 1018 West Peachtree Street was a weedy piece of Atlanta real estate in an area of cinderblock store buildings separated by peeling clapboard houses, and the Superstation quarters were the same quarters that had housed Channel 17. Turner's second-floor office, reached by climbing an echoing stairwell, was paneled in hardware-store wallboard, had a well-trod rug, and opened not on a spacious view but upon hard-working Dee Woods, Turner's secretary–bodyguard–confidante–bookkeeper–answering service –whipping post–Xerox machine–tape transcriber–chauffeur–coffee machine. And she had no view at all. To enter her domain, visitors first had to thrust open a 100-pound fire door, with the result that everyone who gained access seemed to have a vein throbbing in his neck.

On the other side of the fire door lay the Superstation. The second floor, a maze of nooks and crannies, housed the sales force; the first was a linoleum-floored studio overseen by R. T. Williams and his gang of producers, technicians and directors, most of them dressed as if about to depart for a touch football game. A lone receptionist-cum-switchboard operator guarded the door while routing calls, with the result that the standard incoming wait was thirty rings before anyone answered the Superstation phone. The most notable physical aspect of Channel 17, in fact, was the 1,093-foot antenna looming overhead. It became obsolete the day the Superstation switch was thrown.

Into this ramshackle outpost evidence of the revolution poured. Turner used to go to the mailroom every morning for his fix.

"Look at these letters," he'd shout, flipping through orders for direct-mail merchandise such as *The Roy Clark Guitar Book* or the Knitter. "The postmarks tell the tale!" Then he'd read the postmarks to anyone who would listen and envision with him the gallop of his Superstation across the land. "Texarkana, Texas! Fort Ice, Arkansas! Pocatello, Idaho! Hickory, North Carolina! Jackson, Mississippi! Modesto, California! Princeton, West Virginia! Lake Tahoe, Nevada! International Falls, Minnesota! Bristol, Tennessee! Paducah, Kentucky! These are people who are not only watching us, but buying our stuff. Not too shabby, huh?"

Indeed, earth receiving stations were being installed almost daily from Honolulu to Annapolis, and the local cable system had only to plug in to add thousands more viewers of Atlanta's Channel 17. Strange things began to happen. Housewives in Modesto could name the entire starting lineup of the Braves. The unintentionally campy *Academy Award Theater* became a cult hit Sunday mornings in hip San

Francisco, where young men wrote long letters to Turner praising his "dedication to American cinematic history." Three-hundred-pound wrestlers with yellow hair and Georgia accents received mash notes from the Bronx.

In Nye County, Nevada, in the town of Tonopah, viewership of the Superstation reached 95 percent, according to Edward Lee, president of the cable company there. Prostitution is legal in Tonopah, and the brothels are well stocked with television sets—"everywhere but the bars," says Lee. "The madams found they cut into drinking. Turner's station is real popular because there isn't much to do but watch TV and go to the cathouses, and he has sports and movies and it's on all night. Lots of the girls get to know the Atlanta players quite well from watching them on TV. They're real clean girls. They have to go to the hospital every week to get checked."

At Granite state prison in Oklahoma, Darrell Rand, Fan #96137, was effusive in his praise. "Ted's channel gave us a chance to see the old great movie stars, some of the shows my old man grew up watching. But mostly it gave us the chance to see what was going on in far places like Atlanta, and a lot of the dudes thought that was the best fare on TV."

Turner never apologized for what he was showing because he never had to. If anyone complained that his blend of movies, sports and sitcom reruns wasn't CBS, he would retort that there *already was* a CBS, and his goal was to provide an alternative.

As for news, it was broadcast at 3:00 A.M. by a good-humored young man named Bill Tush. To say that Tush did not take news seriously is to miss the point. He once read his entire program, for example, while holding a photograph of Walter Cronkite in front of his face.

After 1980, Channel 17 took a more serious view of the world, as befitted its owner's personal development as a public figure. But Tush's madcap, demonstrably nonnetwork air was typical of the tone of the Superstation throughout its early history, as it hurtled through the night without looking back, and probably just as well.

A slice of programming beginning at 9:37 P.M. Sept. 23rd, 1979, suffices as example:

* * *

Welcome to WTBS *Newswatch,* a headline service presided over by Marilyn Ringo. Ringo, who somewhat resembles Raquel Welch, informs the satellite audience that antinuclear demonstrators have been arrested in an attempt to shut down the nuclear power plant in Vernon, Vt.

The Amazing Whippomatic! The nonelectric kitchen mixing machine (millions sold at $10.98 yours for only $7.98!) which comes with its own mixing bowl and has an aerodynamic mixing action so incredible it outmixes an electric. Impossible? Watch!

Ringo returns with good news for bean lovers. "Food scientists at the University of British Columbia in Vancouver will start a research program early next year aimed at evolving a gasless bean. The microbiologist in charge of the project says beans are an important source of protein, but probably won't catch on until a way can be found to cut down on the amount of gas generated by them." Ringo's smirk is almost imperceptible.

Now back to the Sunday Night Movie 17—Off Limits, *starring Bob Hope and Mickey Rooney. Oops! Bob has poured a can of paint on the General's automobile!*

"We hope you enjoyed the movie, and welcome to our public affairs presentation on the local-option sales tax for Atlanta," says Bill Tush, introducing six experts with the line "Gentlemen, I don't know much about this, but just what is the local-option sales tax?" As the experts disagree, they are interrupted by an ad for cookware skillets, complete with a toll-free number for residents of Hawaii, who must be fascinated by the sales-tax issue in Georgia.

The next ad begins with an Elizabethan trumpet fanfare promoting Keith Michell—a fine Shakespearean actor whose name is nevertheless less than a household word in either Honolulu or Fulton County—in the British Broadcasting Company's production of Henry VIII, *airing the next night.*

The links of this television sausage are flashy Superstation logotypes frankly inspired by the sexy typeface used to render the title of the movie *Star Wars.*

"Hey, don't hold that public-affairs show against me," Tush said the next day while trying to decide how to interview a marionette. "I interviewed sixteen different people on camera yesterday, and that doesn't leave much for preparation time."

You asked for diversity, FCC. You got it.

But what, exactly, did Turner get? He was exporting Atlanta like Holland exports tulips, but there was one big difference. You had to pay for the tulips. It was easy to see how Ed Taylor could make money with SSS: the common carrier charged each cable system 10 cents per subscriber per month as a delivery fee. If Turner got five million homes, Taylor got $6 million a year. Sidney Topol sold equipment—the kind of equipment you had to buy to receive Channel 17. The cable operators charged about $10 monthly in exchange for wiring homes to receive clear TV pictures and a wide range of programming. Home Box Office, which fed new movies and comedy productions by satellite with no commercials, also billed its clients—that was why it was called pay TV.

But how was Turner going to make money? His plan, in fact, was to charge nothing at first for the Superstation. He wanted to watch cable systems grow and viewers become accustomed to it. "Once that happens," he would say, "they'll never let it get away from them." In the meantime, his local UHF TV advertising clients would get a free ride by satellite to a bonus audience several million strong.

Then he would slam shut the door of the trap—and raise his ad rates. "If you give somebody what they want," Turner promised, "they'll pay for it gladly. But they gotta know they want it, first—both the viewers and the advertisers."

In January 1979, he slammed the rate-increase trap shut—right on his fingers. The ad agencies recoiled in astonishment. It was as if the President of the United States had announced the annexation of Mexico and Canada—and the tripling of taxes to pay for it.

Delta Airlines, the wings of Atlanta's burgeoning local economy and a longtime sponsor of the Braves, dropped its entire Channel 17 campaign. Satellite, schmatellite. "We have a retail approach and a localized message," said Lee Sport of Delta. Besides, Sport claimed, if he paid the new rate a bill of $100,000 would become $540,000.

Nobody at Channel 17 could bring Delta around. But then a funny thing happened. Eastern Airlines, a rival for the New South carriage trade, jumped in and claimed the Braves as its own. It began to look like competition was still operative, after all.

A month after the rate increase, three members of Turner's marketing team met for a somewhat gloomy lunch at the Stadium Club at

Fulton County Stadium. The food was somewhat wilted, the baseball diamond a field of mud in the process of being converted to a motor-cycle race course, but since Turner owned the restaurant, it was considered disloyal to eat anyplace else. Don Andersson was slouched a bit, toying with his salad; Bob Sieber, a research expert capable of warbling Nielsen numbers like Pat Boone doing "Love Letters in the Sand," wasn't singing; and Don Lachowski ("say Lahuski"), the sales vice president, could count only twenty-two advertisers signed on at the new rate.

"Right now, we've achieved very little toward our goal," Lachow-ski was saying. "But remember, we're creating a whole new market where there wasn't one before. We're paving the highway, and then the other satellite stations will tool right in on it. We're like Lewis and Clark. The problem is that right now we don't fit. When you're talking to an ad agency in New York, it's as if there are two doors. One is marked 'Spot Advertising,' and the other is marked 'Network.'

"If we go in the 'Spot' door, they say our prices are too high. If we go in the 'Network' door, they say, 'If you don't have the potential to reach 80 or 85 percent of the audience, you're not a network.' What we're trying to do is use a chainsaw to cut ourselves a new door."

Turner was the chainsaw, and when he smiled you could see his teeth. He became the Red Baron of cable television, plunging into New York and Chicago and strafing the disbelievers there with high-velocity information. In the meantime, he started spending $500,000 a year on promotion. He wanted to drive up the number of cable homes quickly, so he would reimburse cable systems for much of the cost of their ads announcing the arrival of his Superstation. When Channel 17 went on QUBE, the experimental thirty-channel system in Columbus, Ohio, there were a hundred trucks tooling around town bearing signs that said "QUBE Brings You the Superstation." The big multiple cable system operators liked that style of commit-ment, and besides, Warner, TelePrompTer, Cox, Storr, Wometco, United, Viacom and the others had already been graced with a per-sonal visit by Turner himself.

"The little guys are important too," said Roger Williams of the Superstation marketing staff. "There was an owner in Idaho who had only 1,500 subscribers, and just to see what would happen he pulled the plug on Channel 17 one Saturday afternoon. Fifty-six people called up to see what was wrong with their TV sets."

But the best selling tool of all was Turner himself, his scarf flying in the wind as he looped the loop of notoriety.

"You're asking me if Turner has been useful in promoting the Superstation?" Don Andersson remarked incredulously. "A useful tool? That's the grossest understatement I've ever heard. It's a gross misunderstatement. I could take you out there and show you. I could take you to our smallest system, a little town with only thirty-nine homes in North Dakota, and try a name recognition test on the subscribers there. Ted would come close—he might even surpass—the President.

"I'm not saying it's as true in New York City, but across the country he is incredibly well known. The week after the Fastnet Race we couldn't get anything done at the office. Calls were coming in every minute. Is Ted OK? Did he survive? You combine that sort of thing with his appearance on *60 Minutes,* the couple of Tom Snyder shows he's done, the constant newspaper and magazine articles, the America's Cup, the controversy with the Commissioner of Baseball, and it's amazing.

"Ted knows how valuable it is. He has the actor's ability to play to a crowd, and it works for us every time. Like when Johnny Carson said he wasn't going to renew with NBC, Ted immediately offered him a job on the Superstation. The wire services picked it up, and we got calls asking, 'When does Carson start?' "

In the meantime, Turner's sales staff had to hunker down with some very challenging follow-up. Even when the national rates seemed to have gained acceptance—there were more than 150 national clients by the end of 1979—Turner's glorious footprints still tended to fade just before they could be filled.

"Turner's not an easy act to follow," says Gerry Hogan, a veteran of Turner's UHF days who is now general sales manager of the Superstation. "We'd announced the revolution, but the industry perceived that we were having tough sledding. People didn't realize that we had our direct-marketing business to tide us over after the rate increase, and they saw us going down. It's very important how you're perceived in this business, especially by agencies. They smell a rat, they'll turn off. The herd instinct is to walk away if you're having trouble.

"Our first national customers were foreign-owned—Toyota, Panasonic—with marketing strategies not so firmly entrenched. But on the home front strange things happened. I had a guy call me on a Saturday afternoon from Atlanta airport, and he had read in his hometown paper that the Superstation had bombed and that Ted was in great difficulty. He was prepared, he said, to pay me cash in the amount of $10,000 for a $100,000 ad contract, but I would have to come to the airport to pick it up. Ten cents on the dollar, take it or leave it. And he was only going to be at the airport for an hour. The product was Selsen Blue, a dandruff shampoo, and he explained that his company liked to take advantage of opportunities and we looked like we needed cash. It was pretty annoying. We were nowhere close to that desperate."

The perception problem was compounded by the very nature of the advertising business—how do you prove results? If Channel 17 had $200,000 worth of Vitalis hair tonic ads, it was hard to argue that Turner was keeping the cowlicks down, since Vitalis's total campaign was probably $15 million. Toyota, which placed $250,000 with the Superstation, could not trace the sale of any one car to any one ad. But there were hints that something was up. *Time* magazine tried using the station to sell subscriptions, and when its phones rang off the hook, *Time* increased its Superstation buy by 800 percent. Bristol-Myers tried an experimental sponsorship of Channel 17's quality programming hour at 10:00 P.M., offering a consumer booklet by Bess Myerson as part of one commercial message. Demand for the booklets was high, and Bristol-Myers made a substantial commitment.

For the sales staff, however, selling the Superstation was like trying to teach the new math to the PTA. The agencies knew it was important, probably even the wave of the future, but they had already learned to sell soap the old way, thanks.

"Motivation has been a big problem for our people," Hogan concedes. "It takes so much time to teach people all this. The traditional TV sales call takes maybe an hour of preparation. Ours require as much as fifteen hours, and to have someone totally reject your proposal is very frustrating. The primary talent required is tenacity.

You have to go back, start again. Many of our orders are the result of six, eight, ten calls over a span of two or three or four months. Ted himself may soar in, and he's very effective.

"But in the meantime, some of our guys can't take it. They lash out—it's just too much work. We've had turnover. When we opened Turner Television Sales offices in New York and Chicago to push the national rates, we had eight people. Of that original group, four remain, and one of them is having motivational problems. We even lost our president. Bill Ganley had been in Chicago, and he moved to New York to take his place. Ted knows exactly what he wants us to do, but it's more work than some are willing to put in."

Almost as soon as it went on the air at the end of the Bicentennial year, the Superstation began gaining viewers at the astounding rate of 200,000 a month. As the newly unleashed cable television industry rushed to wire the rest of the nation, the strategy map on Don Andersson's wall became a hive of pinheads. Turner stumped his new outlets like a politician following a gerrymander, waving his cigar at his new constituents, kissing babies, hyperbolically announcing that he had reinvented television (if not communication, leadership, and human nature itself), and generally making a great deal of noise.

The noise woke certain parties up. "Hey," said the syndicates who had sold Turner *Leave It to Beaver* for transmission to little old Atlanta and environs. "You're showing our *Beaver* in Hawaii. Who says you can do that?" Organized sports fell out of bed: "Turner, your franchise is the Southeast. You can't just show your teams any old place you want. You're horning in on the other owners' territory, and it's against the law." The movie producers, suddenly noticing that *Mr. Deeds Goes to Town* was going by satellite to hundreds of unexpected towns, yelled for their poolside phones. Fellow broadcasters called Turner a traitor who had sold out to the cable "thieves," and even the networks started scratching at the new flea.

"No wonder the Superstation is getting so big," they thundered in a chorus. "Turner is stealing our stuff, and giving it away for free!"

A battle royal was taking shape, one that would lead both sides to a bitter confrontation in Washington—a face-off between the well-heeled powers that be and a loose alliance of privateers, led by Ted

Turner, out for plunder under a flag of convenience called the satellite revolution.

Turner's response was to go sailing for six months. It was 1977, time for his second try at winning the America's Cup. He left for Newport, towing a $30,000 portable earth station behind his car.

After the day's racing, he wanted to be able to watch the Superstation in his room.

5 "If You Want to Get Rich, Stand Here by Me"

TED TURNER may sometimes rub people the wrong way, but he also rubs off on them. A half-dozen of his associates are already millionaires, and periodically those close to him can be observed declaring their own candidacy for fortune. The Lessons of Turner, taught by demonstration and occasionally by lecture, are not the sort found in tomes on business management, of which he himself has read but few. He tried one of Peter F. Drucker's guides to efficiency in the marketplace, but got bored very quickly. There is nothing to memorize in Turner's method, no rules, no homework. But the final examination is given daily.

It surprised no one at Turner Communications when the chairman of the board, having led his men onto the Superstation battlefield, suddenly abandoned them for six months to take on an entirely different challenge—a naval battle in 12-meter yachts in the waters off Newport, Rhode Island. Like a blindfolded chess champion playing multiple opponents, Turner frequently makes his move quickly, then goes on to the next problem while his adversaries scratch their heads.

Few have played with Turner whose own game has not improved as a result. The requirements are an open mind, confidence in the luck of the draw, and a certain surefootedness on the personal front. There can be only one Ted Turner. The trick lies in figuring out which one.

Janus, the god of beginnings, had two faces, but this subject shows many more. A highly skilled corporate maneuverer, he considers written contracts mere formalities; a fortune-hunter of formidable resolution, he frequently disparages the value of money as a goal; a skillful intriguer, he spills his closest secrets at the drop of a hat. He can be a romantic of quotients and dividends, a Calvinist in love with excess, a bully who demands friendship as his price. The Romans put Janus on a single coin, but the numismatics of Turner do not so easily fit.

A surprising number of friends and others, simpler explications having faltered, have been compelled to conclude that Turner is a business genius.

"A genius? Me?" he replies, reacting to the category like a concert pianist whose "talent" has been admired at the expense of decades of hard work. "That's really baloney, who told you that? Albert Einstein is a genius, not me. I know exactly how smart I am. My IQ is 128. That ain't bad, but it isn't the point. It doesn't help you make a good business deal—that I learned from my father. That and work your butt off, but not from behind a desk like most people do.

"I would say there's entirely too much emphasis on money. People are much more important than money, and anyhow if you think money is a real big deal you'll never make any. You'll be too scared of losing it to get it. I don't need money to be happy, I'll tell you that. Well, just a little. I like to have a plantation, and a boat, and food on the table for my family. But I can be happy with a small boat, maybe even happier. Just let me work, let me do things. You have to try to contribute to society, and even if it's just with a few happy billboards you'll make out OK if you do. That's why a criminal is always miserable, which is easy to see because they put a hat over their face when someone goes to take their picture, right? Stealing money makes you put your hat over your face, so it's no good. Nothing is worth that.

"It's better to be a ditchdigger. A ditchdigger has it all right, and he can be 100 percent happy. Maybe there's not much money, but he's on a bowling team or something. He's got good friends, like in the beer commercial, and some broads to have fun with. There's overtime if he wants some extra cash, and all he needs is a shovel. The trouble comes when the guy wants to be a stockbroker or something else besides a ditchdigger. Then he's a jerk to stay in the ditch, and if he does it's his own fault and no amount of welfare money will make him happy. He's talking about competing at a higher level, and he'd better get out of the ditch and do it.

"See, there's all kind of competition. You choose your own. Business is no different from sailboat racing or any other game you decide to play. You just go out there planning to win, and make sure you do.

"Of course, not everybody's going to be on your side. People make the mistake of asking for help. They get an idea and they ask, 'Won't somebody help me with this, please? Pretty please?' Nah, you got to help yourself. Ninety percent of the people give you the wrong advice anyhow. If it's your idea, you should know more about it than anybody. When I started my Superstation I didn't go around saying, 'Please help me, I'm trying to do this difficult thing.' No! I said, 'Hey, I'm a Superstation, and it's going to be great.' I knew it would be, and I told them why. The smart ones caught on right away, and even the dummies catch up sooner or later.

"Everybody tries to make things hard, but I try to make them easy. Business is full of nitpickers and i-dotters and t-crossers, and a lot of times things get unnecessarily complicated. There are lawyers all over the place, but you don't do business with lawyers. Buyers and sellers are individuals, and an individual always has a big advantage over some committee that can't make a decision. You can't shake hands with a committee.

"That's why people are so important. You can be yourself, you can be colorful. Just don't get a big deal idea of how important you are. One reason that I was able to buy good programming for my little TV station was that I used to entertain the salesmen myself. I took them to baseball games. I had them over to my house, and sometimes they stayed for the night. And I was the top guy. Normally the program purchases are handled by a guy making $20,000 a year who's a real sourpuss. He likes to be taken out by the salesmen, who always pick up the tab. Whereas I would fight them for the tab. I used to astound them, because here they had the expense account, but I insisted on paying. They had assumed they would be doing the selling.

"Oh no. I made it clear that they were important. I said, 'I'm only a little UHF station and your programs are my lifeblood. The other clients you have are network affiliates, working for big companies. But this is life and death to me, personally.' The salesmen got to like me, because I appreciated them. A lot of times they would even tell me what the other bids were, and a peek is always worth three finesses. They could let me know. 'If it's $1,500 an episode, will that make it?' I would ask. 'Try another hundred,' they'd say. In other words, a lot of good came to me from not playing the big cheese."

Turner, who studiously avoids being perceived as a cheese, is nonetheless not averse to appearing from time to time as a coconut. A pretty girl still stops him dead in his tracks, requiring the more businesslike members of his party to wait until his ogle is completed. For years he had the habit of answering other people's business phones when he dropped by, beating the receptionist to her receiver and launching into a flamboyant sales pitch for whatever his host company happened to sell. He delights in blitzkrieg visits to business associates, entering their appointment schedules through a tiny opening but leaving a gaping hole behind. In fact, his standard entrance into any room has the effect of a bowling ball on tenpins for those within.

On one of his forays to Washington with Terry McGuirk, the two went from office to office on Capitol Hill, lobbying a half-dozen Congressmen in one morning. At one office Turner requested an aspirin from a secretary. Later on she accosted McGuirk.

"She wanted to know what kind of drug Ted really took," McGuirk says, scandalized at the recollection. "She said he must be using some kind of uppers to have all that energy." The notion of Turner on pep pills made McGuirk laugh. It would be like feeding a kangaroo jumping beans.

Turner's enthusiasm is natural, and it races at the speed of a fully developed tidal wave, pushing everything before it. Along the front of the wave, crests continually form and reform. Some are strong enough to cascade momentarily down its speeding face, while others, after a promising start, lose momentum and are reabsorbed. This is not the usual shape of American business endeavor. The problem for Turner's staff is to tell which crests will break and which won't.

Riding the Boston–New York shuttle recently, Turner fell into a discussion of television with his seatmate. He was full of admiration for a British series Channel 17 was running called *The World at War.* As it happened, the man next to him was the author of a slightly dogeared outline for a massive television project called *Vietnam: The Whole Story.* By the end of the forty-five-minute flight, Turner was convinced he wanted to produce it.

Back in Atlanta, he brought the thirteen-part series to the attention of R. T. Williams and his general manager, Sid Pike. "Nobody has ever told the whole Vietnam story on TV," Turner said. "Five years ago people would've puked. But *Coming Home* just won the Academy Award, and it's time to tell the tale. It's going to take guts, because we lost the war, and I hate to lose. But we're going to do the whole story, find out what went wrong, talk to the Viet Cong, interview the generals on our side, whatever it takes. You guys figure out how. But I want it on the air in six months."

Williams and Pike rolled their eyes. "We ought to be able to do it for $1 million," Turner said, walking out of Pike's office.

A tidal-wave warning was sent to Will Sanders, the financial vice president, and Williams was sent to New York. He looked up Isaac Kleinerman, a veteran television producer who had put together the famous *Victory at Sea* series of the early 1950s. "Turner wants this in six months?" Kleinerman said. "For $1 million?" Kleinerman, a bear of a man whose white hair and mustache give him an imperturbably avuncular look, had recently quit smoking. He reached for the cigarettes that weren't there.

In the next week, R. T. Williams plunged into the Vietnam program with the same enthusiasm that had led him up the 1,093-foot antenna; Kleinerman, fascinated, mobilized his production company to work up a projected budget, timetable, and twenty-six-page scenario. The author of the Vietnam project, somewhat stunned by the rapidity of these developments, plunged into a crash study of available Vietnam film footage, locating more than 100 million feet. Days later Kleinerman's study of the production of a thirteen-part TV series on Vietnam was in: realistically, the project would cost $2,763,-423 and require eighteen months.

R. T. Williams did not want to be the one to tell Turner. That was Will Sanders's job. "Ted," Sanders said, "we've got the Superstation just launched. If you go ahead with Cable News Network that will be a $35 million start-up cost. The Vietnam project is fine—but you can't afford it."

So on the day Kleinerman's bill arrived—it was $8,000 for the scenario, the budget and the consultations—Turner slowed down briefly in the hallway. "By the way," he said to R. T. Williams, "we ain't going to do that Vietnam series. I love the idea, but Sanders says we'll go broke."

Williams asked Turner what to do with Kleinerman's bill.

"Pay it, dummy," Turner said.

It was a typical Turner crest, and no one was surprised when it failed to break.

On a rainy morning in August 1979, Turner woke in his Marietta house to a ringing phone. Janie, answering it, asked if he had made an appointment with a realtor that morning. Yeah, he had. He was going to look at a new house.

"You mean, a house for us all to move to?" Janie asked as the realtor's Cadillac Seville pulled into the driveway an hour later.

"Yeah, maybe," said Turner.

"Do I get to look at it?" Janie asked.

"Nope."

The house was a sprawling ranch on large acreage nearly an hour from downtown Atlanta. It had a pond and plenty of room for Nevis, the beloved horse of Jennie, his ten-year-old daughter. The price was $900,000. Turner tramped through the rooms while rain poured over the vast lawns outside and an elderly real estate salesman, who'd thoughtfully brought along an attractive woman as his aide, yammered on about how the ranch would perfectly fit Turner's style. Furthermore, Janie and the kids would enjoy it, he added.

"I decide," Turner said.

That crest also merely foamed. Janie was relieved, since Turner had purchased the plantation near Charleston not two years before, having paid about $2 million for it, and she had not even gotten used to that. He had also recently bought a 600-acre farm with a small lake on it an hour outside of Atlanta, which he had visited no more than half a dozen times. His son Beau liked to fish there, with Jimmy Brown or Chief Nok-A-Homa, the Braves mascot, serving as companion and guide.

Turner had also acquired an island on the Carolina coast near Hilton Head, an hour or so from Hope Plantation. The island was several thousand acres of sand and mosquitoes, and could be reached only by boat.

The day after looking at the $900,000 ranch, Turner took a small detour on his way to the office at 8:30 A.M. He slowed down the Toyota, turned off the mansion-studded lane that led toward downtown Atlanta, and parked in a steeply sloping driveway that plunged into a line of pines. He strolled down the driveway, breathing deeply of the misty morning air, humming a little tune based on the McDonald's jingle. After 500 yards the driveway leveled out in a quiet hollow that contained a small pond. The modest one-story house was hidden partly in the trees and had not been lived in for some time.

"I picked this place up pretty fast a couple of weeks ago," Turner explained. "Maybe I'll build a place on it. That house over there would be perfect for Jimmy Brown. You know, there was a doctor also interested in buying this land, and when I beat him to the punch he cried."

Turner was asked how his kids would appreciate the steep driveway, which would make arrivals and departures on foot a challenge worthy of Tenzing and Hillary. "Good exercise," he said.

Turner's urge to acquire is well known, and it means that he is constantly assaulted by sellers of various commodities. He can be a willing victim, but he has to be willing. He will pay $5,000 on the spot for a ship model. At an auction for Ducks Unlimited, an organization of hunters concerned about the protection of waterfowl populations, he bid $10,000 for one shotgun. He is crazy about dogs, and will pay hundreds of dollars per puppy.

His joy in these purchased things, and in their disposition, is obvious. One night Terry McGuirk visited his house to adopt one of Turner's cast-off hounds. "He's a great dog, Terry, you're going to love him. Only thing wrong is that Max here has no killer instinct. But he'll be great for you. Even the kids want you to have him. McGuirk, you got yourself a dog. The dog already loves you, look at him."

Actually, McGuirk could not look at Max the dog because Max had run away to hide. "Let me show you my new dog," Turner said.

It was 11:00 P.M., but Turner got his new dog, a trained retriever, out on the lawn in the drizzle. The dog would fetch a thrown object on command. He would fetch two objects thrown in opposite directions, one first, then the other. He dropped these objects at his master's feet. Turner was so happy that he eventually had Janie, McGuirk, and several visitors standing in the rain, applauding the new dog's talent.

Max eventually was located and returned to McGuirk's house, where he learned to jump over any fence McGuirk could devise. "Boy, did Ted sell me a bill of goods with Max," he said a week later, as the dog tumbled down his back porch stairs like a slinky toy gone berserk.

From house to house, dog to dog, Turner is seldom satisfied. In the middle of the Irish Sea, dining with the offwatch on his 61-foot ocean racer, he dreamed of building a J-boat. The J-boats were the 130-foot America's Cup sloops of the 1930s, gone now like dinosaurs. The crew egged him on. Who wouldn't want to sail on a J-boat?

"We could do it, really," Turner said. "Jobson, you can be tactician. It would only cost a couple mil. We'd get the money someplace. Holy cow, it took sixteen guys just to raise the sails on those boats. 'Bring back the J's'—that could be our slogan! 'Course we'd have to find somebody else to build one too, so we could race. Baron Bich can afford it. Hey, we got to do that!"

If Turner likes something, bigness does not deter him. The larger the scale, the better it tips in his favor. Twice he has been a guest on Tom Snyder's *Tomorrow* program on NBC. Twice he has offered Snyder a job. Johnny Carson and Walter Cronkite have also had offers. There is hardly a winning free agent in baseball whom he has not tried to seduce onto the humble Braves.

The lure of bigness can be geographical, too.

"Years ago he was going to move to Australia," Janie Turner said one night while riding home after appearing at the stadium in the role of Wife of the Owner. "He'd gone down there for a sailboat race, and then he had me down to look at it. It was scary, because even though I was trying to be enthusiastic, it seemed pretty far away. I wouldn't see my parents much in Australia. But he said there were riches to be made there. It was a good country, but he couldn't find any McDonald's franchises or any Kentucky Fried Chicken. Ted thought if he got those franchises, he would make a lot of money, and I'm sure he would have. This was back when the television stations weren't doing very well. We talked it over with the children and everything. We were actually going to do it. But then he changed his mind. He said, 'I'm really an American. This is my country. I really belong in America.' "

A man who seriously considers relocating to Australia injects certain uncommon factors into the daily business life of his associates. If he also has a history of going sailing half of every year, starting more projects than Franklin Delano Roosevelt, and insisting that he be completely in charge, the factor is multiplied. It was Will Sanders, who opened his own overseas investment firm in 1979 but remains on Turner's board of directors, who did most of the multiplying. Like all of Turner's best men, Sanders's view of the world-according-to-Ted is a rough mix of admiration and candor.

"Turner is an excellent contract guy, an excellent marketing guy, and an excellent salesman. He's also an excellent leader, but he doesn't care to spend much time with details or acquisition agreements and things like that. He leaves that to people like me and Tench Coxe. Ted's not a real manager. He can do it, but he doesn't like it much. He'd rather give people general directions. He delegates a lot of responsibility, but at the same time very little authority. If it's business as usual, take care of it. If it's saving money, OK. But anything that requires committing additional funds to, you have to check with him. His style is never to let go of anything, to always stay in touch.

"Of course that's fine, but here is a guy who ought to have five people, maximum, reporting straight to him, and he probably has fifteen. Having a president didn't work because he would go into a meeting with buyers and leave the president sitting in the waiting room. He runs his company the same way he runs his boat. There's only one captain.

"And yet, in a lot of ways his people have great latitude. You're left alone to do your thing, and you can do it your way, in your style. He gives you the goal, and you get the results. Don't make many mistakes. Don't do what you're not supposed to do. Keep the ball rolling."

Sanders was not much taken aback when the chairman of the

board departed for Newport immediately after the Superstation was launched. He was used to that sort of thing, and it had benefits.

"Well, Ted would call once a week or so. I made up a list of questions, and he would give answers. He doesn't hem and haw. He knows he can go away, because good people will run things. In a sense, Ted tends to be a disruptive influence anyhow. He causes turmoil. He creates projects, maybe 75 to 90 percent of which we eventually disregard. That takes away from production, of course. When he's out of town things go smoothly. Sales go up, a lot of interesting things happen. I get a lot of work done, I get time to think. You've got to be able to think, and not spend most of your time, perhaps 150 percent of your time, reacting to new projects he's dreamed up.

"So I'd say there's a positive benefit from his prolonged absence. The jobs may get done more thoroughly, with more study, perhaps at the expense of glamour. Ted is the most important ingredient, but there's certainly a benefit to the company when he occupies himself elsewhere."

As a result, Turner's employees seem to understand the importance of their roles, for success depends more heavily on their performance than it might under a less eccentric administration. The Turner style relies on intuition—in fact, it relies on brilliance—rather than analysis. He has little patience, for example, with marketing studies, the new voodoo of American enterprise. Such studies abound in today's corporate life. A new soap, or antifreeze, or laser-light home video system, is now routinely "tested" on a cross section of potential buyers before going into production. The commissioning parent then pores over the results, seeking confirmation that the fetal concept is without defect.

Human response to humans can be easily tested too, and a central rating system already exists to record the likability and recognition factors of movie stars, television entertainers and news figures as well. Programs, films and music recordings also visit the oracle— which takes the form of a roomful of volunteers with one hand on a "how much do you like it?" electronic response dial. Even tough-minded newspapers have jumped on the bandwagon, commissioning elaborate studies of themselves and how they are "perceived" by readers. The resulting plastic-bound market survey, complete with demographic charts and a scientific margin of error of 3 percent, is very persuasive. It shows what people like. The implication is that they should be given that.

"Where's the fun in making a bunch of studies?" Turner says. "I usually know what I want to do, and you have to have confidence in your own ideas. I never even did a marketing study on Cable News Network, which is going to cost me every penny I've got. Wait, actually we did do one on that. It cost $4,000 and it was done in Sarasota, Florida. But that was just for advertising. If everybody in that survey had said they hated the idea, I wouldn't have given a damn. There's never a reason for a study if your idea is conceptually sound. If I had decided to move to Australia and open those McDonald's franchises and bring the good Australian people Kentucky Fried Chicken, you bet I wouldn't have done a survey there either.

"I do my own marketing analysis," he says, blowing a smoke ring from his cigar. 'Hey, where is the Colonel's chicken?' I asked a guy in Australia. When he didn't know what I meant, I knew I could make a million within a year."

Turner's staff has also learned that he does not put a great lot of stock in the multipage written agreements.

"I've heard Ted say lots of times that a contract is absolutely useless unless both parties agree to it," says McGuirk. "So he signs contracts fast. I think he feels that he can maybe get out of them later, if things change, or the contract can be revised. It can get scary. We signed a contract for a transponder on the satellite for Cable News Network in one day. We got it, I read it once, and he signed it. It never went to any of our legal people, it never went anywhere. When our lawyers finally got hold of it, they were shocked. It's a several-million-dollar obligation, and he had signed it without reading it."

Turner's personal acquisitions have been deals made equally fast, leaving Will Sanders to pick up the pieces.

"Ted would say to me, 'Hey, Will, I agreed to do so-and-so. I agreed to buy a piece of property over in Carlson County, Georgia, and it's a great deal and I only paid $600 an acre or whatever it is. Here's the guy, give him a call and work up a contract.' So I make notes on what he says and then I at least try to document the deal to his best advantage. Sometimes he's done it so fast there's no room left for negotiation."

Occasionally Sanders would advise Turner to back off after his investigation.

"Ted was very interested in buying an island in South Carolina called Pritchard's Island. He was thinking in terms of paying $2 million. So I started checking it out, talking to real estate people in the area, who pointed out things that could go wrong. Like the average terrain was one foot above sea level and sometimes the island was completely flooded. You could inspect the place and see palm stumps sticking out of the surf. Was the place disappearing, or what? There's no bridge; how do you get to it? There's no fresh water. These are the kinds of things Ted wouldn't have thought about in his initial enthusiasm. Basic things that I could look into, and which kept the deal on the back burner a little.

"Then, four months later, we heard that the owner had lost control of the property and it was being sold on the courthouse steps for foreclosure. So we cranked up again. How much shall we bid? Do we want Ted handling this in person, or should we set up a two-way radio and have somebody else go in for us? We had already ridden a little boat over to walk up and down the entire beach. So by the time of the sale we had a lot of information. We had the walkie-talkie set up, with Gary Jobson actually making the bids. Ted backed out when the bidding got to $1,017,000. I was kind of surprised.

"He eventually bought a different island, but the question was, Does he ever back down? I think if you made a study of it, went back and counted the number of things that we've gotten into, you'd find that we have rejected more than we've gone with. Ted is smart enough to have smart people around him, and he will listen."

One thing is certain, however, and that is that Turner is undeterred by dollar signs. For years, his yearly ocean-racing campaign expenses have been over $100,000. His contribution to the America's Cup defense efforts has been two or three times that amount. After he won the Cup in *Courageous,* he bought the boat, and another 12-meter, too—"just to make sure they didn't fall into the wrong hands" for the 1980 defense.

These expenditures Sanders handled as best he could. Turner could

offset some of the costs by giving speeches and endorsing products—
and he employs an agent to look for such opportunities. His planta- ·
tion, too, is both an investment and a facility for entertainment. For
tax purposes, a few acres around the house are Turner's for recre-
ation, but much of the land represents a timbering business. The
swampy terrain is rich in peat, which Turner is set up to mine as fuel.
And much of the time at the plantation is spent entertaining business
clients, so that figures into the allocation as well.

With so many projects going at once, one feeding off the other like
a fire of green logs which might not burn alone, Turner's business life
could remain shrouded in mystery forever. It never has, and doubtless never will, for a simple reason: he cannot keep a secret. Perhaps
it is braggadoccio, perhaps simple candor, perhaps pride of accomplishment, perhaps psychological warfare, but much of his career is
an open book. Or perhaps a daily newspaper, with screaming headlines.

"Turner buys $2 million in gold!"

"Oh, that," Sanders remarked with a wry grin and a resigned
shrug. "That was going to be our secret."

Ted Turner, beloved of trophies in any form, had seen a Krugerrand and had liked what he'd seen. A Krugerrand is a one-ounce
South African coin of pure gold. You can hold it in your hand, bite
it with your teeth. He bought $2 million worth, at $275 an ounce.
First, he mentioned the idea to Sanders.

"I said, 'Come on, Ted. You're tying up $2 million worth of cash.
The damn stuff could earn $200,000 a year if we just put it in Trea-
sury notes. In other words, it has to go up 10 percent a year just for
you to break even. You're paying $275, which is the all-time high.
I saw it go to $200 an ounce in '74, and plop back to $100 within a
year.'

" 'No,' Turner says, 'it's just gonna keep going. I got to do it now.
I'm worth plenty, and its only a portion of my net worth. It's diver-
sification. I really should get *more.*'

"Well," Sanders continued, "he'd be right if he had had $100
million that he could lay his hands on at that time. The problem was,
of course, that about 85 percent of his worth was in Turner Communication stock, and he would never sell his control of Turner

Corporation. So it's not liquid, forget that. And $2 million didn't work out to 2 percent of his actual liquid money, it was more like 30 percent.

"So we were looking at it two different ways. But what you can't ever do is bet against Ted. If you say gold is going down and he says it's going up, it'll go up. It won't necessarily happen because he studied the situation or even has a good grip on it. He may have talked to some guy on an airplane, or an old buddy who owns a bank in Indiana. Anyhow, he bought it. And not after any long study. We decided, at my urging, not to tell anyone.

"So we get the gold and put it in the vault," Sanders said, "and the next day somebody comes into my office and says, 'Boy, all that gold is something.' I said, 'Huh?' Well, Ted had gone to lunch and told everybody in the restaurant he just bought $2 million in Krugerrands. That's how long the secret lasted."

Turner could have purchased warehouse certificates for the gold, but that would not have been his style.

"No sir," he explained, while driving his jeep through Hope Plantation and decorating the nearby foliage with expertly aimed globules of tobacco juice. "I met the armored car at the bank. They had guards with guns and everything. The gold was in bags, just like money. They gave me a key to the vault and a special combination. I was thinking of actually digging a hole here on the plantation and burying it, but I guess not. I also thought about having some of it melted down and having a goldsmith make some plates and goblets. We could dine with gold! Pretty strong, huh? I hate to see the stuff just sitting there in some bank. How about we build a solid gold replica of the America's Cup! Theirs is only silver, but mine's gold!"

Within a few days Turner had lost the key to his vault, and mislaid the combination. He took to carrying a gold Krugerrand with him everywhere, and flipping it for all to see. Before long he had misplaced the Krugerrand, and had to draw another from his supply.

Within a year, however, gold had hit $800. And Turner had cashed in half of his Krugerrands for a very nice stack of American dollars.

His openness serves him in curious ways. It is quite literal. His office desk phone is fitted with a two-way loudspeaker box, so that callers fill the room with their voices, often unbeknownst to them.

Many of his calls are from hustling businessmen, whose voices are low and secretive, whispering easy profits. Sometimes as many as six Turner associates listen and mug as Turner, winking madly, strings the unwittingly amplified entrepreneur along.

One caller thanked his friend Ted for advising him to buy Turner Corporation stock, which had recently gone up, and added that he was thinking of buying some for his aging father. Turner put down his pipe. "Hey, listen. Your money's one thing, and you're real smart going with me. But I don't want to have to worry about losing your old man's shirt for him. Take my advice and get him into some real safe, nonrisk portfolio, huh?"

The ask-me-anything exterior, however, does hide a fox-in-the-henhouse craft that is always present beneath the talkathon. He bought the Braves with its own money, and after he got the basketball Hawks as well, he was told the Atlanta Chiefs soccer team was off limits. That would be too many teams for one owner.

"Yeah, but I wanted soccer for my TV station," Turner says, "so I loaned every penny of the purchase price to a friend of mine, so he could buy them. I mean I loaned him every dime. There was nothing in there said you couldn't loan money to other owners. The league knows. They said, 'Oh, you *loaned* the money, well, we can't do anything about that.' Ha! See, they can't stop me. I'll be like the Man Without a Country one of these days. He went on living, but just from different ships."

Turner makes it clear that anyone, or anything, that throws in with him shall flourish. His perception of his leadership role in business is almost biblical—Moses, or at least Charlton Heston, teaching the children from the commandments he has received atop the mountain. Thou shalt be loyal to thy friends, and to thy products.

"Ted is amazing in that regard," says Dick McGinnis. "He's actually come into my home and opened the refrigerator to see what brand of milk we're using. It had better be one that's advertising with us. I mean, it's no small thing to him. He would almost fire you if you bought a car from a dealer that wasn't advertising on the station."

He wears an Atlanta Braves necktie almost every day; he sings the praises of his Toyota car, for Toyota was an early Superstation client; during the summer of 1979 the Hobie company gave him one of their

18-foot catamaran sailboats, and he effused in favor of Hobie Cats from Maine to Charleston. Soon Hobie had given him three more. His enthusiasm is born, most often, of simple delight in the people and things that attach to him.

Dining at the Stadium Club before the start of a baseball game, Turner turned pensive for a moment, then excused himself from the table and drifted away. He was beaming like a lighthouse when he returned five minutes later.

"You know that waiter who came over to me a minute ago?" he asked. "He impressed me. I asked him how come he wasn't acting happy, and he said to me, 'Mr. Turner, there's no opportunity for me here.' So I said, 'Will you work? Will you listen, and work hard?' And he said, 'Yes, all I want is that chance.' So I said, 'Report to my TV station Monday in your best suit.' I'll give him an opportunity—and that's all. Boy, was he surprised."

When Turner gives people a chance, they sometimes do not recognize what a chance they are taking. The response must be quick, or the opportunity may fade. And as there is no backing in, there is no backing out.

Once Turner took on an executive, anointed him with a big job, and provided him with 20,000 shares of Turner Corporation stock. The executive was being relocated as part of his promotion, and Turner went so far as to buy his house from him and actually take up residence there himself. The executive performed well, but after three years he came back to Turner and explained that he intended to cash in his stock and leave the company.

Turner was flabbergasted. This was the ultimate disloyalty—to want to leave the fold. Furthermore, the 20,000 shares of stock were worth $1.5 million, and Turner had to pay it out. Bitterness ensued.

"That situation was probably the severest blow to Ted's sense of loyalty," says McGinnis. "He had made this guy a millionaire, and then the guy had kicked him in the butt." The executive's new position, furthermore, placed him in direct competition with one of Turner's enterprises.

"Ted didn't have a no-compete clause, like they usually do," McGinnis says. "He thinks those contracts are useless. If somebody's not happy, what good is a contract? You don't want them there anyway."

These bonds of fealty, as knotted as the social landscape of the Middle Ages, can bind hard on those closest to Turner. His stance is often imperious and distant, and yet by turns overwhelmingly personal. He makes enormous demands of fellowship, loyalty and even love from the eclectic brotherhood that surrounds him. If challenged at this game, he is fully capable of letting fly a shard of Richard II, admonishing his companions, "You have but mistook me all this while: I live with bread like you, feel want, taste grief, need friends; subjected thus, how can you say to me, I am a king?"

His allies at Turner Corporation cope as best they can with this problematical, dramaturgical man. They try to maintain survival distance. In a quiet place, mulling the mysteries of Chairman Ted, even his closest associates may recite the parable of the moth.

"Some moths fly in a wide orbit around the flame, illuminated barely and circling mostly in the darkness. Other moths pass closer still, and fly in brightness so that their colors glow prettily in the light. And then there are the moths who come very close to the candle flame indeed, so close that for an instant they shine as brightly as the light itself. But only for the instant. Then they are consumed, and only the light remains."

Another veteran employee puts it a simpler way. "All close relationships with Ted are potentially destructive."

Most of the members of his team cope with this factor of life like door gunners in combat helicopters: they sit on flak jackets to make sure their balls don't get shot off. The danger is ever present. Turner is a master of verbal abuse, and it vents from him periodically like steam from an overheated boiler.

McGuirk concedes the issue, his grin unfailing. "Yeah, it's a fact that if you screw up, you're going to get yelled at. But there're different kinds and degrees of abuse, and the people around him can tell the difference. Some get it heavier than others, and they seem to live with it. A lot of times they haven't really done anything wrong, they're just targets. And Ted will come back praising them on his next visit."

The ammunition that Turner fires in these fusillades is armor-piercing: he will cite any physical infirmity, past indiscretion, personal failing, spouse problem, IQ deficiency, contradictory opinion, business defeat or vulnerable aspect of race, creed or national origin. "Don't ever let Ted find out anything about you that you don't want broadcast," says one longtime friend. "A harelip, your wife's stretch marks, or your kid's grades in college. It'll get thrown back at you later. And probably before a group."

Turner receives citation of these indisputables with detachment. "A lot of times I'm joking, that's all," he says. "I talk too much sometimes, that's always been a problem of mine. On the other hand, I'm a good talker. I say what's on my mind, and that's not bad, is it? Also, I hate dumb-ass mistakes and I think they should be pointed out to people who can't see them for themselves. I'm just as hard on myself. The worst thing people will say about you is that you're colorful. I like being colorful. I'm a folk hero, don't forget. Most people like me just fine. Mainly, people who don't like me are either intimidated in some way or they're competing with me or they're jealous. They may have gotten a bad impression because of something they read. If they got to know me they would probably like me. That happens a lot."

The fast course in getting to know Ted Turner occurs on his boats, for it is there that the colorfulness is at its most vivid, and livid. His shipmates often sail entire races with their shoulders hunched—not against the elements, but against the torrent of taunts and outrage their skipper showers from his post at the wheel. He jumps up and down, he pounds his feet, he pummels nearby crewmen with his fists, he hurls insults that skewer whole crew teams like shish kabobs (advising his crew to be less talkative during a crucial racing maneuver: "Everybody on the windward rail is a jerk! Shut up, you jerks!"). But he will also apologize for "getting upset back there a while ago." The effect is charming, since the effect—as the direct result of the sharp-edge attention and determination so elicited—is often victory in the race.

Everybody gets his share, even Gary Jobson, who after the *Courageous* America's Cup defense in 1977 emerged as Turner's right hand and alter ego aboard ship. "The people who sail with Ted regularly just shrug it off, mostly. One of our guys, Richie Boyd, gives it right back, and sometimes he and Ted wind up just screaming at each other from bow to stern. That's not too great, you know? But sometimes you have to tell Ted to knock it off." Does it do any good? "Not usually," Jobson says. "The best time to give Ted advice is when he asks for it."

The pattern in Turner's career has been for those persons who cannot abide his rampant humors in the office or on the racecourse to disappear in haste. If the departure takes place before the knots of loyalty have drawn tight, there is no vindictiveness on Turner's side. He seems to leave room for honorable withdrawal, and even sometimes to admire it. The press, on the other hand, is a different story.

Seldom in the history of journalism have so many been excoriated so much and come back begging for more. Faced with a reporter, particularly a print reporter, Turner seems determined to taunt the fates of publicity. Faced with Turner, print reporters seem determined to prove that "objectivity" is an impregnable shield against insult. Almost every day Dee Woods logs in a new request for an interview by the *Wall Street Journal, Parade, Playboy, Esquire,* the networks, or America's peripatetic sports reporters, hundreds of whom dog Turner's steps each year.

Reporters as a class are unable to resist colorfulness. Too many of their subjects turn circumspect in the face of the press, or arrogant in presumed self-defense. Professional newsmakers—actors, politicians or advocates—respond to questions like cues in a play they have performed many times before. Most of the time a reporter finds himself outside the castle wall, hoping that Rapunzel will let down her hair. This Rapunzel jumps on your head.

Don West of *Broadcasting* magazine was interviewing Turner in the lobby of Washington's Mayflower Hotel. *Broadcasting* is a powerful organ of the industry, and Turner was being considered for a cover story. Good, Turner said, agreeing that he was a perfect subject. *Broadcasting,* however, he described as severely flawed and obviously run by jerks. West himself he announced to be an ignoramus and a dummy. Soon Turner was yelling at West, and a crowd began to gather. West turned off his tape recorder and Turner resumed normal conversation. West flicked it on, and Turner called him numbnuts.

West turned it off again, laughing. Why not? He was getting a good story.

"I can't imagine taking that seriously," West said later. "You just figure Ted's turned on. And he's definitely cover-story material, yes."

In Atlanta, a distinguished AP columnist named Will Grimsley stopped by to see Turner at his television station. Grimsley's column is distributed all over the country, and he had known Turner for nearly a decade. He was en route to a speaking engagement at Auburn University, but hoped to drum up a column on the way.

"Shoot," said Turner.

"Well, you own the Braves, and you also do a lot of sailing, and I wondered which, uh, which one you like better."

Pause. "That's just the stupidest question I ever heard," said Turner, seemingly astounded. "Jesus, really. That's incredibly dumb. I mean, people are starving in Africa and the level of topsoil in the United States has fallen from 16 inches to only 9 inches, and you're asking me which is better, sailing or baseball?" Turner berated him for ten minutes, and Grimsley, horrified, fled. His column the next day said that Ted Turner was sitting in his office pondering the salvation of mankind, rather than wasting time on such nonsense as baseball or sailing. "Turner was not being impolite," Grimsley wrote.

In Newport, Beau Cutts of the *Atlanta Constitution* was watching Turner practice for the 1980 America's Cup. Cutts bore a stigma: he had recently written a brief article which suggested that Turner might be a difficult fellow to be friends with. Turner was cool and suspicious. He had Cutts banned from the press boat one day. Cutts followed his subject around as best he could, trailing a photographer, while Jobson and others spread the word not to talk to him much. A hatchet job was presumed.

But Cutts's piece, when it appeared, was a labor of love—carefully crafted, full of high sentence, often flattering.

Turner's poison-tipped attacks on network TV have resulted not in his being ignored or scorned, but in full-length video treatments, including two on Walter Cronkite's *CBS Evening News.* When he was profiled on *60 Minutes,* the television equivalent of the cover of *Time* magazine, Harry Reasoner accompanied him to spring training and took the obligatory jeep ride at Hope Plantation. But even Reasoner wasn't spared.

> REASONER: There's been some criticism of Channel 17's programming. I noticed *The Flintstones* was on there a minute ago.
> TURNER: There's been some criticism of CBS programs. . . . I remember when I first took over the station, everybody said, "Well, your programs lack quality." Well, I could go to New York now and say to the top advertising people, "Do the networks' programs have all that much quality?" And I don't get anybody that argues with me anymore. I don't need any more money, I really don't. I've got more money than I ever dreamed that I'd ever have in my life. Our station is going to stand for something a little bit better.

The press usually gives Turner the benefit of the doubt. Reasoner concluded his show with a testimonial which probably exceeded in value the entire $500,000 Turner Corporation promotion budget:

"I left that baseball field liking Ted Turner," Reasoner said in his fatherly tone. "I'd hate to have to keep up with him, and I'd hate to be that driven myself. But I liked him. He's a talented man with a very large ego, not unheard of in American business and show business. And when you look at his accomplishments, maybe you can't blame him. He's just convinced he can do almost anything he sets out to do. And so far he's been right."

"Pretty strong, huh?" Turner says each time he views the tape.

So the image builds and grows, almost out of control, and Turner's power with it. In the meantime, he continues to cut his own hair.

"Oh, he's been doing that for years," says Janie. "He uses one of those razor comb things. He does it real well, and I help him get the back, where it's hard to reach. I guess it saves $8 or so every time, and it must be important." Janie, however, does not seem to have her heart in the razor comb. "He does the kids' hair too, when he can catch them, and they look kind of butchered sometimes. Once I took them for regular haircuts and it was $7 each, I think. Ted found out. Boy, was he mad. It's just extremely inconsistent, you know. He's so frugal around the house—we can't have the air conditioning on, we can't have the heat on, we can't even have the lights on. Then he goes off and buys a boat or something for some astronomical, unbelievable price. The household expenses can't exceed $100 a week, but then he takes the whole boat crew to dinner and it's thousands of dollars. That bothers me a lot. That really gets me mad sometimes."

Will Sanders also knows about the razor comb. "Well, you can't get rich if you don't save money. I was telling this young barber the other day about it. I didn't mention the name, I just said I knew somebody used a razor comb on his own head and hadn't paid for a haircut in eight years. What did he think about that?"

"He said, 'Oh, that'll ruin your hair. It'll leave all kinds of hack marks. You can't fix it, either, once they do that. This guy must be a real disaster.'

"He wouldn't have believed me if I'd told him it was Ted," Sanders said.

Turner has several times lost substantial fractions of his wardrobe by leaving his suitbag behind in taxicabs or airplanes. "I used to try to keep him looking nice," Janie says, "but I've more or less given up. He just doesn't care." Turner wears black Gucci loafers, the standard footwear of ambition in American business. If he knew they cost $150 the pair he probably would not.

He has a private airstrip on his plantation, but it is grown over with weeds. He flies only on commercial airlines, and always tourist. Traveling with Turner, who is at home at 35,000 feet as he is anywhere else, is both a challenge and an education. Rule One is never check a bag, and woe unto him who does. Here is Turner at Boston's Logan Airport, waiting at baggage claim with a hapless companion: "You ever want to travel with me again you leave that suitcase home. We could have been out of here twenty minutes ago and now we're waiting for your dumb suitcase. Notice that I never carry a suitcase. You get a carry-on bag, in which you put your socks and a shirt. You get a suit bag which you can hang up as you enter the plane. Never check anything, idiot. I'm not waiting much longer, pal. It's toodle-oo to you. Boy, I can't believe you're keeping me waiting like this."

The Turner airport system: Arrive one hour before departure time. Obtain the forwardmost tourist-class seat on the aisle, asking that an adjacent seat be left open if the plane does not fill. This position, in addition to guaranteeing that its occupant will be noticed by all the

other passengers, also assures a fast exit. Only first-class tickethold-
ers will be able to deplane earlier, and since they are usually infirm,
overweight or laid back, they can be easily outrun on the airport
ramp. With any luck this puts Turner in the first taxicab—and away.
Just don't forget your suitbag.

"You know, of course, that professional athletes always fly first
class," Turner says, shaking his head. "It's in the contract and they
think it's a big deal. I'm the owner, and tourist is fine for me, but they
got to make a big show. I wanted to offer all my teams the option—in
other words, if they flew tourist I'd pay them the difference. Just so
as not to waste the money. But I was told it's not a negotiable thing.
I could see a basketball guy who's 7 feet tall wanting the extra room,
but not a shortstop. Certainly not an umpire, with his feet dangling
over the seat. First class on airplanes is almost always pure bull."

Six months after making the mistake of checking a suitcase on a
flight with Turner, the same companion met him in Atlanta for a
flight to Charleston and a few days of hunting and hiking at Hope
Plantation. The companion had the drill down pat: socks in his pockets, toothpaste in his sport jacket, two pairs of muddy shoes crammed
into a suitbag along with a light-blue seersucker suit.

Turner, however, checked a suitcase.

"It's got my machete inside," he explained sheepishly. "You try to
carry a machete through the X-ray machine, they'll think you're
hijacking your way to Cuba."

If Turner's brain is ever dissected in the laboratories of Harvard
Business School, it will probably reveal but little. His phrenology is
a mysterious terrain, and it might take Harvard years to discern the
origin of the haircut alone. But to be with Turner, ah! To watch him
in action, chin to chin and arm in arm, chiseling the blank rocks in
his own image, is a course in millionairing for which no tuition is too
high. A recent matriculant is Gary Jobson.

Jobson is a tall, loose-limbed young man produced by the public
school systems of central New Jersey, where his father, Tom Jobson,
is managing editor of the *Asbury Park Press*. The Jobson family still
lives in Toms River, a growing community on the western shore of
Barnegat Bay.

Jobson was a prototypical kid, wised up and wide-eyed, who as a high school wrestler went 7 and 4 his senior year and never forgot the sting of being pinned in a championship match before his hometown crowd.

He became the steady crew, in the mid-1960s, of Sam Merrick, a pugnacious veteran of the regatta wars who later served as director of the United States Olympic Yachting Committee. "Yeah, I taught Gary everything he knows," Merrick cracks. "It wasn't too hard, because back then Gary didn't know anything. He used to fall all over the boat. It amazes me when I look at him now."

At New York Maritime College, Jobson got hot. He was three times named an All-American Sailor, and after graduation his buoyant, ain't-life-grand personality made him a successful coach there, and later at the United States Naval Academy at Annapolis.

But when Turner tapped him as tactician aboard *Courageous* in the 1977 America's Cup defense, his education really began.

Three summers later, Jobson was relaxing in his neat office overlooking the antique charm of Church Circle in Annapolis. His secretary, Karina Paape, fielded a steady stream of telephone calls to Jobson Sailing Associates. On the wall, a pinboard recorded more than a hundred engagements for his yachting slide-and-lecture show, which he jetted cross-country to deliver in a remarkable exclamatory style that drew audiences of 600 or more for a single night. Posters for his two books on sailing, one written with Turner, were framed on the wall, and he had contracts for two more. He had eight advertising accounts, including Michelob beer, *Yachting,* AMF Sailboats, Hood Sails, and International Marine Wear, for which he promoted equipment, set up regattas, or assisted otherwise in the sailing world. He had been recently named an editor of *Yachting* magazine, admitted to the New York Yacht Club (his eleventh club membership), and had standing free passes to Washington's largest sports arena and the Broadway shows of New York. His new house on Charles Street featured one of the first hot tubs in old Annapolis, where he bobbed amid friends and rum and Cokes at a constant temperature of 92 degrees.

Jobson, at twenty-nine, had developed the Turner touch. When he walked down the crowded Annapolis streets, it was with a smile and a greeting for all—whether they recognized him or not. He had become a hero during the America's Cup of 1977 and learned how to handle it. He would fill any lull in conversation with an enthusiastic, innocent recitation of his latest accomplishments, often closing with Turner's own favorite phrase—"pretty strong, huh?" He put on neither airs nor Gucci loafers, yet his addiction to *Time* and *Newsweek* kept him ready with an opinion on any topic. He had survived three years of intense exposure to Robert Edward Turner III, the crash course.

On the afternoon of December 19, 1979, Jobson passed his final examination. He was crossing Duke of Gloucester Street when it happened.

"Hey," he said to a companion. "You ever think about becoming a millionaire? I've decided I'm going to become one. I've already got a head start. My house is worth, what, $130,000 or something. My business has a value, and I'm probably going to make about $100,000 this year. I think I can do $200,000 next year, if things go right. Yeah, I'm going to do it. Why not? I'm going to be a millionaire."

So does the Turner army march, growing like Alexander's along the way.

6 The Name of the Game

It HAD been raining for days and days in Atlanta, and the city was taking it badly. The tennis courts at the carefully groomed private clubs were sodden, the golf courses puddled, and in the half-light of singles bars, athletic young men and women touched glasses of draft beer, their interoffice softball games for the moment postponed. It was a good Monday night to stay home. The Dallas Cowboys were playing the Cleveland Browns on television, with America's Team fated to lose. Eventually the rain would clear and Atlanta, the San Diego of the New South, could go back outside and play.

Ted Turner, however, had a baseball game to attend. He was known as an indefatigable competitor, and there could be no thought of abandoning his Braves now. Had he not studied leadership with old Leonidas, who fell, killed with his 300 men at Thermopylae, rather than yield to 100,000 Persians? ("Go, stranger, and tell the Lacedaemonians we lie here in obedience to their laws.") No, Turner was the one who accepted every challenge, threading the social labyrinth of the America's Cup, pricking the olympian networks, and locking horns with the professional leagues of baseball, basketball, hockey and soccer. Now that he was called a folk hero, there was more reason than ever to remain obedient to his own laws.

The doubleheader with the Houston Astros was scheduled to begin at 6:15. The Astros were battling for a playoff berth, but Turner's Braves were finishing out the season in last place in their division. Even so, a team party was set for after the second game, and Janie and the three youngest children would be driving to Fulton County Stadium from Marietta to fulfill their roles for the evening. In his office at the Superstation, Turner worked steadily along, flipping through the pile of papers Dee Woods had stacked on his desk and

/ 135

yelling into his telephone voicebox at the steady stream of callers. At 5:00, Woods called the baseball field one last time.

Cupping her hand over the receiver, she called out the news to her boss: "Ted, they say the field's pretty dry under the cover and it looks like the game will start more or less on time."

"OK," Turner replied flatly. Then, as if dissatisfied with his own tone of voice, he began to hum. "Take me out to the ball game, dah da dum dum dum dum. Buy me some peanuts and Crackerjacks, I don't care if I—hey! Aw right, we got a ball game to go to! Dee, call Janie and make sure she's coming. I'm going to have dinner at the Stadium Club. There's a tobacco-spitting contest before the game, if that ain't the most disgusting thing you ever heard. There's a buffet for the players afterward. Make sure everybody knows what's going on."

At the stadium, Turner's Toyota zoomed into its underground parking spot at exuberant speed, and he couldn't resist poking his head into the Braves' locker room for a moment.

"Hey Eddie," he called to Ed Miller, a muscular newcomer wrapped at the moment in a towel. Miller had stolen seventy bases with the Braves' Triple A farm club in Richmond, and was batting .340 in his first major league season. "I'm the one who wanted you here," Turner shouted to him. "And I was right, you're doing great!" Miller nodded shyly, but Turner was already gone.

After dinner, during which he viewed the tobacco-spitting promotion with distaste, he was soon working his way through the stands toward his habitual seat behind the Braves dugout. The few hundred people in the sprawling bleachers recognized Turner instantly. He moseyed in, grabbing hands as they were offered, grinning back at the cries of "Hey Ted!" and "Hi, Mr. Turner!" and "Yo, Terrible Ted!" When an ungainly woman in hair curlers several rows away hollered, "Yoo-hoo! 'Cutie-pie!" Turner stopped so suddenly that two people piled into him from behind. Observing the source of the greeting, however, he moved quickly on. This stroll brought him hard by the Astros' bench.

"I love you guys," he called down to the waiting players. "All of you. But of course you know I can't offer you a job on my team on account of Commissioner Bowie Kuhn would suspend me again for tampering." Grins broke out among the Astros.

The seat toward which Turner was headed was well known to the fans of Atlanta, and to television millions as far as the Superstation reached. For four years he had held forth from it like a tenth player on the team. But the personal microphone, which he once used to address the crowd directly, is now gone. This night, Turner did not even cram a handful of chaw into his mouth, but lit a long cigar instead as the first of the games began in a steady drizzle. He did not leap onto the field to help his curvaceous ball girls sweep the bases clean between innings, nor did he abuse the umpires, nor displace Chief Nok-A-Homa, the team's pseudo-Indian mascot, from his warpath atop the dugout. He just sipped a beer while the Astros, clutching, lost the first game 5-6. Turner clapped as best he could through two tears in the garbage bag that entirely covered his body— a rainproofing gift from several similarly protected fans in nearby seats. When Eddie Miller came to bat, Turner shouted encouragement. When his highly paid, highly talented third baseman, Bob Horner, took the plate, he called, "Go, Bobby." But under his breath he mused: "I always wonder if that guy really likes me. His agent sure tries to bust my butt at contract time."

The drizzle kept up all evening, soaking the bleachers and driving most of the fans under cover. Turner stayed doggedly in his seat. ("You guys go up to the club. I'm going to stick it out down here.") From behind the befogged windows of the Stadium Club he could be seen far below, nearly alone in the empty arena, a small, green-plastic-covered figure smoking a cigar. The image was bizarrely touching—Winston Churchill, thrown out with the trash.

The Braves unaccountably won the second game too, 8-1. Having blown away Houston's playoff shot, they headed for the showers and the end-of-the-season buffet upstairs. Turner was there first, positioned for small talk, the greeting of the players' families, and exuding friendship and enthusiasm. The players did not seem inclined to fraternize, however. Perhaps it was because Turner was standing with John Mullen, his burly general manager, whose Vitalis-induced frontal hair wave marked him as a veteran of the pro ball wars. Management and ownership, shoulder to shoulder.

"I'm sorry that guy had to call you at your office this afternoon," Mullen confided, referring to a member of the team who was being sent back down to the farm club at Richmond, but who had insisted on hearing the bad news from Turner himself.

"Oh no, John," Turner said. "They can always talk to me. I want them to know me."

"It complicates everything," Mullen said.

"Always, always let them talk to me," Turner said.

How hard it was, Turner had found, to maintain control. Since he had purchased the Braves they had not had a winning season, but that did not bother him as much as the team's frustrating imperviousness to direct action. Professional baseball was swathed in multilayered blankets of bureaucracy, and the closer he got the more the blankets enveloped and smothered him. He was used to standing at the helm, whether of a superstation or an ocean racer, sweating, cursing and shouting orders, win, lose or draw. That was the way he approached baseball, too—at first.

When Turner bought the Braves he did not know the difference between a balk and the infield fly rule. But he plunged in with gay abandon, traveling with his players, throwing parties for them, inviting them to his home, even learning to chew tobacco at his first spring training. The players warmed immediately, even as the other owners of the other teams cooled.

Turner told the sportswriters that he was merely living out every American boy's fantasy. "I ought to be allowed to take batting practice," he said. "Not only do I need it real bad, but I paid $11 million for my ticket." National League President Chub Feeney fidgeted for a while, then directed Turner to knock it off. Most especially, Feeney said, Turner must stop playing poker with his team—it was clearly improper for a millionaire owner to ante up with schoolboys. "Hell," Turner says, "that was just nickel-and-dime stuff for fun. Nobody ever lost more than $30 a night, unless it was the guy from Delta Airlines, who used to drop $100 all the time." But Feeney was adamant. Furthermore, Turner had to quit running onto the field during the game to congratulate his players. The other owners were complaining that it was bad for baseball—indeed, hadn't Bob Howsam, the chairman of the Cincinnati Reds, ordered Turner arrested if he jumped the railing at the Cincinnati stadium?

Turner, calling up his military school training, obeyed these various dicta, although he grumped that "a baseball owner's got less rights than any regular U.S. citizen—it's like all of a sudden being shipped off to Russia. I may be kind of weird, but is it against the law to have a good time?"

His freewheeling style got him in hot water from the start with the Baseball Commissioner's office. He had his eye on Gary Matthews, a star hitter for the San Francisco Giants, and at a cocktail party turned to Giants owner Bob Lurie and said, "Anything you offer Gary Matthews, I'll offer more." That comment, which ranks among the least offensive utterances in Turner history, eventually resulted in Turner's being kicked off his own team for a year. Lurie complained to Bowie Kuhn that Turner's challenge constituted an illegal contract negotiation, and Kuhn so found. Turner signed Matthews anyhow, and with him pitcher Andy Messersmith, each for a contract worth $1 million or so.

It was the Messersmith case that first introduced Turner to the world of professional sports contract negotiations. Messersmith had fought through several appeals to achieve free-agent status from the Los Angeles Dodgers, and Turner was determined to get him on the Braves roster. At one point he had already had dinner with the young golden-haired pitcher to discuss Atlanta's bountiful future—and warn Messersmith that any other team he joined would undoubtedly make him cut his hair—but found he could not reach the player's *agent* on the phone. Turner, used to spontaneous combustion, was burning his fingers holding the match.

He told the *Atlanta Constitution,* as the details of the pitcher's contract became more and more complex, that "this whole thing is like having your wife's attorney come up to you on the day you're getting married and tell you that your wife can't cook breakfast on Sunday, and has to get a $150-a-week allowance, and needs a new car every two years. It's a heck of a way to get started."

Agents, he said, were leading the players astray. "These guys love playing ball, but they know it's still a game. They don't need to make fifty times what a high school principal does, do they? Twenty times what a U.S. Senator is paid?

"I always said, in all the sports I'm involved with, that owners and players shouldn't fight each other. But still everybody has to have meetings constantly. The owners get together and say, 'We'll show those players who's boss.' And the players get together and they say the same thing about us. We have special strike funds and task forces and everything. And I'm saying, 'This is baseball? How come we're fighting with our own teams? Why can't we be friends?' "

Horner, the Braves' third baseman, was a case in point. A tiger on the field, he had shown the same claws in contract disputes that by 1979 had left Turner limp with frustration.

Horner had played well against the Houston Astros, and after his shower he slipped into the Stadium Club, skillfully circumnavigated the Turner-Mullen greeting party and entered the buffet line. Caught there, plate in one hand and ladleful of potato salad in the other, he listened once again to an account of Turner's point of view.

"I know Ted wants to be friends with the players," Horner said with a shrug, glancing about to assure the privacy of his conversation. "He says he admires me? Then I'm pleased. But he forgets that there's more to baseball today than playing your position on the field. You have to be smart. For example, I'm twenty-two years old now, but how about when I'm fifty? Will he be my friend then? How about when my batting average goes down to .275 and I only hit eleven home runs one year? The players are well aware that in the major leagues you have maybe three and a half years of top earning power, and when your time is up, you're out. But the owner, he's still in. See, that's why I got my agent, Bucky Moy. It's no problem, I'll be back next year. But on this contract we just did, the hard feelings came because Ted didn't know me, and I didn't know Ted, and Bucky didn't know Ted, and we're all pretty aggressive guys. It's a tough game."

(True enough. At the beginning of the 1980 season, when Horner's batting average slipped and his fielding errors increased, he was unceremoniously demoted to the minor leagues for a few weeks. Horner was furious and threatened to quit, but Turner said, "If you're paid like a star, you should play like a star.")

"Hey," Horner said, his buffet journey completed. "I got a family, a Porsche car, and a nice house outside Atlanta, and parents back home in Phoenix who watch me on cable TV. If things are going OK for me, it's because I look out for myself."

By midnight, Turner was back in his Toyota, heading home in the rain after another seventeen-hour day. His eyes showed fatigue, but although his voice had gone grainy, it was still strident and full of volume. His mind ticked over the events of the day, scanning for evidence of progress, and ranged also into the history and future of his enterprises. This 20-mile commute often produced valuable ideas and projects, and for that reason a tiny tape recorder lay at the foot of his manual gearshift lever. The thoughts that came to him in the car were transcribed by his secretary and dispatched as memos and orders the following morning. If he had a listener, though, Turner seldom bothered with the tape.

"I've had so many unparalleled successes," he said suddenly as the slick highway hissed beneath the wheels. "Now that the baseball season is finished and the Hawks are playing, we'll get going again. I just can't tell you how excited I am about the Hawks, they're a great young team. We've got a Rhodes Scholar, Tom McMillen, playing for us, and that's pretty strong. But the Braves have always been the one thing people could cite—nah, nah, what about the Braves. It's like sticking a knife in my stomach every time." He paused to recover control of the car after a minor skid induced by his simulation of disembowelment. "I started off saying we'd have a World Series in Atlanta within five years, but I've had to move the date up a little. We'll Prove it to You in 1982, yeah. I just have to have time to learn the hard way, like always.

"And I've tried. That first year I was really active. I devoted half my time to the Braves, which is a huge amount. I went around to every National League ball park, met all the general managers, discussed ticket pricing, how to develop players, even how you print up a program. I didn't have any idea how complicated it all was. It was a nightmare. Take football or basketball—you draft players right out of college. All you have to do to see who's good is watch the college games on TV. But in baseball, you sign most of the kids right out of high school. Then to polish them up you have to have a whole system of farm teams. I mean, we've got 250 people working on the Braves' payroll, and we've got farm clubs running in Richmond and Kingsport, Tennessee, and Bradenton, Florida, and Savannah and Raleigh, North Carolina, and on top of that there's six weeks of spring training too. You sign up a kid and put him through all that and then maybe in six years he pays off. Six years! It takes a long time to build a winning team, even if you buy players, too. But of course, being me, I didn't want to wait. At first I tried to shake every hand in the stadium. That was before I realized there were 162 games a year. I even fired a midget. Now that's colorful. This midget's name was Don Davidson, and he'd been with the Braves for forty years and was only four feet tall, and I fired him. Because he didn't like the way I was running the team. The sports writers almost killed me. 'This *great man* fired by a *little man,*' they wrote. I also had a disagreement with Eddie Robinson, who I really, really liked. He was the general manager.

"Robinson had a Cadillac and he flew first class everyplace and stayed in suites. But the team was losing millions of dollars a year. I said, 'Give me a break.' But he felt that was what the big leagues were all about—staying in suites. I said, 'What? I'm in the Little League? I always fly tourist class.' He went off to the Texas Rangers, and he's doing great.

"We did a lot of promotions, too," Turner said.

Such understatement does not do justice to Turner's first Braves' season. It began with his entering the world of professional baseball astride an ostrich, as part of a pregame amusement cooked up by his imaginative stunts director, Bob Hope, now an executive with Coca-Cola. Turner, promising great events, opened his very first game by leading the fans in a 35,000-voice chorus of "Take Me Out to the Ball Game," then turning a scheduled five-minute greeting into a half-hour peroration worthy of Fidel Castro. When the Braves scored their first home run, the fans were astounded to see the owner waiting at home plate to shake his batter's hand. Before long, Braves games took on the look of daytime television shows, with weddings in the batter's box, Karl Wallenda tight-roping across the stadium, on-field easter egg hunts, mad scrambles for windblown dollar bills, and free distribution of scanty halter tops designed to show off the best attributes of female Atlanta. Turner also had a $1 million electronic scoreboard installed capable of transmitting any zany message, and also of instant replay—to the chagrin of the umpires.

The owner pitched in personally. He entered the motorized bathtub races, he served as a bat boy (after the failure of a chimpanzee to handle the job), he chased the ball girls from base to base between innings, once performing a somersault, the first he had ever tried, on the way to third base. He let his players put nicknames on their jerseys, and since Messersmith's number was 17, he became "Channel." It was a natural television ploy—until, once again, the league said to knock it off. When he was not leaping the rail to cavort on the field, Turner held forth by microphone from his seat behind the dugout—once apologizing publicly for his team's bad showing, and promising free tickets to anyone who would come back the next night.

Not since the proudest days of Georgia Tech had Atlanta felt the pull of the glory locomotive. Attendance doubled, for even if the Braves still seemed disconcertingly disaster-prone, Turner was good entertainment. And no one had ever shown more desire to win. When the publicity office announced a contest to see who could roll a baseball around the bases fastest by use of nose power alone, Turner volunteered for the Braves (since no one else would). The other parties to this escapade were the visiting Philadelphia Phillies, who offered resident corkscrew Tug McGraw as designated nose roller. But McGraw never had a chance.

Turner, on hands and knees, nosed his way around the diamond with such ferocity that he scraped the skin off his face from forehead to chin. There is now a framed picture of the victor in the Braves office, looking like an accident victim awaiting helicopter evacuation. The baseball, still daubed with blood, is also permanently enshrined there.

"That all seems like such a long time ago now," Turner said, uncomfortable with the memories. "I didn't have any choice, but it worked at first. We filled up the stadium that first year. Then we got snakebit. Messersmith only pitched sixteen games before he got hurt, so his salary really came to $18,750 a game. Then we got on the damnedest losing streak, and after we'd lost sixteen in a row I told my manager, Dave Bristol, to take a vacation. I wanted to manage the Braves myself, why not? I figured if I could just get down there up close, I could figure out what was wrong, and then Bristol could come back. I didn't think it would be that hard. So after my first game in the dugout, and we only lost 2-1 so I didn't do that bad, this telegram comes from Bowie Kuhn saying get back in the stands where you belong. I read the telegram and I called him up—get me the Big Chief at his teepee. Commissioner Kuhn said he didn't think it was in the best interests of baseball that I manage my own team. Even though I had paid for it. He told me to act like the other owners, but I said the other owners aren't in last place. It seemed like the bigwigs were really tough on me. I just eventually said forget it. Basically, I don't like being an owner. By nature, I'm a participant. It's not for the limelight, it's because it helps the team, and it helps my TV station, and it doesn't hurt anyone. I'll tell you, if there was ever fools' gold, it's the limelight."

The limelight, however, tracked him closely, illuminating in his dealings with baseball a dramatic, often hilarious clash of styles and war of words. Turner invariably called Chub Feeney "the chief," while referring to himself as "the little Indian from Atlanta." Kuhn he labeled "super chief." If Kuhn regarded baseball as part of an American trinity that also included motherhood and apple pie, he must have regarded Turner as Mork from Ork—with his flying saucer illegally parked on the baseball diamond. The more Turner tried to patch things up, the bigger holes he made. On January 18, 1977, he appeared in Kuhn's office to plead against his suspension. The transcription attests that he sounded more like Chief Joseph of the Nez Perce Indian tribe than your average major league owner with a point to make.

TURNER: Give us a way out of this thing, if you can, as the guy who is supposed to be the Big Chief of baseball. The little Indians. I am like the little Indians out in the West. You hear about the Big Chief back in Washington, the Great White Father who says, "You've got to move off your reservation."
We kept moving the Indians back and back and back until they had to fight. A few of them had to fight. I do not want to fight.

Great White Father, please tell me how to avoid fighting for what little we have left. The buffalo are gone. The white man came and killed off all the buffalo.

They drove the trains through what we were told we would have—this land, you know? The Black Hills. Now this gold you want—the yellow metal—you want us to leave and go to the dust bowl of Oklahoma and these are our homes. We must fight for them.

Please go back to the Great White Father, Soldier Man, and tell him to please help us. . . .

I am very contrite. I am very humble. I am sorry. I would get down on the floor and let you jump up and down on me if it would help. I would let you hit me three times in the face without lifting a hand to protect myself. I would bend over and let you paddle my behind, hit me over the head with a Fresca bottle, something like that. Physical pain I can stand.

KUHN: Well, I think you have said some very unstatesmanlike things. . . .

The upshot was that Bowie Kuhn slapped Ted Turner with a one-year suspension from baseball and a $10,000 fine, as punishment for his tampering with Matthews at the cocktail party. Kuhn said in his decision that the action "broke his heart," because Turner had "done so much to generate enthusiasm for the game" in Atlanta. Turner's supporters appealed, soliciting the support of Governor George Busbee and Mayor Maynard Jackson for a 10,000-signature petition in favor of the Braves' owner. The suspension stood, but Turner let none of his boosters down in the turbulent court hearings in Atlanta. Under close questioning by one of Kuhn's attorneys, Turner threatened to deliver the lawyer a "knuckle sandwich" if he didn't back off. The press loved it, and the limelight brightened.

The ruling, however, effectively knocked Turner out of the Braves' prompter's box, since under its terms he was not even allowed to enter his memento-strewn office at Fulton County Stadium.

"Hey! Look at that, we beat Janie home and she and the kids left before we did," Turner said, pulling his car up to the garage of his two-story Colonial home in the Marietta hills. But the chat about baseball had left his personal engine in high gear, and he could not switch it off. "Organized baseball is incredibly screwed up," he continued. "It succeeds on arrogance, not progress. The other owners are fat cats and bigwigs, except for a few guys like George Steinbrenner, who's a fighter like me.

"The real issue is, can they keep me down on the farm? They've divided up the country among themselves with this franchise system they have, and they don't want anybody rocking their boat. They give themselves New York, and L.A., and Chicago, and I'm supposed to be grateful for Atlanta, with less than two million people in the metropolitan area. Stay there, little fella, they say. You bet I'll stay here. I love Atlanta. No more Losersville, U.S.A., now. We're going places.

"What they can't stand is that my teams are going out on my television stations everywhere, not just in the network package deal they set up for themselves, and there's not a thing they can do about it. They thought I was a dumb rich sucker who stepped up with $10 million to buy a losing franchise with only one-tenth of the people to draw on as the big cities. But I'm giving Atlanta to the nation—to the world!

"It's such a brilliant stroke, what I've done. Take a few dollars and turn them into millions. The Braves, the Hawks, and the Chiefs—they'll have fans all over the country. Franchise hell! We're building a Fourth Network, and it just confounds the other owners. You should hear the heated debates at league meetings, people almost screaming at each other. I just sit there quietly, trying not to break out laughing. I say, 'Gentlemen, the law of the land takes precedence over the law of the league.' They've got their own franchise rules, but the rules of the country take precedence in areas of conflict.

"I'll tell you a secret. People love the Braves already, because of what they are—colorful, and trying real hard, and getting better. When they start to win, and get into some playoffs, they're going to take America by storm. It's going to be like my boat, *Tenacious*, which doesn't have a home port on the stern. It just says, *'Tenacious,* U.S.A.' The Braves and the Hawks, because of the wonderful Atlanta fans and my wonderful Superstation, are America's first *national* sporting teams."

Janie and the children arrived thereupon. Janie's hair was still perfectly in place, and her black dress unrumpled. Only a slight drooping of the shoulders indicated fatigue as she aimed the kids toward the kitchen door.

"Hi, sweetie!" Turner yelled in response to her demure wave of greeting. Janie started, as if by the flicking of a familiar light switch she had accidentally set off all the machinery in Dr. Frankenstein's laboratory.

"Oh, Ted." She sighed. "Aren't you tired yet?"

The fact is that however much Turner may rebel against the conservative traditions of baseball ownership, he loves being a baseball owner. From the beginning it gave him a new forum, a new toy, and most important of all, guaranteed television rights to the sport for his Superstation. He held the future of sports in Atlanta in his hands, and Atlanta was grateful. Naturally, he plunged in for more.

On January 4, 1977, the day after Bowie Kuhn announced his suspension from baseball, Turner acquired 98 percent control of the Atlanta Hawks basketball team. This time he promised not to put on a uniform personally, and appointed Mike Storen, former commissioner of the old American Basketball Association, his president and general manager.

The Hawks, last in their division of the National Basketball Association, had also been in grave danger of moving out of town—and Turner had had the same nightmare that had jolted him into taking on the Braves. "What would Atlanta be without a basketball team?" he asked the hordes of sportswriters dogging his every step. "What would the Superstation be without the Hawks?" Also, Turner confided, he wanted to win an NBA championship, and his advisers had told him he couldn't do that without a team. Furthermore, the NBA had never in its history kicked an owner off his own team.

Storen, asked to comment, said, "It's really fun to sit down with your new partner and learn he's been suspended for the good of sports."

The Hawks, a young team, took to Turner immediately. By 1979, under coach Hubie Brown they had made the playoffs, and had even come close to knocking out the battle-scarred Washington Bullets, world champions from the year before. In 1980, the Hawks got in the playoffs again.

Turner set up his friend Al Thornwell as owner of the soccer Chiefs, having been warned by the league that he would not be allowed to become the Ma Bell of professional sports in the South.

Turner theoretically has no say whatever in Chiefs soccer, but he does remain in touch.

Walking down the corridors of Atlanta's stadium, Thornwell informed Turner that he intended to discharge one of the soccer team's high-ranking employees. It had to be done, Thornwell said. Events made it necessary.

"What?" said Turner. "But he's such a nice guy. He's brilliant, he's a prince. What could possibly be the matter?"

"Well, it's the foreign players," Thornwell said unhappily. "He doesn't relate to the foreign players."

"Then let the foreign players relate to him," Turner said. "Really. I don't want you to go any further with that unless you talk to me again."

"OK, Ted," Thornwell said.

Within a period of less than a year, Ted Turner unveiled the nation's first superstation, purchased two big-league professional sports teams, and won the America's Cup. His previous escapades—the pinball journey through Brown University, the seizure of his father's company, the rebuilding of the broken-down UHF TV stations, the takeover of international yacht racing—had made his name hard coinage in diverse circles. But the country as a whole hadn't really caught on. For the most part, the tales of Turner were still relegated to the business page, or the sports columns, or to the specialized magazines of the communications industry.

It took an amateur sailboat race to change all that. It was at the America's Cup of 1977, in what had previously been an arcane and highfalutin contest between thoroughbred yachts off Newport, that the folk hero was born in a flurry of hurriedly aimed TV cameras.

Turner has it figured out.

"The reason that I became really famous, and the reason why the America's Cup became really famous, was that Bowie Kuhn suspended me from baseball that year. I'm not kidding, it's true. When I went off for the Cup trials, it was an innocent man serving time in the Commissioner of Baseball's jail. There's nothing like injustice to make people pay attention."

Turner's underdog status had been assured in 1974, when he first bid for the right to sail in the Cup matches with a new design from the drawing board of naval architect Britton Chance, Jr. Turner and Chance had known each other for years, and had worked together trying to develop various fast sailboats, but *Mariner,* as the new 12-meter boat was named, changed all that. The $1 million yacht was sailing for the first time when Turner and his crew noticed the turbulence in her wake—and began to worry. The path a sailboat leaves through the water is supposed to be as unruffled as possible, but Chance's innovative design left swirls and eddies. In *Mariner's* first scrape with another 12-meter yacht, it was clear that she could not even keep up with the obsolete competition.

Turner, watching the other boat sail away, commented, "Well, it looks like it's going to be a long summer." The observation proved true. Bitter recriminations ensued, with Chance claiming Turner was inadequate as helmsman and Turner protesting that it wasn't his fault. The *Mariner* syndicate—into which Turner himself had placed $10,000—ordered drastic changes in the yacht which took most of the summer to complete. When that didn't work, they changed the helmsman. Turner's tactician, Dennis Conner, was given command of *Mariner,* and Turner relegated to the helm of *Valiant,* a 12-meter used for practice.

"Sure it hurt," Turner says. "It hurt bad, I mean I was in tears. Of course, Dennis was good, that's why I picked him as my tactician. But I kept a stiff upper lip. I stayed around, sailing the other boat so Conner could have his chance with *Mariner,* and being a good loser. But Conner couldn't get *Mariner* going either, that was obvious. Brit had made a big mistake in the design, and he'd been a jerk about it. He blamed everybody but himself. He didn't admit his mistake."

By the time 1977 rolled around, Turner was ready again. The tears were gone, and his eyes, always wolflike, took on a distinctly carnivorous look. This time the syndicate he had joined was sponsoring two 12-meter boats, and the theory was that both had an equal chance to win the right to take on the foreign challenger. The two skippers were Turner, the brash Southerner who had been humiliated in 1974, and Ted Hood, who had gone on to successfully defend the Cup that year.

Hood, the soft-spoken founder of Hood Sails, was regarded almost as a deity by the sailing fraternity. He would sail *Independence,* a new boat of his own design, using sails from his own loft. Turner was assigned Hood's old boat, *Courageous,* to sail.

Three American 12-meters entered the final selection trials, each effort having consumed more than $500,000, each syndicate aware that since the United States had never lost the trophy, winning the right to defend would probably be more of a challenge than the defense itself.

But Hood, it quickly became apparent, couldn't keep up with that year's Turner, and he and his new *Independence* faded remarkably, losing twelve of the fourteen races against *Courageous.* Lowell North, skipper of *Enterprise* and a sailmaker whose lofts battled Hood's for the lucrative yachting trade, fared no better, and was replaced at the helm of his boat by Malin Burnham, who couldn't catch Turner either. *Enterprise* lost six in a row to *Courageous* as the trials wound to a close.

Newport was aghast, but fascinated. It was aghast at Turner's boisterousness (rare among the circumspect helmsmen of Cup boats), and at his shoreside psycho-combat. All summer, when not thrashing North on the racecourse, he had been hectoring him about sails. Turner said that North had promised to sell him racing sails. North countered that although he might want to himself, his syndicate had later ruled it out of the question. Turner's fury was extraordinary. He harped and howled and continually excoriated North—a quiet man from California whose style was hot tubs, not hot words—with lengthy strings of scarifying adjectives. Newport had to learn to enjoy it all, and eventually did. By July 4, Turner's picture had hit the cover of *Sports Illustrated,* and he had been named the American defender against the Australian challenge.

"I mean, there was no way we could lose, we wanted it so much after 1974," Turner says. "We were the best sailboat crew in the history of the planet, and we knew it. You have to be amazed, too, when you realize that I had just gone on the air with the Superstation when I left for Newport. I had just bought the Braves, got suspended, and bought the Hawks. It was a marvel, really."

So, as the public was discovering, were the boats. Twelve-meters, the graceful, 65-foot sloops that became the weapons of America's Cup competition in 1958, are the most photographed boats in yachting today. Through a telephoto lens, they often seem lovely gull-like creatures, posed demurely on a placid sea.

Yet each of these mighty yachts, so regal from a distance, rings on board with the shriek of grinding winches, thunder of flapping sails and bark of commands. All America's Cup races are one-on-one, and the strategy is "stay close." So two 65-foot sloops, each with 60,000 pounds of momentum, time and again head directly toward each other in the age-old game of chicken. When one yacht turns, in a roar of spray and snapping jib sheets, the other follows suit. On both yachts, eleven-man crews sweat and curse, manhandling winches and bar-taut wires. A mistake means precious inches lost against the competitor—or worse. With backstays tensioned to 4.5 tons of pressure, a crew error could send the $100,000 mast crashing over the side. A collision means disqualification, and possible injuries. To be caught by one of the flying lines is to risk losing a hand. The forces of the spinnakers, which seem to pop effortlessly as the boats make their downwind turn, are enormous, and one mistake by any of the team can easily mean a close race lost. With each tack, the dizzying progression of adjustments leaves the crew more and more skinned and worn, and then the command to tack comes again—as many as a hundred times a race. For three hours or more, if the other boat battles closely, the two crews will fight on a moving piece of ocean no larger than a football field, watching the whites of each other's eyes. The rules are excruciatingly complicated, and the vagaries of wind introduce an element of luck which, though it is almost never discussed, is certainly greater than in any other widely practiced sport. It is a strange game, and a difficult one to win.

The pressure creates tremendous loyalties and tremendous strain. Both showed at the final press conference at the Newport Armory, a half-mile walk from Bannister's Wharf. After the defeat of Australia, the crews threw each other in the water, traded shirts and turned the dockside into a tableau that resembled a *Mad* magazine centerfold. The Swedes, eliminated earlier, passed Turner a full bottle of aquavit. By the time he made it to the Armory press conference, the aquavit bottle was half empty. That afternoon, everybody took a back seat to Turner. No one was spared the release of six months of tension—not Janie, nor the syndicate members, nor the Australians, who were trying to figure out how to lose gracefully, or at least get a word in edgewise.

That final press conference of the 1977 Cup remains the most memorable scene in America's Cup history—more so than any photo of white-winged yachts or wind-ruffled sea. Turner, buoyed by delirious, worshiping crowds, came late—and plastered. He was accompanied on the dais by two bottles of rum.

It was widely reported that Turner, during the course of an attempted victory speech, passed out and slipped under the table, bottles in hand. That is not precisely what happened, according to R. T. Williams, the Channel 17 producer, who had arrived at the Armory slightly earlier along with the station's general manager, Sid Pike.

"We got there an hour before Turner did," Williams says. "As Turner went down the street, everybody passed him something to drink, and by the time they got there he and Jobson were sloshed. When Turner finally sat down, someone gave him a bottle of rum, which he started chugalugging. Pike and I were sitting right in front of the table, and Pike is saying, 'Oh my God, this is terrible.' He's a television general manager, remember. He knows the TV lights are coming on any minute.

"So Sid quick stands up and grabs the bottle off of Turner's table and puts it underneath, so the cameras won't pick it up. Just then the cameras go on, though, and as Turner is shouting, 'Pike, give me that, you dumb cluck.' (On the tape used in the CBS *60 Minutes* sequence on Turner, the first half of Pike's name is obscured, and Turner seems only to mouth the vulgarity.) What happened was that Ted ducked under the table and grabbed the bottles—I think there were actually two—and then he popped back up and set them back in front of him. He must've called him every name in the book. Meanwhile the Australian is saying what a great competitor Turner is and stuff like that.

"When it was over, Pike and I are walking along and he says to me, 'Did I do something wrong? I was only trying to protect the guy.' " 'Shoot, Pike, you can't protect Turner from himself,' " Williams remembers replying. " 'Everybody knows that.' "

Eventually, several members of the *Courageous* crew, deciding enough was enough, carried their skipper in mid-monologue from the head table. Turner broke free from his captors outside, and was last seen running off through the back yards of Newport, leaping fences that appeared in his way. He collapsed in his quarters, somewhat scratched from the brambles of his journey, at 8:30 P.M. Jobson partied on, "basking in self-esteem" (as he puts it) at the Ida Lewis Yacht Club, then making an appearance at the Candy Store, a popular dockside eatery and disco. The last thing he remembers, as an adoring crowd of females embraced him there, was the fading words of his wife, Janice.

"Gary, you're an idiot," she said. "I'm going home."

The Cup can be very hard on spouses, friendships, bank accounts and humility, for the narcotic effect is all but overpowering for ordinary mortals caught in its thrall.

"You can't believe what a Cup summer does to you," said a thirty-two-year-old veteran, recalling his crew days ten years before on a winning 12-meter. "I was just a kid, and it was almost too much. It was better than being a Beatle. It was better than being God. We used to stand inside the chain-link fence that kept the spectators out and just look over the girls with their chests up against the links. We had on our white uniforms, and the boat was there, and people would just gaze at us like we were movie stars. All you did was walk over to the best-looking girl of them all and say, 'Would you like to see the boat a little closer?' And then they walked down their side of the fence, and you walked down yours, and the gateman would let her in. Just her. Sometimes the others would applaud. Boy, if you couldn't get laid as an America's Cup crewman, you weren't ever going to. That can be kind of hard to handle when you're only twenty-one."

The flotilla of suntanned beauties that hovered around Turner at Newport in 1977 did little damage to Turner's reputation. He had always succeeded with women, and he liked people to know it. His comrades watched this part of the Turner show with equal parts of admiration and mortification, as they always had. And they learned to keep their girlfriends and wives at a distance, for Turner's idea of flattery was physically direct. Somehow, though, he got away with it. If women rushed to feed his competitive vanity, that was their problem—for his vanity was less formidable to those close to him than either his ego or his id. He was privately delighted when *Playgirl* magazine put him number one in their list of ten sexiest men, featuring a pensive photograph in the cockpit of *Courageous*. But it was the caption that he liked: "Ted knows how to win."

If there was anyone vulnerable in this game, it was his wife. Like Mrs. Robert Redford, Janie Turner seemed to sense that her husband was, for publicity purposes at least, a bachelor—and she stood aside while he took his bows. When Janie was asked a question that summer, it was usually impossible to answer. What did she feed Ted to make him so handsome? Did Ted's reputation as a womanizer bother her? What were the possibilities of divorce?

"I always try to ignore those people and hope they'll go away," Janie says. "There are a lot of mean people in the world, and jealousy has always been Ted's worst enemy. He brings a lot of it on himself, by being such a magnet for publicity. He loves it, he just eats it up. But to me, it's such an invasion of my privacy, you know? Ted has had reporters overnight at the house and they've actually gone through our closets, looking for I don't know what. Every once in a while I put my foot down. 'For Lord's sake, Ted, let's do something as a family for once.' He loves his family, so that really gets him. The America's Cup is great, I suppose, but what he really loves is going down to the plantation with the children. Home-cooked meals, taking the boys fishing or hunting with his friends. Nobody sees him like that. Nobody knows him as I know him."

Janie has lately taken a more active role in Turner's public life. Last year he brought her along for all his major sports endeavors, although that often means sitting at his side through endless basketball or baseball games, or waving goodbye as he sets sail on *Tenacious* for an ocean race. Her confidence, friends say, is growing, and she now joins in the freewheeling, every-person-for-herself conversations that swirl around her husband.

At Newport's most ambitious watering hole, the walnut-and-brass-dominated Inn at Castle Hill, she recently launched into a tale of social survival at a California reducing spa Turner had sent her to. (Janie's weight had not been the issue; the issue had been Turner's dread that she might get "soft, you know, flabby, you know, out of shape.")

"This place was called the Ashram, and it was incredible," Janie related. "Near-starvation rations, and mountain climbing, and brutal massages, the whole thing. The fourth day I was about getting sick, and hanging back from the others, and so was this other girl. She said, 'Where're you from?' And I said, 'Why, Atlanta, Georgia.'

" 'Oh,' she said, 'do you know Teddy Turner?' But I just said, 'Yes,' because I was in a mean mood, just mean, I was so tired.

"Then she said, 'Well, what do they think of him in Atlanta, Georgia?' And I said, 'Oh, they think he's sort of a folk hero there. What do they think of him in California?'

" 'In Malibu Beach they think he gets away with a lot,' she said. But she meant it friendly, and we both laughed. Then she said, 'Well, what's his family like?'

"I said, 'Oh, he loves his family a lot, he goes hiking and fishing and so on.' 'But what's his *wife* like?' she asked me. 'How come she never goes with him?'

" 'Oh, she does,' I said, 'it's just that the press never writes about it.' And I carried on like that for a while about what a great person his wife was, and then I just had to say: 'But it's me. I'm his wife.'

"And she just *screamed.* 'Oh no!' she said, and then we hugged, and she started telling me about her husband, and how he was gone a lot too, and so forth. So I said, 'Who's *your* husband?'

" 'Sly Stallone,' she said. " 'Sylvester Stallone, the producer and movie actor.' And I almost died."

The near-embarrassment made Mrs. Stallone and Mrs. Turner fast pals, altogether appropriate, since the theme from *Rocky,* Stallone's boxing saga about a heroic underdog, was the *Courageous* theme song.

Its value as a forum for colorfulness and recognition notwithstanding, the Cup is indeed a ruthless money drain even for Turner and his fellow syndicate backers. As the 1980 race grew near, Turner had to help in the scramble to raise the more than $600,000 needed to support his return as incumbent. As a practical matter, that meant that when the phone rang in his Atlanta office, he had to try to explain to potential contributors why they should fund his glory. As usual, the amplified voice box on his telephone permitted no secrets.

CALLER: Hi, Ted. Say, about this 1980 Cup thing. I was thinking about maybe participating, you know, for some fun.

TURNER: You want to use it to kind of do some entertaining and so forth, bring a boat up there and take customers out to watch, that sort of thing?

CALLER: Yeah, for the trials and the races too. Just to be on the inside looking out instead of the other way. If we got involved with the syndicate we'd be walking in that circle, instead of as a tourist.

TURNER: You're absolutely right. I put in a quarter mil last time, I paid my own way. We're trying to spread it around now, though. Are you going to bring your own boat up there to the races?

CALLER: Maybe, yeah. I have a 43-footer at home, and I was thinking to leave that alone, and buy another one for Newport. I heard there was a place to keep it near the 12. Not like a tourist.

TURNER: That's right. At certain levels you can do that. We might be able to work you out a spot at the dock at certain levels. It's all tax-deductible, too. What a rotten deal for the taxpayers.

CALLER: Terrible.

TURNER: You don't pay any taxes anyhow, do you?

CALLER: Well, we are in the oil business, and we draw most of it off. We enjoy a fine tax-deductible situation.

TURNER: My trouble is, with the teams and everything, I don't have any deductible income left. I end up with a loss. Deductions I can't use.

CALLER: Neither do we, Ted. With all our tangible write-offs. We do all right in the oil business. This would just be for fun. We want to pay our fair share, and I don't know what level that I should share with you. Somebody should just indicate that to me.

TURNER: I just don't really know. If you're going to do a lot of entertaining of clients, it's different from just watching, as I understand it.

CALLER: Just a couple of people.

TURNER: You might not need your own boat. At a certain level we could get you on a boat that gets inside the spectator lines, as a full syndicate member.

CALLER: I want the inside group, whatever it takes.
TURNER: It's really a lot of fun. I been in it win and lose, and it's fun. We're going to have some parties, and you get access to the dock, and we have cocktails down there every afternoon and all that kind of shit.
CALLER: I'd enjoy getting involved.

Turner was very enthusiastic about this potential syndicate member, a successful ocean racer whom Turner was fond of. "I smoked him up pretty good, huh?" he said, leaning back in his chair. "But I don't know the prices—is dock space a fifty or a hundie? The syndicate should set a price, but I don't know what it is."

Sailing syndicates are not very different from the syndicates that own professional basketball or football teams, with the exception that if your football team makes good, the investment can pay off. That is never a possibility in yachting, yet expensive challenges continue to be hurled and met. In preparation for the 1980 Cup, for example, Turner helped mount a full-scale effort in Six-Metre boats —yachts designed to a meter formula, and which come out about half the size of a 12, with half the crew.

This venture took him to San Francisco and Seattle for more than a month of sailing in the fall of 1979. The boat was named *Ranger*, a 36-foot-long knife in the water built by Eric Goetz from a new design by the race-happy naval architect Gary Mull. The *Ranger* syndicate was based in Fort Worth, Texas, and most of its heavy contributors were on hand for *Ranger* and Turner's battles in the National Six-Metre Championships, the World Championships, and the Australia–America Challenge Cup.

On a bobbing tender in Puget Sound, while Turner and his mates fought for second place in the World Championships, syndicate member Lee Smith tried to explain what he was doing there, writing checks far from the heart of Texas.

"Well," said Smith, drink in hand, "you know, Ted used to have a boat company in Fort Worth, and I met him in the early 1960s. By 1974 we were pretty good friends, and Ted joined our boat club, and about five of us decided to help finance the *Mariner* campaign. Then we got in heavy with *Courageous,* too, and after 1977 we picked up on

Ranger as a way to keep the 12-meter crew together. It keeps us off the streets, I guess. Besides, you have to have a syndicate for stuff like this. We probably put $175,000 into the Six-Metre alone. A guy can't really afford to do that himself."

Smith and his partners show little interest in publicity, nor do they bring clients around to show off Turner and the boats he sails. They take their background roles seriously, and with more than a bit of regional pride. "The age-old question is," Smith said, "if you're from Fort Worth, which only has a little lake to sail on, what are you doing in Six-Metres and 12-meters? But we are one of the finest inland yacht clubs in the United States; we turn out a lot of good sailors. We like to have a little attention for Fort Worth."

Financial backers of such racing-only sailboats are welcome everywhere in the effort, with one exception: they are seldom invited to set foot on the yacht itself, and never entitled to race.

The prospect of the syndicate racing to come did not, however, deter Turner from having a bit of family fun as the summer of 1979 drew to a close.

One hot August day he rose early at his plantation, threw some sailing gear into his rust-riddled South Carolina station wagon, and set off with son Rhett and Janie for Charleston, an hour away. He had promised Rhett that they would race together in the annual regatta of the Hobcaw Yacht Club, an informal barbecue and boat race on the city's Wando River. They were entered in the Hobie 18 class, and would be competing in a new breed of fast catamaran with which the winner of the America's Cup was almost totally unfamiliar.

As the car hummed down the blazing highway (air conditioner off; "This country is an energy disaster, and I'm not going to be part of it"), Janie wondered aloud what the weekend would be like. "I hope it's just fun," she said. "I hope people aren't going to be there just for a crack at you, Ted."

"Couldn't happen," Turner said. "Nobody even knows I'm coming. It's just Rhett and me, going sailing, like I did with my father. Right, Rhett?"

"Yes sir."

Turner arrived at the club at 9:00 A.M. By 9:30 A.M. he had seen the Charleston paper, and the story and picture on the front page of the sports section entitled: "Turner May Race." By 10:00 A.M. a reporter had arrived to observe Turner's every move. By 11:00 A.M. a television crew was on hand, setting up its equipment and making light-meter readings of Turner's somewhat piqued face.

"What is your goal in this race?" asked Jim Laise of the *Charleston News and Courier.*

"My goal?" came the caustic reply. "I'd say my goal was not to be humiliated. I never even sailed one of these boats before, dummy."

A committee member helped explain Turner's frazzled mood. "We only had two boats in the Hobie 18 class until word got out that Ted might come down. Now we've got five. I guess everybody wants a shot at Terrible Ted."

Turner's mood was dark as he realized what was up. One of the recent entrants in his class was the local Hobie Cat champion, who eyed Turner as if to measure him for a notch in his gun. "Damn, the cat is out of the bag," Turner muttered.

But the Hobcaw Regatta was the stuff of which sailing memories are made. A burning sun climbed in the summer sky as sixteen separate classes of small boats, more than a hundred competitors in all, rigged on the sandy club yard and beach. In the shade of some Southern pines, the barbecue committee set up its equipment, and a brisk, hot wind was springing up over the Wando River. It was a scene from Turner's own past, with rich Carolina and Georgia accents casting a spell of a different texture than that of boat races in the New England axis. "Hole thet halyid up taght, boy," fathers ordered sons. "Hey, Penrod, swang yo' stern around hyere so ah kin catch it. That's the man." "Teddy Turnah! Ah haven't seen you around here in a dog's age. Looks like we going to have a pretty day, keeps on like this."

So Turner jammed his engineer's cap on his head, raised the sails on his boat, helped his son hook into the trapeze hiking harness, and roared off into a three-race series. He never could catch the local champ, but he turned in a strong second-place performance that left Rhett feeling proud. The defender of the America's Cup had met defeat on the mighty Wando, but he was magnanimous. When Laise, notebook in hand, asked Turner how he was coping with the status differential between Newport and Charleston, Laise was treated to the entire *Richard II* excerpt: "You have but mistook me all this while, dummy . . ."

On the way back to the plantation, Turner was enthralled. He had never had more fun sailing, he said. "I just as soon do that for the rest of my life as go off to England with *Tenacious,*" he proclaimed. "I've seen the bright lights. Sure, that guy beat me fair and square, but I've got such a fast learning curve. A couple more races, I'd be as fast as him. I know I could do it. As a matter of fact, I think I will."

But the Six-Metre sailboat championships in Seattle kept Turner from the catamaran wars, and in Seattle he met up with another factor of fame: analytic forays into the always interesting realm of What Makes Teddy Run. The source of the probe this time was Werner Erhard, founder of the self-motivation cult est, a lowercase corporation with uppercase revenues.

Erhard, born the bouncing baby boy of Joseph and Dorothy Rosenberg of Philadelphia on the fifth day of September 1935, is himself a millionaire who races Formula Super-Vee automobiles and owns a yacht too. His est consciousness transformation seminars became famous in the 1970s for their no-holds-barred methods of increasing clients' self-esteem, and Erhard himself was quasi-immortalized as the character Friedrich Bismarck in the satiric film *Semi-Tough.*

Erhard and Turner met on a motorboat between races, whereupon Turner inquired if it was true that Erhard did not permit seminar members to go to the bathroom.

"Ted, we found that people will make up any excuse to avoid feedback about themselves."

"Yeah, true," replied Turner. "But you gotta go to the bathroom, don't you?"

That evening, after a day of racing which had lasted from 8:00 A.M. to 9:00 P.M. and left the fleet exhausted, a dinner invitation arrived. Turner and Janie, along with several other of the supercompetitors at the championship event, were invited to dinner at the Other Place, a gourmet restaurant owned by a friend of Erhard's named Robert Rosellini.

Turner found himself seated next to Tom Blackaller, a robust world-class boat racer from San Francisco who is known also for his wild gray hair and megaphone enthusiasm. The two had admired each other—without overdoing it—for years. Various hotshot crewmen also were among the twelve at table as Erhard took his seat opposite Turner and Blackaller.

"I think you will enjoy this meal," Erhard said quietly as everyone tried to figure out what was going on.

Rosellini then appeared, introduced himself, and said:

"Your meal tonight will begin with a crayfish bisque, the crayfish arriving live from Clear Lake, north of Seattle. The richness and intensity of flavor has been achieved by producing a carefully made sauce Americaine from the puréed shells of the tails of the crayfish, roasted in a hot oven, deglazed in cognac, steamed down in milk, and reduced with a fish stock. Next will come a terrine, or pâté, of duck, which should present itself well because we raise, in a natural environment, all our own wild mallards, and because we have access to fresh livers, which is the foundation of the velvety texture. The sable fish which follows was caught this morning; from the viewpoint of delicacy, of texture, it is the most refined fish on the West Coast of North America. It will be served poached in its own stock, deglazed in white wine, blended with a cream reduction, and a hint of sorrel. The sherbet you will find was produced from fresh plums in the Yokima Valley. We shall also bring sweatmeats, taken from twelve-week old calves on a milk-based diet, and using only the thymus, for its little membranes and evenness of texture. The salad, gentlemen, was produced from wild and organically grown plants and flowers, hand-picked by our staff and sprinkled with local fresh blackberries in a very delicate dill herb dressing.

"The meat will be elk. Your elk was shot in Colorado by an associate who hunts for us, and it has been marinated in red wine, vegetables, and herbs for about three days. A stock, very intense, was produced from the bones, then both the stock and the marinade were reduced, deglazed in cognac, blended with sour cream, and finished with puréed fresh red and black currants. No flour has been added. Enjoy your meal."

Rosellini withdrew. Erhard remained implacable, a tiny smile forming and reforming on one side of his face.

"Holy shit," said Turner. "I can't believe it's already ten-thirty and we have to eat all the way through that. Back where I come from, it's simple, wholesome food."

"Hey, Bob?" Blackaller called to Rosellini. "Could I get a Big Mac?"

Turner was reminded of the frequent feasts of fresh game that characterize the table at his plantation. He replied, "Well, yeah, we eat good. But we don't talk about it so much."

While the courses were being prepared, Erhard quietly declined to provide any specific reason for the banquet, saying only that he was sure his guests would enjoy Rosellini's menu. This caused a wave of fidgeting to sweep the table, as Gary Jobson, Turner, Blackaller, veteran racer Steve Taft and Gary Mull sought unsuccessfully to relax. Turner was the first to give up.

He brought out his Krugerrand and began flipping it. "Feel it—real, pure gold," he advised. "No fair biting it, you'll get little chips of gold in your teeth and sell them." The coin made its way from hand to hand, and was eventually returned by Blackaller. But the coin Blackaller returned was a quarter.

"Har har," said Turner. "I don't care, I've got a farm and a plantation and a TV station and billboards and—hey, listen to this, my plantation's built on solid peat. You know what that's going to be worth in a couple of years? It's better than oil, it's a great fuel. When you're driving a peat-burning car, I'll have the market cornered."

"I got a fortune too, Ted," countered Blackaller, mugging. "But I got it tied up in Dacron. A huge amount of Dacron at my sail loft in San Francisco."

"Well," said Turner, "you can't eat Dacron. You can't have a Dacron sandwich. Boy, are you going to be hungry, Blackaller."

Erhard smiled slightly as the table broke down into a series of small, well-placed insults. Gary Mull started on an analysis of the sail settings of the race leader—the Swede Pelle Petterson, who was outsailing both Turner and Blackaller in the championships.

"Wait a minute, wait a minute," said Blackaller. "Mull, you're on Turner's boat. Pelle was first today and I was second, and you guys couldn't possibly even have seen the leaders that close."

"Ow," Turner said. "Ow, ow. Blackaller, come on, give me a break. You're beating me, so give me a break."

"I don't want to beat you, Ted," said Blackaller, unable to contain a gigantic grin. "Nothing personal. I want to beat everybody."

"You're just not used to it, that's all," Turner said.

"Sure I'm used to it," Blackaller said. "I'm used to beating you all week."

Turner said, "Well, Blackaller, you're right. Beating everybody—that's a worthy goal. It really is. Dennis Conner once said to me that he didn't care about the rest, as long as he beat me he was happy. I told him that was bull. The whole idea is just like you said—you try to beat everybody, that's what makes it fun."

By 1:15 A.M. the dinner was over, and the competitors, having chided each other mercilessly for three hours, staggered back to their rooms overlooking Puget Sound. Before retiring, Gary Mull put in a wake-up call for 6:00 A.M. Not for himself, but for Blackaller. "It's very important that you wake him," he explained to the desk. "Keep calling back every five minutes, no matter what he says." Mull, satisfied, reclined on his bed. "I wonder what Werner Erhard really wanted from us?" he asked, hugging his pillow. "That meal must have cost a fortune."

What Erhard wanted, he explained later, was to further his study of the competitive spirit. And what better way than to place the most competitive men he could find in one small room and see what would happen?

"I was on my way home from Portland, where I'd been racing my Formula SuperVee car," Erhard said. "That was something I had set out to do—race cars—even though the year before I hadn't even had a driving license. To learn what it takes to win I tried it myself.

"Anyhow, I found Ted to be absolutely fascinating. The study of motivation is something I love, but people are often misled by the surface. For example, you think of Ted as ambitious, driven, single-minded, cold-blooded, things like that. But that's not what I saw. What was really noticeable right away was his, well, his humanity. Yes, he has the capability of being piercing and intrusive, and that seems impolite. But that's an important signal of selfhood, which I always look for. That edge, that dig, that avoidance of certain social ritual. Very successful people are just not trying to fit in with everybody else. They have an independent sense of things. They're not looking for anyone's approval.

"You look at a man like Ted and you think, well, he's inner-directed. But that's not it. It's really the reverse. He's outer-directed. He sees the world as it is. He's getting feedback from the outside, and making use of it. Most people make the mistake of looking inside themselves for the answers, but they're not there.

"It's very Zen-like," Erhard said, almost apologetically. "The trouble is that Zen is expressed in most people's minds as a meditative thing, as life in a monastery. They think of Nirvana, which is the Eighth Picture of Zen. But in fact there are two more pictures after that, and the final one is of an old man on the road of life, just living. He's out in the real world. Right where Turner is."

Turner's spontaneous travels down the road of life do, in fact, fit well the familiar phrases of Zen—its characteristic *mo chih ch'u* ("going ahead without hesitation") and *wu-shih* (simplicity, the absence of affection). Even Turner's response to this analysis ("Bullshit!") is worthy of a Zen master. He liked Erhard, but there was something that bothered him: "He shouldn't have changed his name," Turner said. "He was born Rosenberg, he should've stayed Rosenberg. You never, ever change your name."

By the way, how did Erhard do at the Formula SuperVee national championships in Portland, after his personal experiment in the Winning Way?

"I won it," Erhard said.

Ted Turner did not win the America's Cup of 1980. In fact, Turner and *Courageous* were the first American contenders eliminated from the trials. In fact, he was defeated time and again by a yacht named *Clipper*, sailed by young Russell Long, a twenty-four-year-old hotshot whom Turner had adopted as a partner boat for tune-up races. Both Turner and Long were decisively beaten all summer by Dennis Conner, sailing a new 12-meter named *Freedom* and backed by a reported $2 million syndication effort. In fact, Turner was actually expelled from the elimination trials at one point—as punishment for taking on his boat a member of the challenging team from Australia. It was Dennis Conner who eventually defeated Australia to keep the Cup safe for another three years, and it was Dennis Conner who was thrown into the water from Bannister's Wharf wearing a grin of triumph. By that time, Turner was back home, and his *Courageous* had been put up for sale.

All summer, as *Courageous* lost race after race, one explanation had circulated for the change in Ted Turner's fortunes. That explanation was that Ted really didn't want to race this time. His mind was always someplace else.

It is an explanation he denies.

"I was justing starting Cable News Network, yes, and we'd had tough times. Yes, I'd thought about pulling out of the race. I discussed it with Gary Jobson as far back as the previous fall, and then again in the spring. I said, 'Look, business comes before sailing.' I wanted Gary to be mentally prepared in case he had to take over. But as it happened, I was able to sail. And it is not true that I didn't want to, or that I was distracted by business problems.

"I figured that we had an excellent chance to win without building a new boat. I also figured that we had an excellent chance of being beaten. To race *Courageous* cost about $600,000, of which I guaranteed about a quarter of a million. I understand that Dennis Conner and *Freedom* spent about $2 million. They went through a tremendous crew-selection process, and they sailed every day for more than a year before the races. I think that is why they won. I think *Freedom* had a more powerful hull than *Courageous,* and I think their sails were better than ours."

What usually happens when an America's Cup boat is not going well is that the skipper is replaced. That did not happen on *Courageous* during the summer of 1980.

"It crossed my mind a couple of times," Turner said, "that maybe I should relinquish the helm. Maybe. But I wasn't sailing the boat badly, it was just that we were slower. I discussed it with Gary. He thought I should stay if I could. What finished us off was losing two masts. We would never have caught *Freedom,* I don't think. But if we hadn't broken the masts we would have had a better record than *Clipper.''*

When Turner started to lose, *The New York Times* yachting writer still made him the lead: "Yesterday's news in Newport," the *Times* man wrote, "was that Ted Turner is a gracious loser."

"I think I've always been a gracious loser," Turner said. "I'm not going to stop sailboat racing. I'm not trying to prove anything anymore, I don't have to. I'm going to race my little Hobie 18. I'm going to have a hell of a lot of fun.

"And—You know what?" Turner added, brightening. "Next year —or maybe the year after—the Braves are going to win the pennant."

7 The Battle of Washington

TED TURNER'S coast-to-coast ride across the United States in the saddle of his satellite may have heralded a new age of television, but it also made him the masked man of communications in the decade of the 1970s. At first he managed to keep one town ahead of the gathering posse of program owners, independent broadcasters, professional sports leagues and the bigwigs of advertising and network TV whose lucrative marketplaces he had trampled along the way. In the spring of 1979, in the federal city of Washington, D.C., the posse caught up to Turner.

The first indication of trouble came in a telephone call from Tom Wheeler, now president of the National Cable Television Association. "Wheeler said to look out," Turner recalls. "The fight was on—we were coming under attack. I said good. Sometimes the best thing that can happen is all-out war. It makes you stronger, if you survive. I had seen this confrontation coming all along anyhow. It was the old versus the new, and at least I was on the side of the new."

The posse was made up of the Powers That Be in television, who had correctly identified Turner as their chief superstation antagonist. By 1979, there were four operating superstations, but Atlanta's Channel 17 was the only broadcast station on the satellite by choice. The others, like WGN, the giant independent in Chicago, were known as "reluctant" superstations. By federal regulation, they could not prevent common-carrier companies from transmitting their programming to cable companies all over the country. The common carriers could make money by charging for the delivery of the programming, but there was no money in it for the superstations. Only Turner had raised his advertising rates in an attempt to take advantage of the newfound audience. Only Turner was on friendly terms with the common carrier (after all, he had founded one—Southern Satellite Systems—himself). Among broadcasters, only Turner stood to gain from the survival of superstations. And he would be the only noticeable broadcasting victim if the infant service died.

Turner had an exceedingly simple perspective on superstations: most of the country shared only three large networks, and anywhere his Channel 17 was brought in gave viewers an alternative to those three networks. What was wrong with that? he continually asked.

The Baseball Commissioner, for example, contended that Turner had no right to broadcast Atlanta Braves games all over the country just because he happened to own the team. No, that presented the specter of disaster—in the form of a glut of baseball. It devalued the "product," which required careful protection from overexposure if the networks were to continue to pay big money for national telecasts, and if individual team owners were to be able to sell TV rights to their local stations. Turner's indiscriminate airings of Braves games, Bowie Kuhn's lawyers claimed, even threatened the heart of baseball's marketing strategy—the local television blackout provision that presumably kept stadium gate receipts safe. Too much baseball, Kuhn seemed to be saying, would be the ruination of baseball.

This argument was echoed by the owners of the most familiar shows on television today—the syndicated reruns of *All in the Family, Gilligan's Island, Star Trek,* and the rest. Before superstations, these copyright holders were able to sell their programs individually in more than a hundred viewing markets in the United States. Reruns were the real money anyway—a premiere showing on a network was lucky just to recoup the $250,000-an-hour production costs of a program like *All in the Family.* But if Turner showed these programs to five or ten million viewers at once, the syndicators claimed, their market would be destroyed.

But the most outraged of all the members of the superstation-chasing posse were Turner's own former colleagues—the owners of independent television stations like his own WTBS in Atlanta. Metromedia, which owns a string of TV stations across the country, fired off an inch-thick petition to the Federal Communications Commission. What was the secret behind the satellite's ability to provide programming previously available only through local stations? The answer, Metromedia said, is that a superstation "does not bother with troublesome details like obtaining rights to the programs which it sells. The basic principle, known to thieves down through the ages, is that you can sell for less if you steal your product."

But Turner replied—gleefully—that he wasn't stealing anything. Every time a syndicated program was aired, payments were made to a little-known agency known as the Copyright Royalty Tribunal, in compensation. When the syndicators sputtered that they were only token payments, Turner turned his palms up and innocently asked who had set the rate. It had been the syndicators, of course. But before they had figured out what Turner was up to.

So the offended parties set out to change the rules. Congressman Lionel Van Deerlin, California Democrat, was that year engaged in a rewrite of the 1934 Communications Act, a vast undertaking that kept his House Subcommittee on Communications buried under tons of paper and conflicting testimony. Into this complicated bill was inserted a seemingly innocuous provision called "retransmission consent." The nut of the provision was that before anyone sent off TV programs to the new markets made possible by satellites, permission had to be obtained from the owners of the programs.

Fair is fair, said the Motion Picture Association of America, the National Association of Broadcasters, the baseball, basketball and football leagues, the Independent Television Stations Association, and the head of the White House's expert agency on telecommunication.

Retransmission consent was designed to protect the status quo in the television marketplace. Its advocates did not deny that it was also likely to put Turner, and the infant superstation industry, out of business.

Given the right of consent, program syndicators were certain to withhold it.

Spring comes early to Washington, and it is a pretty season. The damp, 40-degree weather of February yields in fits and starts to the blossomy days of March, when the cherry trees of the Tidal Basin and the downtown parks burst into their first color. On the sprawling lawns of the well-groomed city men in three-piece suits walk outdoors again, arguing, cajoling, bullying, lobbying and reasoning together over the affairs of the world. It is an intriguing game, and if its moves and goals are sometimes abstruse or mundane, they seldom seem so on a playing field bordered by the Supreme Court, the Library of Congress, the giant office buildings of the bicameral legislature, and the imposing dome of the Capitol itself. Washington's game is played in the loveliest stadium of all, and Turner was ready and waiting for the game to start.

"I didn't mind going up there to fight," he said. "It looked like fun. I like meeting Congressmen. I like meeting all kinds of people. Besides, I had been to Washington before."

Indeed he had. It was in the Bicentennial summer of 1976, at the invitation of Representative Van Deerlin's same subcommittee, and he had scored a memorable triumph of style. That year, the House had been looking into the future of cable television, and Turner had been called to testify as a maverick TV broadcaster—the only one who could be found who did not see cable as a Godzilla seeking to devour America's free market in communications. There were no superstations then, but there was a Ted Turner: brash, embattled, amusing, loquacious, and a good show. It was his first chance to perform on Capitol Hill, and he plunged in with a typically colorful marathon sentence.

"I think you're going to hear from some gentlemen who are a little upset, quite frankly, about my appearing here," he said dramatically. "I wear so many hats that I am not quite sure which one I am wearing at the present time, but I am one of those guys in the independent, UHF, television business, which, five years ago when I went into it, was noted as the lunatic fringe of the broadcast industry, and as far as exorbitant profits are concerned we, believe it or not, are making a profit in independent UHF television which surprised even me, because in the beginning we were losing millions literally, but luckily we turned it around just before we ran out of some very carefully harvested money that I had made in the outdoor advertising business, which—you know, stop billboard blight—I figured I ought to diversify a little bit because that business lived under such regulatory problems that every night when I went to bed I had nightmares that the City Council or some federal commission would put us out of business the next day by making us remove all our signs from the high-ways."

Turner plunged on, advising the Congressmen that he had not graduated from college, and if he had, "and been very smart, I would not have gotten into the UHF television business at the time, so I am kind of like the bumble bee who does not know that he cannot fly, that aerodynamically it is impossible." Still wearing his verbal straw hat, he allowed as how he had come into television "because I believe that there should be more voices heard than the network voices out of New York."

Van Deerlin, amused, fed him a gold-plated question: "Mr. Turner, given the evidence that you have cited in your own experience, what do you think accounts for the continuing opposition of your fellow broadcasters to cable development?"

"Well, in all fairness," Turner fed back, "broadcasters do lead a relatively sheltered life from competition . . . and that is true of all industry, unfortunately, because the less competition you have, the more you can charge, the more you can make." He added, "If I cannot do a good enough job to attract the viewers to my station in the free and open marketplace, then I do not deserve those viewers. I do not think that I should, by government regulation, be protected. . . . Very few broadcasters would be that open and honest, but most of them work for big companies, and if they said something like that they would get fired."

This apparently fearless broadcaster held great appeal for the pan-el, who liked his jokes and his call for diversity. Charles J. Carney, Ohio Democrat, was prompted to say, "The gentleman from Atlanta, Mr. Turner—he said that he is without the benefit of a college educa-tion. Maybe that is why you had to learn how to think, Mr. Turner."

TURNER: I did go to college. I just didn't finish.
CARNEY: And maybe that is why you had to learn how to think.

Eventually the Congressmen got around to the possibilities of superstations, and Tim Wirth, Colorado Democrat, inquired if it wasn't true that Turner's Atlanta station was already known as "Su-per 17."

"It got that name six years ago when we were losing $80,000 a month and were watched by no one," Turner replied, to the amusement of the audience. "We had a young girl down in promotion who did not last very long, but she had one great idea. I said, 'We need to jazz this place up a little bit.' We had a bunch of hippies, some of which were on heroin, running the programs, and they ran the few commercials we did have in black and white, upside down, but nobody was watching, so it didn't matter. And she said, 'Why don't we call this place Super 17?' I said, 'That's a great idea.' You know, in other words, it was a real tongue-in-cheek thing, long before the superstation concept."

WIRTH: Do you have any reaction to the notion of a superstation?

TURNER: Well, I would love to become a superstation. I would love desperately to create a Fourth Network for cable television, producing our own programs, not just running *I Love Lucy* and *Gilligan's Island* for the fifty-seventh time. And I intend to go that way, if we are allowed to.

You have to remember that there are three supernetworks who only own four or five stations apiece that are controlling the way this nation thinks and raking off exorbitant profits, and most of these local stations that everybody is crying about are just carrying those network programs that are originated out of New York. They have an absolute, a virtual stranglehold, on what Americans see and think, and I think a lot of times they do not operate in the public good, showing overemphasis on murders and violence and so forth.

So if we do become super, it will be another voice. Perhaps it might be a little more representative of what we think the average American would like to see. A little less blood and gore on television and more sports and old movies and that sort of thing, that we think might encourage children not to go out and buy a gun and start blasting people, like in *Taxi Driver*.

WIRTH: Mr. Chairman, I personally find that a very healthy and productive approach to this. I wish that were reflected all across the board.

The Ted Turner of 1976 hardly seemed a threat to anyone. On the contrary, he was a refreshing change from the witnesses Van Deerlin's subcommittee was accustomed to hearing—men speaking from deeply dug-in positions along their own profit perimeters. Here was the owner of the country's most profitable UHF TV station saying that his own market should be opened up to a future of unpredictable technological revolution. Besides, he had a sense of humor—rough and ready to be sure, but entertaining. From Turner's point of view, the outing in Washington that Bicentennial year had been a lark. The Congressmen were nice guys; and like the geese of his plantation, they had learned to like him.

So when Wheeler's call came three years later, Turner saw nothing to fear amid the cherry blossoms.

"We were real busy in Atlanta that spring," says Terry McGuirk. "The Superstation was trying to sell national ads for the first time, and it was taking a huge amount of our energy. We had known for about three weeks that Ted would be testifying before the House. When the day came we had breakfast with our Washington lawyers at the Mayflower Hotel and talked over the thing a little, and then we went over to the Rayburn Building right away, because we were supposed to go on at ten o'clock.

"Well, these hearing rooms are arranged so the Congressmen sit above you, like judges almost, and shoot questions down at the people at the witness table, which is on a much lower level.

"We got into the room, and you could see that Ted was duly impressed, and I think kind of nervous. Everything had gone so fast, and suddenly here we were. Ten o'clock came and went, with us just waiting while other people took the stand. Bowie Kuhn testified how superstations were hurting baseball. He actually took the stand twice, before we did. Ted and I just sat there, and every minute as the day wore on Ted wound a little tighter, until he was curled up in his chair like a spring. He must've smoked thirty-two cigars, just waiting. The last three hours I didn't have any input at all, Ted was just sitting there, legs crossed one way, his body twisted the other way from the tension.

"About four o'clock they called him, and he went up and things started to go wrong. I was left sitting there, and all of a sudden it hit me. We were totally unprepared. We had no idea what questions they were going to ask him. There were eight Congressmen up there, some Democrats and some Republicans, some conservative and some liberal, and we didn't know which was what. We didn't know who was friendly and who wasn't, and you can't always tell by the questions they ask. Bad stuff had been said about us all morning, and now it was our turn. But we were babes in the woods."

The Communications Subcommittee was the same group Turner had enjoyed so much in 1976, but much had happened since then. Now the satellite was a reality, Turner was famous, and the broadcasting establishment was bellowing like a wounded giant. Retransmission consent was rolling, and it looked like it might flatten superstations for all time.

The seriousness of the situation had grown on Turner all day, as he impatiently waited his turn to speak. Now, as he finally took the witness table, he was astonished to find that there were virtually no Congressmen left in the room. They had listened to the Commissioner of Baseball politely, and shown deference to Henry Geller, who had dreamed up the notion of retransmission consent ten years before, and as the head of the National Telecommunications and Information Administration was its best-informed advocate. But when Turner's turn came, the Congressmen were gone.

His spring uncoiled immediately. No sooner had Turner thanked Martin A. Russo, Illinois Democrat, for acting as chairman in Van Deerlin's absence than he added, in words full of pique, "I am disappointed that so few of the Congressmen are here when I testify, since it is a life-or-death matter to me and also to the public we serve." Plunging into a written statement, he harshly attacked retransmission consent as anti-American and certain to leave viewers "with the alternative of watching only the three monopolistic networks, or no commercial television at all."

As Turner spoke, however, the members of the subcommittee began to file in, one by one. My God, McGuirk realized with horror, the Congressmen hadn't abandoned them at all—they had just slipped away for a roll-call vote on the House floor. And returned to hear themselves unjustly accused of willful absenteeism.

Having started on the wrong foot, Turner continued to hop to the music of his own different drum. The members of the subcommittee, all men accomplished in the ways of Capitol Hill, were accustomed to a traditional circumspection. The bitterest political enemies still addressed each other in formal, flowing language—"Will the gentleman yield?" They had intentionally called witnesses from both sides of the retransmission consent argument, and they expected those witnesses to adopt a similarly sophisticated oratorical style. Turner had his own style, however, as Mark Marks of Pennsylvania discovered first.

Marks seemed to have difficulty with the precise reason for Turner's prediction of doomsday. "What is your problem?" he asked. "You somehow managed not only to survive, but also to accumulate quite a reputation for survival of the fittest."

Turner came back strong, as usual. "I don't care that much what happens to me," he said with histrionic emotion. "I am more for the consumers and the public and the smaller towns of America that can only see the garbage that is on the commercial networks, and we offer an alternative that the film companies and sports interests don't want. And the National Association of Broadcasters are trying to deny us."

Turner's aggressiveness made Marks uncomfortable. "Whenever I hear about the 'garbage' you mentioned, and some of us have been talking a little bit about that 'garbage'—I am a little concerned," he said. "Your statements, as affirmative as they are—well, I wonder if you actually can cite us some examples as to where you have had problems in securing programming. . . ."

Turner, however, informed Marks that he would address these points in the rest of his presentation, "if I could just continue, sir. I think it is really fun, sir."

"That is what we are here for, and to do," Marks answered caustically. "Provide you with fun."

But Turner read on, telling his success story, until interrupted by Chairman Van Deerlin. Van Deerlin observed that it seemed to him that Turner was doing very well, and in fact was an example of the system working just fine.

Not if the bill under discussion passed as written, Turner countered. Not, Turner said, if his program suppliers "had to go through the retransmission consent proposal that Mr. Shooshan wrote into your bill."

With these words a hush fell over the hearing room. McGuirk, in his observer's seat, blanched. "It was the big gasp, all right," he recalls. "Chip Shooshan was the majority counsel to the subcommittee, a powerful guy in his own right and sort of a hostile character to us. Ted was convinced Shooshan had argued retransmission consent into Van Deerlin's bill. Of course Shooshan had done just that, but you weren't supposed to say it. It was saying Van Deerlin didn't know what was in his own bill. It was like saying the worst conceivable thing about somebody's sex life right in the middle of their wedding. Even if it's true, you don't say it. So there was this terrible hush."

Marks broke the silence. "I think you ought to understand that Mr. Shooshan did not write anything into the bill."

"I am sorry," Turner replied. "That is what I heard."

"Well, sometimes even the information you get is not correct," Marks shot back.

"I get a lot of bad information," Turner said.

"And that had to be some of it," Marks added, just for emphasis.

Turner lurched on. He pilloried network TV for producing programs such as *The Newlywed Game* and *The Gong Show,* and attacked "bouncing-around boobs" in prime time, saying such things were offensive to his family. He noted that his station, on the other hand, had recently produced a three-hour special entitled *The New Religions,* which analyzed a culture through which "hundreds and thousands of young people's minds are being enslaved by Reverend Moon and a bunch of other nuts running around."

Representative Russo, however, asked if it was true that Turner's Channel 17 aired its basic news program between 2:00 and 3:00 A.M. "Is that accurate, or inaccurate?" Russo asked, seeking a direct answer.

"That is accurate," Turner replied, grabbing the opportunity for one of his favorite gags. "We have 100 percent share of the audience then."

The room exploded in laughter, with Turner mugging and beaming. Russo, however, did not join in.

"Just let me ask you another question," Russo said when relative quiet returned. "This is like some of the comments made earlier, it does not turn me on at all. I think that the facts have to be laid out before the committee. We are not a joke."

The Turner luck just didn't seem to be working, and it let him down once more before the afternoon was through. Representative Wirth of Colorado, after some discussion about the growth of the cable industry, asked Turner what he thought the subcommittee ought to do next. The question was an easy lob, but Turner caught it and threw it back much harder than anyone expected.

"It is being taken care of now," he said. "The current FCC regulations are working, and are adequate. You have a fine group of people over there that are trying real hard to balance everything out. They have a tough job, but they work at it full time, and you all only do it part time because you have other, bigger problems to worry with."

What should Congress do? Turner had been asked. Simple, he had replied—leave matters to the Federal Communications Commission, an agency that knew what it was doing.

At 6:15 P.M., Turner and McGuirk walked into the taproom of the Mayflower Hotel, joining some friends there who were waiting to hear the outcome of his day on the Hill. Turner was giddy with exhaustion. "You better bring three vodka and tonics and line them up in a row right here in front of me," he told the waitress. "And then go get three more and line those up in front of McGuirk."

"How did it go?" one of his friends asked.

"Not well," Turner said. "It was a complete disaster."

Back in Atlanta, a brutal reassessment began. Turner, who at first thought he had scored a few hits and at least come out even, concluded that he had screwed up. McGuirk was on the phone the next day to Leighton, Conklin and Lemov, Turner's newly hired lobbyists in Washington, who had helped prepare the House testimony and pave the way to the hearing.

"I just blamed them for everything that happened," McGuirk said. "I told them they had let us down. But a big part of it was they had been intimidated by Ted, I think. They just had no way of dealing with him. At that point Ted put me in charge of our Washington relations. He had determined never to make the same mistake again."

Dick Leighton was also upset, as was his partner Michael Lemov. "Yeah, the House stuff was bad," Leighton said. "Ted bristled all through it—he was mad because they'd kept him waiting all day, and he seemed to want to challenge the Congressmen every chance he could. Even the ones who we had already talked to, and who were friendly to him.

"There's no question that our firm created some of the problem," Leighton said. "We'd just met Ted. He told us he was a debating champion, he told us he was good at talking before a group—that we should just sit back and watch. So we really didn't force him, like we do all our other clients, to go through real tough practice sessions, with us asking devil's advocate questions. We figured he was a pro, that his charisma and dynamism would carry it through. But it turned out that he had a bad day, that he wasn't really in his element.

"We stewed about it quite a lot, and then we decided to go down to Atlanta and start over, because Turner was also going to testify before the Senate on the same matters. By this time we had learned to yell at him. We told him it wasn't as easy as it looked, and he agreed. The stakes were pretty high, and we thought he might just duck the Senate altogether—say the hell with it. But he wasn't afraid. He just doubled the ante."

"Ted had taken a new perspective," McGuirk says. "We set up a plan whereby we would study his House testimony and figure out what went wrong. Leighton and Lemov marked the transcript up, underlining places where he'd lost points, or offended people, or been too blunt. We had practice sessions in Atlanta and in Washington, just hammering Ted with this stuff, and he got better and better at handling himself.

"Plus," McGuirk continues, "this time Ted wanted to meet each Senator beforehand, so he could feel some simpatico. He wanted to be fully briefed. He wanted to know what colleges they went to, their background, and he got a briefing card for every guy. A lot of grievances were aired. Back when we took Ted around to see the Congressmen on Van Deerlin's subcommittee, Ted had pressed them real hard right in their own offices. He would try to dominate them. Mike Lemov was with us, and if Mike tried to interject something, Ted would say, 'Let me handle this.' This embarrassed Mike, and he said so.

"The difference about the Senate was we all knew preparation would be the key," says Leighton. "Ted was much better, and we saw everybody in two days. He listened to the Senators, and he stayed on topic. When he met the Congressmen he had tended to go off on the Middle East, with strong views that were perhaps not based on very careful study. Now he was much more in control, and they loved him. Both the Senators and their staffs saw him as a marvelous personality, almost like a movie star, and we made real headway. We managed to get him scheduled to testify on the first day of the Senate hearings, on a panel with big guns—Gene Jankowski, the president of the CBS Broadcast Group, and Henry Geller. This scared everybody just a little, because we knew television would be there, and a big audience."

Turner, however, was not particularly scared. He was in fact following his traditional path—he was in seemingly far over his head, he was clearly the underdog, and he had no intention of giving up.

"When you're doing as many things simultaneously as I am," Turner says, "you just sort of crash along at full speed until you hit some obstacle. A lot of times you make a mistake, and everybody says, 'Oh, he's out of it now.' You let them think that, then you come back and whip them good. They don't know what hit them. Because by then they have written you off."

By the time the day of the hearing came, Turner, McGuirk, Leighton and Lemov had the tingly feeling of contestants absolutely convinced that they had worked harder for victory than their adversaries. After a leisurely breakfast, Turner went over to the Senate hearing room, which happened to be paneled in walnut, and seemed much more intimate than the chamber he had occupied in the House. Instead of enemy witnesses, it turned out that the first speaker of the day was Charles Ferris, chairman of the FCC, who singled out Turner in his testimony as a good example of a broadcaster intent on creating more services for viewers.

Turner's turn came directly thereafter, and he had a few tricks up his sleeve. The witness table had three chairs, and two microphones. The instant Commissioner Ferris stood up, Turner, by prearranged plan, darted forward and occupied the chair at the extreme right. He grabbed the nearest microphone and positioned it in front of himself, keeping his hand on it. Henry Geller, an old hand at this business, took the left-hand chair. Jankowski of CBS was left with the middle seat, sharing a microphone.

"Leighton and Lemov had that figured out," said McGuirk. "You don't sit in the middle, because then the people on each side talk right through you. Also, because of the way the questions and answers tend to run, the witnesses at each end are either first, or they get the rebuttal position. The guy in the middle gets kind of glossed over."

Senator Ernest F. Hollings, who happened to represent Turner's "second home state" of South Carolina, started things off by introducing Geller, who said it was very important that the "marketplace" be free to operate in television economics. Retransmission consent, he said, was merely a synonym for "marketplace." According to Geller, Turner and cable had been given an unfair advantage by government, since they were required to pay only copyright fees for distributing nonnetwork program material. They should be required to deal directly with the program owner, Geller said.

Jankowski, by virtue of his middle position, came next. Low of voice and pinstriped of suit, the president of the CBS Broadcast Group observed that commercial television had done well for America, and that "what began with a crystal set has evolved in a short time into a system in which virtually everyone in the country has a wide choice of varied entertainment." But Jankowski, too, recognized a "fundamental unfairness." Broadcasters, he explained, had to pay substantial rights fees for the use of program material, while "cable interests use the same program material by paying a token statutory fee."

Geller and Jankowski had positioned themselves precisely as the Atlanta team had hoped. On cue, Turner immediately struck what was to be the theme of the day: who do you feel sorry for, the networks or the viewers?

Quoting a news story that put the pretax profits of CBS, NBC and CBS at $560 million that year, Turner observed with a grin, "It is hard to feel sorry for the big organizations . . . does this sound like an industry that is having trouble in the marketplace? Are these the defenseless entities that need your intervention to protect them from competition?" He also carefully pointed out that the movie industry had set a record of $2.6 billion in box-office receipts that year, and reported $550 million in profits. As for the eight major production companies in the film and television business, their pretax gains were up 50 percent in one year—to $658 million.

"What alarms me most," Turner added, ". . . is that when a small businessman comes in, works hard, plays by Mr. Ferris's rules and has a few successes, the first thing these huge organizations do is try to use their power and influence to change the name of the game."

In the audience, Dick Leighton breathed a sigh of relief. "Ted had actually stuck directly to the prepared statement, which I hadn't been sure he would do, tell you the truth. The setup was perfect. The plan was going well."

Senator Hollings then asked Geller some questions about the "marketplace," since it had become apparent that all three witnesses held that image of free enterprise most dear to their hearts. Geller seemed to see the irony, commenting at one point, "Mr. Turner mentioned marketplace over twenty times when I stopped counting. I have been criticized on the House side when I testified because I used it thirty-seven times." Geller and Hollings zinged back and forth for a few moments, and then the chairman turned to the witness in the middle.

"Mr. Jankowski," the chairman said, "I loved your statement. I don't want to disturb it." (McGuirk exulted: Wow! Hollings was passing right over Jankowski!). Hollings then proceeded to paraphrase the complaints about Turner, observing, "Ted Turner is not only a good sailor, he is a good burglar; he is good at robbing the airwaves, and he gets a free load. What is your answer to that?"

It was the question Turner had been waiting for, and Senator Hollings's jocular introduction was perfect.

The problem, Turner said, was simply that "the big American companies can't understand the satellite; they can't figure it out any more than Mr. Geller. You know Mr. Jankowski can figure it out, because he wants to stop us."

The audience began to laugh. Several grins broke out among the Senators. What "Mr. Jankowski's buddies" were afraid of, Turner added, was that the networks' television sports packages—and the ratings for Saturday's game of the week—would be devalued if viewers could watch a variety of games, and not just those shown by the networks.

Jankowski could only object that if a network paid a substantial amount of money for the rights to broadcast baseball games, it obviously had the right to object to cable systems' showing them while the network paid the freight.

The issues rapidly became more and more complicated as ramifications of the new satellite technology were explored, the rights of the owners of television and movie programming defended, and the presumed needs of the viewing public waved like flags by all three witnesses. Jankowski was certainly no fool; he had a good case when he said that Turner and cable ought to have to bargain for what they transmitted. And Henry Geller was persuasive in arguing that government had no business creating a cable TV loophole through which the profits of program owners in the private sector might drain away. But Ted Turner, on the other hand, was that most precious of American human commodities: an entrepreneur with a better mousetrap.

The tone in this Senate hearing was vastly different from that of its equivalent in the House. For some reason, the Senators did not seem at all threatened by Turner. (The reason, according to Leighton, was that this time Turner had identified his adversaries as Jankowski and Geller, and not the members of the subcommittee.) The Senators seemed to be enjoying the Ted Turner show; it was at least new. They had heard from the powerful networks many times before.

When Geller mentioned in passing that the networks currently reach 98 percent of American households, Senator Barry Goldwater showed sharp interest. "How big?" he asked.

Geller took the nod, suggesting that he agreed such dominance— "dominance that goes into the American living room—should be broken, although probably over a long period of time."

That exchange made Jankowski uncomfortable.

"I think what troubles me, Senator, is that it implies that there's something improper about what's being broadcast on the networks. . . ."

"There are times when some people have felt that that is true," Goldwater replied.

Jankowski tried to explain that television was really controlled by its local affiliates, and was heavily regulated by government, and was in no way a malignant force. Goldwater immediately asked Turner if he wanted to comment.

"I could spend the rest of the day commenting on it," Turner replied. "CBS, NBC and ABC have a complete lock on what happens in this industry . . . I mean, look at these guys. They're sitting there making billions and they're here concerned—they're trying to stop me. This Mr. Jankowski even brought up in his testimony that he proposes retransmission consent because he's worried about the authors and program owners.

"What he's worried about is a fourth or fifth network getting started, actually, sir. Which is exactly what's happening. A network who puts on quality programming and what the people want to see above just ratings and putting on the lowest-common-denominator junk shows that the networks cram down our throats."

Looking directly at Goldwater, Turner added: "One reason you don't get the support of the people out there is that television networks haven't given the coverage to the big issues. They'll cover an airplane crash or a Senator getting in trouble, but they don't cover the good Senators. They don't cover the good things, the important issues about fuel and everything. They pass them over because they don't want General Motors to not sell a lot of cars and be sponsors of the Super Bowl.

"I know what they do," Turner went on. "They want to stop all competition and keep the little club the same way it is, just the three of them monopolizing what the American people see and hear. And Mr. Geller is stringing along with them."

Geller countered quickly, defending his National Telecommunications and Information Administration as having a "deep commitment to diversity." But Turner, he said, "misses the point of what's involved here."

Goldwater, however, was intrigued by Turner's argument. "This is a very important point, Mr. Jankowski, that a lot of you people at the top of the television networks fail to see," he said. "We who sit here supposedly in this Land of Oz where the news is made often go home at night and watch our television sets and say, why didn't they mention that? Why do they keep harping about that? I've heard about the DC-10 crash so often I know how many nuts and bolts go into a DC-10. There are more important things than trying to destroy an industry because of one crash. That's just an example I'm using. Do you want to comment?"

"May I?" Jankowski asked. "First, I think that with all due respect, Mr. Turner had more emotion than fact packed into some of his statements. . . ."

Titters immediately broke out in the hearing room, punctuating a general shuffling and grinning among the spectators. While Jankowski spoke, Turner had unveiled one of his longest cigars. With elaborate precision, he struck a match and lit it, sending clouds of smoke billowing up from the end of the witness table.

Jankowski was trying to inform the subcommittee that the three networks together spent more than $100 million a year in a search for new programming ideas and material, but Turner's smoke was blowing in his face. The very air currents of the room seem to conspire in Turner's favor. Jankowski dodged the smoke, maintaining his composure as best he could, but made noticeably uncomfortable by Turner's mugging at his right. Jankowski also defended network news programming, contending that its unfettered role was integral to the American Way. "And I think that the fact that our country is as strong as it is is proof of the fact that the system that has operated so successfully for fifty years is still the best way to go."

Goldwater turned to Turner and his cigar, offering him the rebuttal, and Turner sprang to the attack:

"Our country has never been weaker than it is now, not in the last forty years to my knowledge, and I think it's the networks' poor treatment of the national news they spend twenty-two minutes a day covering. I've already announced starting a twenty-four-hour-a-day satellite-fed cable news network . . . and we're going to give you gentlemen an opportunity to really air your views up here and spend hours discussing with the American people what's going on, so the people will be informed.

"The networks, in their talk about quality programming, creative ideas, they don't try to come up with creative ideas for their programs," Turner continued, boring in. "They try to come up with programs that will get the biggest audience, not the best. There's not hardly any consideration of quality anywhere in there. Their idea of good is big. And if it's crummy, which so much of it is, that's all the better for them. Their creative ideas are not to put on something fine like *The World at War.* . . . It's mostly cops and robbers blowing each other up and girls jiggling around. The teenage programs, soap operas and that sort of thing. That's what they're spending their $100 million on. And they don't dare run hardly anything good because the other network would be number one that night."

Jankowski, wreathed in smoke, saw no gain in joining that particular battle. Instead, he chose to describe and praise the CBS radio network. But the topic was not radio for long.

> Hollings: If you don't mind one minute, let's take judicial notice. You have CBS coverage of the hearings today.
> Jankowski: It should be noted that representatives from other news organizations this afternoon also are here.
> Hollings: And you'll also have it this afternoon?
> Jankowski: I don't know the answer to that, Senator.
> Hollings: How about the previous twenty days of hearings? We haven't seen them.
> Jankowski: Was Mr. Turner here the previous twenty days?

One thing seemed clear to McGuirk as he watched Turner's smoke waft across the room, and that was that the advantage had turned their way. Communications law was not a matter to be decided in one hearing. But Jankowski, having been set up as the defender of commercial network television, had found himself in a classic no-win situation.

Senator Larry Pressler, South Dakota Republican, eventually put his finger on the problem facing the subcommittee.

"It is difficult to piece this together," he said. "If we have retransmission consent, then, as I understand it, that would make the local broadcasters stronger, theoretically, because you wouldn't have cable coming in, and theoretically forcing them out or hurting their programs. And if we don't have retransmission consent, it would strengthen cable, which brings in national programs and sports

. . . but which can't do local reporting. That's my one stumbling block with your thesis, Mr. Turner. How do you get around that?"

Without hesitation, Turner cited an economic inquiry study done by the FCC which demonstrated that so far, cable had not caused any significant harm to any broadcaster anywhere.

This simple debating ploy—pulling the right 3 × 5 card out of memory at precisely the right time—proved the turning point of the hearing. When Pressler asked Jankowski if he agreed with that conclusion from the economic report, Jankowski ducked in a curious way.

"In terms of the network," he said, "I think I ought to emphasize that we don't feel the impact of cable. The reason why we're in a position of [wanting] a retransmission right has to do with the local station and the supplier of the program."

This seemed to interest Pressler. He pushed on: "Do you support retransmission consent?"

> Jankowski: I do.
> Pressler: So it doesn't make any difference to you—
> Jankowski: Not as a network, it does not.
> Pressler: So you're supporting it on general principle?
> Jankowski: On general principle.
> Pressler: . . .Are you familiar with the FCC study that found no economic impact?
> Jankowski: No, I'm not.

"When Jankowski said that," McGuirk recalls, "a murmur swept through the room. I mean, all this testimony had been taken to the effect that Turner was going to kill free enterprise and everything, and that the diversity we were offering would bring the house down, and then the president of CBS admits that it really doesn't make any difference to him. He's just there on general principle. All you could think was that the general principle involved was fear of competition."

The swing continued. Geller volunteered that he also was unaware of the study, but assumed that it was accurate as reported. "But we would say that is not relevant. . . . What we're advocating very strongly is that you should sweep aside the government intervention for the cable systems."

Jankowski, who was to appear before another hearing in the House later that day, was excused early. This gave Turner what was in effect the last shot.

"I really think that if the American people are ever going to get more divergent views, the only way that can occur is through cable television. And cable television offers the promise of perhaps ten, twenty, or thirty networks at some point in time. News networks, various ethnic networks, programming that the three mass networks currently cannot and will not serve.

"And if Mr. Geller and, obviously, the president of CBS don't want to see three or four more networks—he wants to see it remain just the way it is because he's in business to make billions of dollars, and that's exactly what he's doing. . . .

"I hope that the American people have a lot more choice, because— I mean it would be a horrible country if there were only three magazines, wouldn't it, gentlemen? That's what we have now. And these guys are trying to maintain that monopoly. . . .

"I think you agree with me, and any thinking person would. All you've got to do is go ask people back in your own constituencies, 'Would you rather have thirty channels or three?' and you'll find out how the people feel about it.

"We're part of that new technology, and they are here trying to stop us because they're scared. Because I've come out and said I'm going to put program quality ahead of ratings goals. Maybe I'm crazy, but I'm sure having a lot of fun with it.

"And obviously, they're scared to death or they wouldn't be here. So thank you very much."

Senator Goldwater, closing down the hearing, sounded rather like Harry Reasoner concluding his encounter with Turner on CBS's own *60 Minutes* program.

"Gentlemen, on behalf of the chairman and this committee, I want to thank you for being here. I'll have to say, Mr. Turner, there's a lot to what you said. I sat in this room not so long ago when, for the first time in the 200-year history of our country, the abuse of the constitutional privilege of the President was being discussed relative to abrogation of a treaty. And there wasn't one camera in here. There wasn't a reporter from any big Eastern newspaper. So I don't know. Maybe if we had something else, it might have made the news."

Turner was still talking as the hearing folded its tent around him: "Boy Scouts never get covered, sir. How many times have they said that Eagle Scouts are on the increase? They never cover that. But let a heroin-soaked kid hold up a little store somewhere and shoot somebody, that makes the news. . . ."

When Turner emerged from the hearing room he was walking approximately 2 feet above floor level. He knew he had done it, and done it good. It was just like the old days back at McCallie in Chattanooga, when he had won the state debating medal by twisting the issue into a pretzel of his own design. People crowded around, asking him about sailing, about the Braves, about his new idea called Cable News Network.

"It was a positively amazing performance that he put in," says Leighton. "He took the battle to CBS, and he never let them off the hook. He was peremptory, but just enough to throw everything off, and into his favor. People were literally clapping and laughing for him through it all—the cigar, the competitiveness, the appearance of a little guy up against bigness. At the end he got rolling and swaggering so much we thought he'd go too far. We thought he would get up on the table or something. But he stopped himself just in time. You go back to those Senators' offices now, and they still talk about 'the day Ted came.' "

Shortly after Turner's testimony in the Senate, the House dropped the retransmission-consent section from its rewrite of the Communications Act of 1934. The provision never even got written into the Senate bill.

The Motion Picture Association of America pulled back. "Realistically, what we can expect now is a revision of the Copyright Act by Congress," commented Fritz Attaway, MPAA vice president. "Personally, I think cable is too big a business. It's able to put tremendous grass-roots pressure on Congress."

The National Association of Broadcasters and the nation's independent television stations continue to identify Turner as a broadcast pirate, but have put retransmission consent on the back burner. "You have to admire Turner's ingenuity," said James T. J. Popham, assistant general counsel of the NAB. "The law is completely wrong, but he's taking complete advantage of it, and it's legal."

At Henry Geller's office, there was hardly time to look back. "Those issues will probably come up eventually before the copyright committee," commented Stuart Brotman. "Meanwhile, we're investigating a new wrinkle in which pay television comes directly to your home from the satellite. Sears, Roebuck is talking about marketing the receiving dish for about $200 each. If you think network affiliates are mad at Turner, wait till they hear about this."

At the office of the Baseball Commissioner in New York, it was decided to fight fire with fire. Bowie Kuhn's testimony before Congress had not had the desired effect, so baseball had gone into the cable TV business itself.

"It's the God-given right of every American to protect his property," said Tom Villante. "We couldn't do it in the legislature, so we've tried a marketing counter. We're now offering our own cablecasts on Thursday nights. It's much better than Turner's Superstation, because with ours, the local cable operator can sell his own local ads." Turner, Villante confirmed, will get his share of these revenues, along with every other baseball owner.

As for Turner himself, he lost no time in proclaiming victory over them all. Up and down and back across the country, as his harrying schedule carried him hither and yon, he reminded friends, foes and anyone else who would listen that the bell of change had rung in Washington—and in his favor. He made no pretense about his method.

"You just got to be a folk hero, that's all," he told a roomful of people in Atlanta. "It's like I told the cable operators, they've got to be heroes too, real Paul Bunyans.

"Face it, without me the cable operators would be up the yazoo. I'm the one who has baseball and basketball. I'm the one who outmaneuvered the broadcasters before they knew what was up. If any station other than Super 17 had been the first to go on satellite, the leagues would've moved the teams off that station so fast it would've made your head spin.

"But everything my enemies have said is true!" Turner yelled, breaking into a zany laugh. "We won in Washington on an emotional issue! I just decided to attack the rest of television. The logic was that it was in the best interests of the American people to steal those no-good bastards' programs anyway. And that's how we won. And that's how come Channel 17 is still on the air, and still growing, and making a profit by providing people with at least an alternative to networks. The cable industry couldn't have done it without me!" He laughed uproariously.

This speech completed, Turner careered off down the corridors of the Superstation building, flipping a Krugerrand and singing a victory chant: "The battle of Washington's done! We've won, we've won, we've won!"

8 The Fastnet
of Death

TED TURNER lay on his bunk in the owner's cabin of his 61-foot yacht
Tenacious, looking at the ceiling. The small stateroom was dark, except
for the red glow that issued from the instruments of the navigator's
table near the door. At the table sat Peter Bowker, hunched over and
listening to the radio through headphones jammed over his thatched
white hair. Turner could not sleep, but he forced himself to lie in the
bunk anyway. Inches from his ear, on the other side of the aluminum
hull, the Irish Sea swirled by at 10 knots, its steady progress interrupted more and more frequently by urgent slamming sounds. The
new sounds did not puzzle Turner. He knew that they meant the
wind and sea were rising.

It was 9:00 P.M., August 13, 1979, a Monday. Two and a half hours
before, *Tenacious* had rounded Fastnet Rock, a craggy lighthouse station off southern Ireland that served as the turning point in the
600-mile Fastnet Race. It had been just then, as the yacht was making
her final turn for home, that Bowker had delivered an unexpected
weather report: gale warnings. Winds of Force 8–9, imminent.

Now, as he lay listening, a series of pictures crossed Turner's mind.
They were the sequential photographs in a double page of *Bowditch's
Practical Navigator,* a thick tome that was the centerpiece of every
yacht's library. After Bowker's forecast, Turner and his two watch
captains looked up Force 9, though each knew the Beaufort scale of
windspeed well.

The first picture in Bowditch illustrated Force 1, the number assigned to breezes of from 0 to 3 knots. The photograph showed a
destroyer operating on what seemed to be a mill pond. Force 2, 4 to
7 knots, was much the same, but for a few ripples. In the picture
illustrating Force 5, there were many whitecaps on the sea. Force 9,

47 to 52 knots, was accompanied by a photo of a ship rolling wildly on a gale-whipped sea. Force 10 indicated a hurricane. The photo was blurred. Waves rose as high as the destroyer's bridge, and one broke heavily on her gray steel bow.

Maybe it would not come to that, Turner thought. There had been no warnings of a large-scale storm two days before, when the race had started amid the holiday merriment at Cowes on the Isle of Wight. Overhead, he heard the sounds of pounding feet as the crew took another reef in the mainsail. He had confidence in the men aboard—all eighteen of them. He had whipped them into shape pretty well, he thought. Again he felt the urgency of the sea outside, reverberating through the aluminum. Again he fought the urge to rise, pull on his foul-weather gear and boots, and climb into the cockpit to assume direct command.

He had already briefed the 8:00 watch as it clambered on deck after dinner, warning that a gale was en route, and probably a vicious one. This night, he had said, men would die. He thought of the other 302 boats on the long and difficult course, and he was sorry for them. Most were smaller than *Tenacious,* and with crews of lesser experience.

"Bowker," he said to the navigator, "what've you got now?"

"Still Force 8 to 9. Could go to Force 10 in this sector," Bowker replied from the table.

At that moment a cresting wave broke heavily over the bow of *Tenacious.* The boat shuddered, then rose like a surfacing submarine, a hundred waterfalls erupting from her decks.

"When would you like me to wake you?" Bowker asked in his calm voice. The Englishman's bemused air, in combination with the rumpled black turtleneck sweater and the headphones he wore, lent him a remarkably cinematic appearance. Bowker was already something of a legend in sailing circles. He had either thirteen or fifteen transatlantic voyages to his credit—he couldn't remember which.

"Don't worry," Turner said. "I'm not planning to sleep."

The sequence of events that put Turner in the middle of the Irish Sea that bleak night was not accidental, but plotted as carefully as a novel. And since Turner saw himself as the protagonist, not the author, he did not expect to know the ending of the story in advance.

He was no unfortunate, fate-crossed mariner, but a willing player in the well-studied game of ocean racing. If the game went rough, he had no one to blame but himself.

The sequence had begun two weeks before, when a taxicab dropped him and Janie into the humid summer night outside the Air India terminal at New York's Kennedy Airport. The broad terrazzo lobbies sprawled almost empty, but for a few knots of travelers dressed in the robes and kaftans of the East. Near the ticket counter, however, stood familiar cargo—a 6-foot-high pile of bulging duffel bags, linked by pairs of black rubber sea boots and ornamented with colorful articles of offshore foul-weather gear.

To the right of the pile was a small taproom, made up in plastic stained glass and imitation wood to resemble an English pub and overflowing with conversation and the clink of beer mugs. Shoulder to shoulder in the room, well-tanned men could be seen shaking hands in reacquaintance. Many of them wore similar blue blazers and brown leather boating shoes, a uniform which served, in the absence of prior meeting, as its own introduction. Each, the blazers denoted, was headed for the same destination: the Isle of Wight off the south coast of England, and the international yacht races there.

Turner, however, did not join this group, but went directly up a wide flight of stairs and into a telephone booth near its summit. Janie followed, wearily it seemed, and slipped into a line of chairs not far away.

"I just don't believe it," she repeated again and again as members of the taproom crew, word of Turner's arrival having reached them, gravitated to her side. "Can you believe Ted left his briefcase in the cab, and he can't remember which cab company it was? Why does this always happen—why?"

Turner continued to dial phone numbers for half an hour, then strolled over to the gathering of familiar faces.

"Hi, gang!" he called. "Hey, it's a disaster! I've lost my entire briefcase, and I don't know what to do." With that, he slipped quickly into a VIP lounge nearby. The lounge was guarded by a pretty attendant, who explained that airline regulations permitted the entry of Mrs. Turner and two guests.

Soon there were twelve crewmen inside, and the attendant had lost her patience. She attempted to block the door with her body, but quickly thought better of it as new waves of Turner buddies surged by. "But he's lost his briefcase," one explained, pushing in.

"Gentlemen, if any more try to come through this door I'll call the airport police," she said, lip trembling.

"The bar's in here!" Turner called gaily from behind, waving his arm.

By midnight the VIP lounge attendant had been reduced to tears, the 747 was climbing into the sky over the Atlantic toward England, and Turner was bedded down across three adjacent seats under a pile of Air India blankets. Atlanta was far behind, and with it the Superstation, the hearing rooms of Washington, the billboard companies, the Braves, the Hawks, the Chiefs, the Flames and the alligators of Hope Plantation. In the coming weeks, all of Turner's concentration would be taken up by the naval battles at hand. Rhett Butler would give way for the moment to Horatio Hornblower; Turner could switch personas as easily as he could switch wars, and this war would be against Britain's amateur navy. By the time the plane had reached its cruising altitude of 38,000 feet, he was fast asleep.

After four hours aloft, a flight officer made his way back among the dozing passengers to Turner's side. "Excuse me, sir," he said, "but we have received a message in the cockpit that your briefcase has been located. If you like, we will have it placed on the next flight to London."

"Huh?" said Turner, peering up at the officer with one eye. "I don't care what you do with it. Tell them to send it to Atlanta."

The Isle of Wight for most of the year is a sleepy community of fewer than a dozen towns, each well entrenched on this 15-mile-long chunk of southern England which seems to have broken its moorings at Portsmouth and Lymington and drifted just 2 miles seaward.

As a result of this separation, the Isle of Wight is shielded from the mainland by neither river nor bay, but by a sort of swift-flowing moat called the Solent. There, off the tiny village of Cowes, the sport of yachting had its origins. The date is often given as 1812, that being the founding year of the Royal Yacht Squadron, occupant of a small but proper castle hard on the waterfront. Cowes Castle was originally one of two forts, or "cows," ordered built on the island by King Henry VIII, and from which the village, previously called Shamford, derived a new name.

The normal population of the town of Cowes is 2,500. But each year, invaded by hundreds of sailboats, crews, and their supporters and observers, its number swells for a few weeks to nearly 25,000. For a provincial island far from the bustle of London, the strain is substantial. Many residents, having had their fill in years past of packed streets and night-long revels, pack suitcases and depart. Not, of course, before renting their homes to the invaders—at rates sometimes exceeding $2,500 a week.

They leave their pretty island at the mercy of yacht racers from more than twenty countries, who fill the lanes and restaurants and pubs with deafening arguments and celebrations in French, Polish, German, Italian, Japanese, Spanish, Dutch and Swedish—languages in which, as it happens, the word for "yacht" is frequently cognate. When these hordes are not talking or drinking, they empty the shelves of the tiny groceries to provision their boats; they empty the marinas and chandleries of line, gear and hardware; and they empty their pockets of pounds, shillings and pence.

At Cowes waterfront, and the mouth of the current-swept Medina River, hundreds and hundreds of boats lie tied, swarmed over by crews, spectators and members of the press. They are the very latest designs, the sleekest and richest and fastest ocean-racing yachts in the world, and the visual effect of the array is staggering. In the days before the racing actually begins, colorful sails are packed, electric drills wail as last-minute gear is fitted, and boggling examples of international womanhood recline on the cluttered decks, exposing whatever portion of flesh they dare to the cool English sun which streams down whenever the towering gray clouds split between rain showers and warning gusts of wind.

The Solent may be an imperfect place for sailboat races—its currents too swift, its winds either howling or nonexistent—but Cowes is without doubt the premiere bleacher for observation of this esoteric sport. Most yacht races take place away from shore, seen and celebrated only by the contestants themselves. But at Cowes, where deep water runs within 10 feet of the green lawns and stony beaches, the boats compete in full view. A visitor who finds himself strolling on the walk between Cowes Castle and Egypt Hill during race week may feel all but run down by the progression of sails that hurtle toward him.

Yachts 70 feet long, Dacron straining, charge directly for the beach, seeking to escape the stronger current offshore, and do not tack away until the last instant. Eighty or ninety large boats, with crews of six or more, may repeat this spectacular maneuver directly in front of a stationary viewer. And when the big boats are gone, the day racers come, zigging and zagging up the shoreline, battling for position at the water's edge. Seven hundred of them.

By 1979, Cowes Week had come to represent the acme of glory for yachtsmen. It began with the Channel Race, a 215-mile overnight sprint to France and back; then treated spectators and crews to five separate day races confined to the Solent itself, where the vessels raced in sight of the Royal Yacht Squadron castle much of the time; and it ended, with suitable flourish, in the bidding goodbye of the fleet as it set off on the one endurance event of the series—the 600-mile charge to Ireland's Fastnet Rock, and the return to Plymouth. The English and European press seemed determined to make heroes of as many contestants as possible, and so the Isle of Wight fairly swarmed with journalists of all shapes and descriptions, whose plight it was to watch and record sailboat races for a living, if they did not drown in spirits first. A major sponsor of the race week was Mumm Champagne, and the firm did not tolerate half-filled glasses in its well-attended press tents.

Into this paradisiacal arena came Ted Turner, by hydrofoil across the Solent, dashing onto the ferry ramps without pause after a long bus ride from Heathrow Airport in London. Soon he and Janie were ensconced in the very proper Homewood Hotel and the crew lodged in a rented house or on board *Tenacious* herself. The yacht had preceded Turner to England by a week, having made a transatlantic voyage from Newfoundland under her professional captain, twenty-five-year-old Bud Sutherland. Turner seemed in good spirits, and word was passed that the crew would meet aboard *Tenacious* at 8:30 A.M. on the day of the first race, ready to go.

When the *Tenacious* crew arrived onboard, however, they found their skipper already there, resplendent in white Lacoste shirt, khakis held up by suspenders in the style of Mork from Ork, and trademark railroad engineer's cap. Women crowded the dock, drawn by the familiar mustached profile—with which Turner signaled like a lighthouse from atop his cabin top. Whatever happened on the racecourse, Turner had already taken the lead in the psychological wars ashore.

As the big yacht motored out to the starting line off Cowes Castle, joining the dress parade of competitors, Turner seemed uncharacteristically calm, even though two crewmen still dangled in bosun's chairs aloft, making last-minute repairs to the rigging. As the starting cannons fired, *Tenacious*'s spinnaker filled beautifully, and the race to Europe was on.

The crew, shaking off its jet lag, looked to its stations. Each man was a veteran of many blue-water races, but it was apparent there were cobwebs in the air. Though *Tenacious* had quickly taken her place near the head of the charging fleet, the men remained as yet imperfectly familiar with the complicated gear, the scores of wires and lines, and the twenty-five sails on board. There were incidents of clumsiness, and of hesitation. Shortly after the start, Turner began to yell.

Three times in one hour he replaced the man assigned to trim the mainsail, in each case specifically describing the gross deficiencies that led to his decision. Then he turned his attention to the team tending to the large jib, firing various of them from their jobs with torrents of scorn and outrage. As *Tenacious* bashed along at top speed, cleaving the steep channel waves, Turner systematically worked over nearly every man on board, sparing not even his two watch captains —the men who actually ran the boat whenever he retired to his cabin. Idiots and stumblebums all, he announced; definitely a marginal crew. Unquestionably a problem bunch. His frustration grew greater as it became apparent that Turner did not, in fact, even know the names of each man aboard.

"Hey you! Stupid!" he would shout at a figure among the twenty bodies on deck. "You on the boom vang! You with the sweater, yeah, you! I don't even know who you are—but you're a jerk! Get somebody on the boom vang who knows what he's doing!"

And so that anonymous person would slink elsewhere on the deck, replaced by a nearby hand whose lot it was to fare no better. For the crew, three hours after the start of this first race together, the order of the day was head down, guard up. As the skipper's most piercing epithets rained down on them, tiny smiles formed—carefully shielded from the helm. There was no thought of rebellion. Certainly this was an adrenaline-charged way to begin what might turn out to be a difficult race, and it was unquestionably an even stranger way to begin an expensive summer vacation. But at least each man was assured he would not be criticized behind his back.

There were other mitigating factors too, factors of pride and justice. Every man on *Tenacious* was conscious that he had departed his home a sort of prefabricated hero, flying off to England to race with Ted Turner. Now the time had come to earn it, to prove to Turner and to himself that he could take anything Turner or the sea could dish up. It was important, for every man aboard, that these races be some kind of a test.

The crew list of *Tenacious* in England showed a rough mix of muscle and experience, its members drawn together by the flamboyance of their skipper and the inclination to have a summer adventure otherwise elusive in their middle-class lives. They represented twelve states and five countries, and more than half had sailed together before.

Gary Jobson, twenty-nine. Watch captain. Tall, lean and inseparable from Turner's recent sailing history.

Jim Mattingly, thirty-five. Watch captain. A veteran Turner organizer and vice president of Derecktor Yacht Builders, Mamaroneck, N.Y.

Peter Bowker, fifty-two. Navigator. An Englishman living in Fort Lauderdale.

Robert H. "Bobby" Symonette, fifty. Symonette's father had been governor of Nassau, and Symonette served as guest expert on the topics of boating and international life.

Richard Collins, thirty-four. An automotive supplier in Stowe, Vermont, Collins had sailed with Turner since 1967.

Courtenay Jenkins, twenty-three. Blond and strong, Jenkins was postponing his career in investment banking by a summer of yacht racing.

Royal Dubois "Duby" Joslin, thirty-two. A retired Navy officer, Joslin had two America's Cup campaigns behind him and was employed by a shipping firm in Philadelphia.

Crosby Martin, twenty-five. A Californian, Martin had signed on for *Tenacious* delivery passage from Newfoundland.

Richard Rodoreda, twenty-two. His civil engineering studies in Perth, Australia, were being interrupted for a year of horizon-chasing.

John Samama, twenty-seven. A development economist from Wageningen, Holland, Samama was a physical giant who had sailed his first Cowes Week at age seventeen.

Greg Shires, twenty-eight. A public relations man from Chicago, Shires had crewed on *Tenacious* since her launching, as *Dora IV*, in 1972.

Bud Sutherland, twenty-five. An expert seaman and navigator, Sutherland had been Turner's paid captain on board since he was twenty-three.

Robert E. "Teddy" Turner IV, sixteen. Turner's oldest son was serving as a paid hand for the summer, assisting Captain Sutherland.

Steve Ward, twenty-six. A shipwright whose family operated a yard in Australia, Ward had crewed on *Australia,* the America's Cup challenger in 1977, and would join the *Courageous* team in 1980.

George Varga, twenty-three, a.k.a. "Jaws." Impervious to pain or exhaustion, Varga was a classmate of Jenkins at UVM, where they had been co-captains of the lacrosse team.

Tom Relyea, twenty-six. A fearless and cocky Californian, Relyea enjoyed being hauled to the top of the mast at midnight during a squall.

Rives Potts, twenty-nine. A boatbuilder from Virginia, Potts sailed his second 12-meter campaign aboard *Freedom* in 1980.

Jane Potts, twenty-six. Cook. The sister of Rives Potts, she had once hitchhiked around the world and now delivered a lecture series on job opportunities for young people abroad.

Christian Williams, thirty-six. A latent recrudescence of the Turner media circus, Williams worked for a newspaper in Washington, D.C.

* * *

This crew, arranged by Mattingly from his New York office after consultations with Turner and Jobson, had other reasons for pride. Unlike many of the grand prix yachting teams at the Isle of Wight, each had paid his own way. That was a tradition on Turner's boats, and it could be attributed to frugality on the part of the owner, or the need for independence on the part of the crew, or both. In any case, these circumstances differed greatly from those aboard a sleek, bottle-blue maxi-racer which often moored alongside *Tenacious*. On that yacht, as on others, many men had a "ticket." Upon arrival, every man received his own set of expensive foul-weather gear, an embroidered coat, and a high-status Lacoste shirt with the yacht's name on the chest. The blue yacht was owned by an international oil magnate, and his crew, when ashore between races, slept in a house rented by him. Turner's crew had a house too, but paid $225 per person to sleep in it. The crew of *Tenacious* looked upon these perquisites of the blue yacht not without envy. But whenever the blue yacht drew alongside during a race, the envy turned to adrenaline. And the blue yacht would be beaten back by almost fanatic concentrations of energy from the Turner "underdogs."

The Channel Race, as it happened, was sailed under virtually perfect conditions. As one four-hour watch gave way to another, day and night, warm sun and bright stars wonderfully illuminated the sea. Cherbourg rose out of the dawn mist ("There's France, squad," Turner called. "You'll never see it prettier than you do now") and declined again, and the yacht slipped back across the Channel to the Solent, where she ghosted to a stop 10 miles from the finish, becalmed among *Ondine, Mistress Quickly, Condor of Bermuda, Boomerang* and several other thoroughbreds, their spinnakers hanging useless in the late morning calm.

Quietly, stealthily, Turner zigged and zagged among them, sniffing the merest puffs of wind, playing his famous chess game. He found the reluctant breezes first, and rode them until they expired. He ghosted and snuck and finessed and held his breath, but *Tenacious* kept moving. Hardly a word was said, but when the breeze filled in at noon, the other boats had fallen behind. *Tenacious* had won her class.

Six-ounce cans of Heineken beer were passed around. Only after the finish line is crossed is consumption of alcohol permitted on board; and never is tobacco consumed belowdecks on Turner's boats.

Cowes Week had begun with a win, but Turner still seemed distant. Late in the first day of the race, he had systematically visited with each member of his crew, in several cases introducing himself: "Hi, I'm Ted Turner. Who the hell are you? If I yelled at you, don't worry about it. You seem like a strong guy. Of course, looks are deceiving. We'll see. You may not make it." As is his custom, Turner instantly departed as soon as the boat touched the dock, leaving the crew to ponder their own performance.

That night the crew hastened to sleep, for tomorrow's day race came early. Once again the yachts cast off and the colorful fleet had its rambunctious start, thrashing along the spectator-crammed shorelines, while Turner, from his position at the helm, taunted and cajoled his own overflowing team. When the yacht moored in midafternoon, the crew, its hands sore and backs aching, fell to the long task of repacking sails and cleaning up. That evening Turner left Janie to have a quiet and elegant dinner with Jobson and a few others while he attended a meeting of the Royal Ocean Racing Club committee.

Joining this group later, Turner mused mysteriously about the races to come. "What do you think of this crew?" he asked Jobson.

"The guys seem all right," Jobson said. "They're working hard. I think it's going to be fine, Ted."

"Still marginal," the skipper replied, walking into the Homewood with his arm around Janie. "Got a way to go."

By morning the wind was up. Steve Ward and his friend Jane Cullen, Rich Collins and Jim Mattingly wolfed down breakfast while Cowes's swollen stream of sailors rushed by outside the restaurant window facing High Street. "We better get down to the boat," Collins said. "Ted said anybody who isn't on board on time is getting kicked off the boat."

No one was late, and by now a pattern had formed in the racing days as one followed the other. The half-hour walk from the crew house to *Tenacious's* berth on the Medina, the scramble as scores of huge sailboats poured out of the river en route to the starting line, the tense moments that began with the ten-minute warning gun, then the boom of the starting cannon.

The crew, after several races together, had noticeably changed. Last names had given way to first names, and first names to nicknames. The hesitations of the first day were gone. Now, when Turner shouted, the appropriate crewman quickly jumped into action. Sails were changed and trimmed with precision almost all of the time. This was an Admiral's Cup Race—one of a series of international team races held as part of Cowes Week.

On a windy day, there is great excitement at the starting line of a boat race, and this day was coming up windy. Turner blasted toward the line as the seconds closed down, cheek by jowl with three other boats. As the crew pumped winches furiously, it became apparent that all four yachts intended to cross the line at the same place. Closer and closer they came to each other until all four sped along, side by side, still converging at maximum speed. Shouts broke out from several of the boats as each claimed right of way, but the cries were quickly lost in the whitecaps and wind.

Two of the boats suddenly slewed away, but Turner, well braced behind his destroyer-style steering wheel, declined to yield. Just below him, a British yacht pressed up hard, both boats pitched suddenly in the Solent waves, and there was a resounding crash. The mouths of the Englishmen fell open, and a great noise arose in the Queen's language.

"You have run right into us!" came a voice from the other yacht, as both screamed across the line and onto the 30-mile-long course.

"Nah, you obviously ran into us," Turner shouted back. "Why don't you guys watch where you're going?"

Any collision on the racecourse warrants a protest hearing, but Turner remained unfazed. In fact, he stuck his chin out and carried a grin through the rest of the day. He sailed well, smoothly in synch with his tacticians in the cockpit and with Bowker's expert readings of current and shoals.

When the course made a sharp turn, requiring the big spinnaker to be jibed from one side of the boat to the other, the crew performed its work flawlessly. Turner had been watching like a hawk.

"Not too shabby," he said calmly. The crew, engrossed with the tasks of their duty stations, did not look back toward the helm. But the following breeze had brought his words efficiently to them. They had heard.

"Hey, Willie," Turner called down to Wilhelmina Samama, a redoubtable young woman who had talked herself aboard this race even though a cook was unnecessary and she was in fact six months pregnant. "You ought to pass these guys some gum. Gum all around for the crew. There's nothing for a crew . . . better than a chew," he added happily.

Tenacious won that race, hands down. Back at the crew house at Egypt Hill, a great feast of lamb was being cooked, and various team members arrived that evening bearing their victuals and cases of wine and beer. The aroma of the lamb was spectacular, and Willie Samama and her friends had set mounds of fresh garlic butter about, and bowls of mint jelly, and piles of steaming vegetables. The crew laughed and joked, waiting for Ted to arrive. But Turner and Jobson were at the protest committee meeting. Seven o'clock came and went. Eight o'clock too. At nine, with apologies to Janie, the lamb was attacked.

Turner and Jobson arrived at 9:30 to find a room full of zombielike figures, reeking of garlic and mint and floating in a sea of empty wineglasses. They brought bad news.

"Hey gang, we lost," Turner said simply. "When you go into a protest over a collision there's only a fifty-fifty chance, and they didn't see it our way. So we won it, but we lost it."

Voices rose in protest, but Turner waved them down.

"Forget it," he said. "Listen, you're not such a bad crew. I know I yelled a lot the first couple of days, but it's because you didn't know what you were doing, that's all. I don't think some of you guys were ever on a sailboat before yesterday anyhow—you just lied to get to come along." A few catcalls broke out. "No," Turner went on. "You may be able to make it yet. You may just turn out to be a real crew yet. We won this one, didn't we? Who cares if you lose a protest once in a while?"

The crew, relieved of tension for the first time since the Air India flight had arrived at Heathrow almost a week before, broke out in a cheer.

Turner seemed almost surprised that a portion of the meal had been preserved for him.

"You saved me some? That's the nicest thing anyone ever did for me," Turner replied as a plate and a glass were thrust into his hands. "I look at this nice group here, all my friends even though I didn't even know who some of these ding-dongs were a couple of days ago, and I never felt better. Let the other people go to the fancy restaurants! I would rather eat here in the crew house with my friends any day!" Then he laughed, adding: "I'm treating you all to the most expensive meal you ever ate. Come to the Homewood Thursday night at 7:30. I'll probably go broke, but we'll have a good time."

Wednesday, *Tenacious* won the Britannia Cup, and the crew, fueled by the lamb feast the night before, performed with confidence.

It was apparent, however, that Turner and his men were getting the test they had signed on for. One boat, a 45-footer named *Madrugada*, had already been holed in a collision, and stood beached in a marina in Cowes with a 6-foot gash in her side that exactly duplicated the shape of her assailant's bow. At the start of the Britannia Cup, there had been a high-speed collision too.

The Australian yacht *Police Car* had been struck by *Indigo* of Brazil with a crash so alarming that heads turned on boats a quarter mile away. As the boats parted, an Australian crewman named John Mooney was dragged into the sea. The wind was gusting and the view unclear from *Tenacious,* but it seemed that instantly a yellow-clad figure dove in headfirst after him.

"That was a guy on *Indigo* who saw me go in," Mooney explained weeks later, sitting out a dance in a British discotheque, his arm in a cast. "Me arm was broken, see, and I was in shock and going down. If that guy hadn't gone in, I wouldn't be here now. Like he said, he had to swim down and find me before he could bring me up."

The collision had not delayed the start, but as Turner charged on for the line he exclaimed, "See—I told you guys it was dangerous out here. That's something to remember—in order to win, you got to survive!"

There was only one race remaining before the start of the Fastnet, the long-distance event to which these day races led, step by step, like a steep mountain trail to an unknown summit. *Tenacious* finished in early afternoon, which gave the crew precious time for a long gam at the beer tent, where 500 men and women could be counted on to argue over the true wonders of the racing day. The tent, which unlike the mad streets of Cowes was more or less restricted to the sailors themselves, was a bazaar of opinions and familiar faces. Edward Heath, the former Prime Minister, could be seen beer glass in hand, complaining about the broken rudder of his yacht *Morning Cloud*. Prince Charles had made a brief appearance. Knots of nationalists— the Poles, Italians and French in particular—broke often into bellicose songs, only to be outshouted by the nearest Australian. A staff of ten bartenders poured pints continually into this melee in a losing effort to staunch the din.

Such deafening celebrations were not really Turner's style, but after the Britannia Cup win he and Collins and Ward and Jobson and a few others dropped by to see what was up and defend *Tenacious's* honor if need be. On the way, Turner observed proudly to his entourage that his crew, at least, was of a certain maturity, and could be counted on to comport themselves as winners should.

Upon arriving at the tent site, it was apparent how comparatively well comported his team was: the beer tent had been burned to the ground. Nothing remained but a peripheral line of black ashes and several large piles of melted glass. "That's awful," Turner said loudly to a throng of firebugs inspecting the wreckage. "Who would ever want to do that to the beer tent?"

"The French," came an anonymous answer from the crowd.

That evening the Cowes police visited *Tenacious*. "Just checking to see what you know about the burning of the tent," a helmeted bobby explained. The few members of the crew who happened to be aboard, most of them waiting in line to shave, took this as an accusation and gruffly sent the policeman away. The French, even more offended by rumors blaming their sailors for beer-tent arson, went so far as to file a protest through their embassy in London.

That night, Turner's crew gathered thirty strong at the Homewood, where a speech was made in the skipper's honor and he was presented with a book signed by all. Turner, overcome with emotion, rose with a flourish to respond.

At the far end of the room, however, another party was going on, and just as Turner rose that party launched into a loud performance of "Happy Birthday to You." Turner tried to speak over the song, but found he could not. He tried a second time, while the crew leaned forward. "This is a wonderful thing, when we can all race hard together during the day, and then . . ."

". . . to you, happy birthday to you, happy . . ."

". . . share a meal together, and then . . ."

". . . happy birthday, happy birthday, happy . . ."

". . . and then, *hey! Happy birthday over there!*"

But the other group did not hear. Turner, supposing them to be Germans, then instructed his long table in a chorus of "Deutschland Uber Alles," which he led in the style of Von Karajan before the Berlin Philharmonic. The effect was somewhat lessened when it became apparent that not only did his crew not know the words to "Deutschland Uber Alles," but the other party was not German.

So "Deutschland Uber Alles" faded quickly, while "Happy Birthday" did not, and Turner had no choice but to sit down. "Even I can't compete with that," he said and shrugged. This surreal moment did not last, however, as a wave of dessert cakes, coffee and cigars swept the table end to end. Within the hour, Turner had retired to bed.

Morning brought scud clouds blowing low from the west, and the air was cool. This last day race was called the New York Yacht Club Challenge Cup, for it was here, in the Solent off the Royal Yacht Squadron 128 years before, that the schooner *America* had first shown the British what a fast sailing boat looked like. It was just another in the day-by-day series of 30-mile races, and the fleet gathered as it had all week at the starting line by late morning.

Something was different, however. There was a real punch in the air, and the sea was in a froth. As *Tenacious* turned the corner of the Medina River, a blast caught her bow and turned her half around. "Hey, it's windy as hell out here," Turner shouted, ordering the sails changed immediately. Sail was taken in on the other big boats, too, as the fleet grew in the starting-line area and the now-familiar seascape of a hundred super-racers took shape. Conditions quickly became wild, as a black rain squall descended just after the start and scores of boats took knockdowns which laid their masts nearly flat in the water and left crews scrambling for handholds.

Tenacious flew off into the chop, spray dousing the deck, and punched quickly around the first mark. With the big spinnaker up, running downwind, the whole fleet was suddenly well astern. Many of them also seemed to be out of control.

Turner stood at the wheel as the wind screamed, with Jobson looking back to warn him of extra-violent gusts. Near the English shore, distress flares burned brightly, and a Royal Navy helicopter made speed toward them. The rest of the fleet was scattered. As *Tenacious* was finding out, this happened to be a full westerly gale, sprung up without warning. Several yachts could be seen abandoning the course, making speed back to the wharfside.

"They're not that stupid," Turner yelled, spinning the wheel this way and that as *Tenacious* foamed along, just on the edge of control. "They don't want to bust their boats with the Fastnet coming up day after tomorrow."

"Here comes a big one, Ted!" Jobson called.

"I can't hold her!" Turner shouted.

"Bear off a little, Ted!"

"Hold on, everybody!" Turner screamed as the windspeed indicator before him jumped instantly from 35 to 45 knots. "We're going oooooovvvveeeerrrr . . . !"

So was the mighty *Tenacious* struck down from behind, having carried too much sail too long. Turner had lost control, and could only hang onto the wheel while he watched the members of his crew grab handholds themselves. The yacht broached wildly to the right, and the gust—catching the sails sideways now—knocked her nearly flat on her side. The crew dangled helplessly as the deck tilted to 50 degrees for what seemed an eternity, and then, with a violent ripping sound, the red-and-white spinnaker exploded into tatters, the pressure was relieved, and the boat bounded to her feet again.

Turner, cursing the indignity, ran forward to help the crew recover the shreds of the $5,000 sail, and *Tenacious* was under way again— several places back from the lead. The race ended as it had begun, in a foaming melee, as five of the surviving boats hurtled abreast down the Cowes shoreline to the cheers of several thousand spectators. The finish line was a bobbing mass of debris, photographer's launches and observation boats—and the sad sight of two yachts which had tangled in each other's rigging, and lay dismasted side by side, plunging up and down in the dying gale. The New York Yacht Club Challenge Cup had turned into a Class A gearbuster. There were no fatalities, but the London Telegraph the next day reported conditions in the Solent "the worst in living memory" for a boat race. Only fifty-two yachts had been permitted to start, and more than thirty of them had failed to complete the course. Damage, the Telegraph said, was estimated to be tens of thousands of pounds.

"There's only one thing to do after something like this," Turner announced back at the dock. "Tomorrow's our only day off all week, so we'll just have time to zip over to Portsmouth and visit the Victory, Lord Nelson's flagship. I been there a couple of times before, but it's real inspiring, believe me."

On the way back from the Victory, however, Turner was put out. First, he had known a good deal more about Admiral Nelson's career than had the young Royal Navy guide that escorted him and Janie and Teddy and a half-dozen crew through the bowels of the old three-decker warship. Second, Teddy had fallen so far behind the 10-mile-an hour strides his father set that the boy had missed the hovercraft back across the Solent to Ryde. The Victory, Turner had neglected to inform his party, was located about four miles inland—by foot.

Teddy caught the next scheduled hovercraft forty-five minutes later, wearing a sheepish teenage grin. He joined his father's party for lunch at a scenic hotel—and was eaten alive by his father.

Cowes Week had its formal end that night in a blaze of fireworks attended by 20,000. The finale of the display was a large waterfront frieze that spelled out "Long Live the Queen" in pyrotechnics. The crowd applauded heartily. To do otherwise would have been demonstrably impolite, as the Queen herself was on hand—as she had been all week—aboard HMS Britannia, moored just offshore.

All that remained for weary Cowes was the bidding goodbye of the Fastnet fleet.

The course of the Fastnet Race is 605 miles long: from Cowes it follows the coast of southern England to Lands End, then shoots northwest across the mouth of the Irish Sea to Fastnet Rock itself, and returns along nearly the same route to a finish line off Plymouth. That is no easy jaunt for sailboats, but even so, since the first race was held in 1925, the number of entrants in the biennial event has grown each time. From the beginning, the Fastnet has had its own mystique, known for the strong currents and unpredictable breezes that test skippers, crews and navigators equally. In recent years, winds on the course have been light to moderate, with frequent episodes of calm, and smaller and smaller yachts have done well. Memories of the bitter contest of 1957, in which three nasty gales reduced a fleet of forty-two to only twelve finishers, had faded into legend and history. Those boats were wood, with spruce masts and sails of Egyptian cotton. By 1979, there was hardly a wooden boat left, and the hardware was of aluminum and stainless steel, and the sails of Dacron.

Three hundred and three of these modern vessels crowded the start this pleasant Saturday, with the smaller boats starting off first through light rain showers toward distant Fastnet. *Tenacious's* turn would come at 2:30 P.M., with the other maximum yachts of Class O. As he waited at the helm, Turner hashed over the same thought again and again.

"Hey, guys," he said. "I set the course record here in 1971 with *American Eagle.* There's only one thing I ask, and that's that we do it again. It's my record, after all, and we can break it if we want. We've had a good time so far, haven't we? We've won some races, haven't we? But this is the big one. I said you guys weren't that great at first, and I'm still not so sure. Now's the time you'll prove it."

He seemed terrifically excited, jumping up and down behind the wheel, as the sequence of cannons boomed down. Among the boats in Class O, in fact, was his old *American Eagle,* the record-setter. She was renamed *War Baby,* and shortly after the start, *Tenacious* crossed her bow.

"That's the way, squad!" Turner yelled. "Only 600 miles to go!"

The pace of an ocean race is different from one in which the crew will sleep ashore at night. The first effect is the result of the watch system—four hours on and four hours off—which halves the crew into eight-man teams. One team, led by its watch captain, works the boat to exhaustion and then tumbles below, relieved by its opposite number. Since the off watch must eat, sleep and change clothes, and the deck watch work continually at sail changing and trimming, there is little fraternization between the two groups.

And yet, after the start of the Fastnet, both watches remained on deck together for hours. This, after all, was what they had come for, and the sights and sounds of the Solent that afternoon were not rivaled even by the fresh memories of Cowes Week past.

As the sun tracked lower and lower in the west, the biggest boats steadily caught up to the smaller ones, so that by early evening all 300 converged in the narrow exit where the Solent meets the Atlantic. Zigging and zagging synchronously into a 10-knot breeze, the fleet lay brilliantly illuminated in a diorama for which the backdrop was the blanched limestone spires of the Needles, the toothy extremity of the Isle of Wight.

The low angle of the sun turned the sea quicksilver, and in the twin mirrors of Turner's one-way sunglasses a buoyant message repeated itself: *Tenacious* was carving steadily through the flotilla, and soon would be among the leaders. No one spoke. The only sound was the gentle rushing of the sea below the leeward gunwale, and the clicking of the winches as the sail trimmers expertly responded to the fractional changes in wind speed.

As the Needles fell behind, *Tenacious* clearly emerged at the head of the race, joining the true maxi-racers there: famous *Kialoa,* 79 feet overall; Australian *Siska,* a bright-orange giant; beautifully varnished *Condor of Bermuda,* veteran of the round-the-world race; *Mistress Quickly,* with her tall rig; and a scattering of the fastest lesser boats. The sight, unimaginably romantic, was made the more extraordinary in that there was no battery of photographers and reporters to plaster it over postcards, calendars and T-shirts. The crew of *Tenacious* looked hard in order to remember.

"Hey," Turner called out, breaking the spell. "The off watch is supposed to be below. You guys better get some sleep while you can, or you'll be sorry."

When the eight-man team emerged again at 8:00 P.M., stuffed with the three-course meal Jane Potts had spread out on the varnished table below, Turner was still at the helm, but the aspect had changed.

It was still light, and several miles off to the right loomed the headland Portland Bill. Portland Bill, a jutland on the West Country coast, is a tactical barrier of the Fastnet course, and off its rocky shore the current ran a full 5 knots in opposition to the fleet. To the hundred boats that simultaneously had this famous headland in sight, the choice was the same: to go very close inshore, cheating the current by sailing through the shallows, or to give the Bill a wide berth, and hope to keep up speed in the steadier wind offshore.

The discussion in the cockpit was lively.

"I say we go right in, right in to the rocks," Turner said.

"Ah, Ted, I don't know," said Symonette in his broad Bahamian accent. "Hate to get too close in there."

"How about it, Bowker?" Turner demanded.

"Um, it looks all right out here where we are," the navigator said. Navigators do not like to be asked for judgment calls on tactical matters. They much prefer to be asked the position of the yacht, or the course to the next mark, or the speed of the current, or the weather report.

Turner was getting impatient. "Let's go in, right, Gary?" He said to Jobson.

Jobson mashed his chewing gum as if to kill it. "Well, the thing is, Ted, we're already a couple miles off, and we'd lose time going into the rocks, and who knows what we'll find when we get there?"

"That settles it," Turner exclaimed. "We're going in."

So the yacht changed course—and in she went. Soon the gray outline of the point grew larger, and the rocks sprouted houses— curious tar-paper shacks, apparently those of local fishermen. *Tenacious* kept on, making a beeline for the coast, until the crew could see more than 500 English families far above, watching silently. When a white line of surf could be seen dead ahead, Turner changed course to parallel the shore.

"See, this ain't so bad," he said. "We've even got some company." Right ahead lay the Australian yacht *Siska*, making slow progress against the tide. And also *Marloo*, a smaller boat but very fast. The three at first made steady progress along the rocks. Then, as the headland loomed, the powerful current stream slowed each to a stop. They sailed, heeled over slightly, a fresh wave at their bows, at 5 knots; the current opposed at precisely the same speed. Stalemate. It began to get dark. From behind, the fleet closed in—having taken its clue from the leaders, and gone inshore too.

Now, as vagaries of the unseen current gripped their keels, *Tenacious*, *Siska* and *Marloo* were swept sideways, away from Portland Bill, their places usurped by scores of following boats. But the newcomers could not stem the tide either, and soon more than sixty yachts lay side by side, close under the rocky point, hollering at one another for right of way they could neither give nor receive, for the back eddy of the 5-knot tide held them in thrall.

"Ha," said Turner. "At least we ain't caught in that mess. We may not be going anyplace ourselves, but look at those poor bastards in there."

At that moment, a strange sound rose from the other side of *Tenacious*, the seaward side, where there should have been nothing but ocean. A splashing. A ragged, ripping sound of water aswirl. Heads turned toward the sound, one after another.

"Oops!" called Turner. As they watched, mighty *Siska* was carried sideways by the tide into a boiling caldron, a mass of stationary breakers that doused her decks and sent her crew scrambling this way and that. "Don't worry, men," Turner said, "it's only the Overfalls. Hold on! We're going in!"

First *Tenacious*, and then *Marloo* too, spun helplessly after *Siska*. By this time the wind had died completely, and without steerageway the rudder was useless. Crew members looked at each other with eyes wide, like sailors on the *Santa Maria* observing the ultimate proof that Columbus had been wrong. In the darkness, as spray peppered the decks, it quickly became apparent that the Overfalls were nothing more than a dramatic but harmless tide rip. They even showed clearly on the chart—as a line of breakers. Soon the three companion boats emerged dampened, but unscathed, on the other side.

"Well, Symonette," Turner said cockily, "you're supposed to have seen everything. You ever seen the Overfalls?"

"Yeah, I've seen them," Symonette replied sarcastically. "It's just that I never sailed through them before."

All in all, *Tenacious's* helter-skelter ride through the currents turned out not badly at all. In a moment a ghostly wind returned, and she carefully made her way off through the darkness toward Lands End.

Portland Bill faded astern, her tide and calms still holding the rest of the fleet in an imprisoning embrace.

For the next two days the yacht sailed on, gradually separating from her rivals so that she sailed alone on a sparkling sea. Eddystone Light passed to leeward, and Sunday evening Lands End itself. *Tenacious* was in the Irish Sea, swooping at good speed toward Fastnet Rock.

By now, shipboard routine was firmly established, and four hours on and four off seemed as natural a way to live as had the pubs and restaurants and pillowed beds of Cowes Week past. Turner was in good spirits, for the sailing weather was fine: just enough wind to keep the crew busy and the yacht moving fast, but not enough to spoil the appetite.

Jobson and Mattingly herded their watches on and off deck with precision, and but few complaints. It was true that Mattingly sometimes was late coming on deck; it was also true that Jobson's watch occasionally left a sail or two to be packed by the fresh crew. Turner visited with each on deck and below, keeping his finger on the pulse of life on the crowded little ship.

Even in these idyllic conditions, the pulse ran fast. The crew's job was to keep the boat going at its highest potential speed at all times, day and night. This meant, in effect, changing sails often, since a sail which was perfectly suited for 9 knots of wind could be replaced— from *Tenacious's* large inventory in the forecastle—with one that would perform even better at 13 knots of wind.

Most sails on board weighed at least 100 pounds even when dry. They had to be wrestled onto the foredeck from below, fastened in place by the light of flashlights held in the teeth, and then hoisted by winch and manpower. Then the old sail had to be lowered, packed, and dragged back to its storage place. For the five-man foredeck teams, one sail change meant a complete soaking in sweat, if the weather was light, and in seawater too, in a blow. The men who made these changes labored under the most abominable conditions: on a pitching deck sometimes awash with breaking seas, or in a steamy, claustrophopic cabin filled with snoring bodies. One sail change often took as long as an hour, with much of that time spent repacking the slippery, dripping Dacron that had just been removed. The fold-ing and stuffing was done in *Tenacious's* elegant main salon, for nowhere else was there sufficient room. Often wet spinnakers—all 80 feet of them—were dragged directly across the faces of sleeping men, who only replied, in dazed tones: "Thank you for not stepping on me."

After four changes in one four-hour period, the entire population of the deck would pour below, gasping for air and grabbing for candy bars and Coke. They occasionally also grabbed for the well-rounded form of Jane Potts, cook, who seemed a vision of unearthly loveliness when encountered strapped before her stove in a powder-blue jogging suit. Potts had large and newly sharpened knives nearby at all times, and maintained a sweet and thoughtful demeanor.

While these exhausted specimens gasped and drooled, reclining in innocent vulgarity on wet sailbags in their woolen underwear, Potts would place before them huge amounts of fresh-baked bread, steaming casseroles, cans of cold fruit juice, and scores of exotic sweets. Hot pies, mounds of fudge, piles of pacifying pudding. And the animals would dine.

Relyea, cramming bananas through his beard. Jobson, talking with his mouth full about the nature of Success. Jenkins, draining can after can of orange juice as if to color his bright hair from the inside out. Symonette, pretending to represent civilization at table. Joslin, neat as a cat, no crumb spilling no matter how the boat rolled under his plate. Varga, otherwise known as "Jaws," a devouring force. And Rodoreda, the living punch line to a joke about Australian gourmets.

No beer, no booze, no tobacco to bring on sleep. No need. Even the porno locker, a dark drawer filled to overflowing with international publications revealing the most monstrous scenes of human degradation, went unopened after these wonderful, salt-encrusted postwatch repasts.

"I have a decision to make," said Joslin after one such enormous meal. "Either I take off my wet foul-weather gear, or I don't take off my wet foul-weather gear." With that, he fell asleep.

Since there were two watches, Potts in effect served two meals, three times a day. Turner alternated informally between them, joined at the swinging table in the main cabin. No matter how waterlogged and aching the crew, Turner always appeared fresh from the laundromat—sauntering out from his owner's stateroom in white ducks and clean shirt, ready with a tale of shoreside business adventure or some freshly imagined challenge on the water. He was totally at home on his yacht, and wore it like a familiar article of clothing. Not surprising, since by his own reckoning he had spent more than 300 days at sea on board.

These interludes belowdecks were of a dreamlike quality aboard *Tenacious,* and doubtless for the rest of the fleet as well, since the wind was fine and the seas gentle, and every hour brought Fastnet Rock nearer for all. There can be great peace during an ocean passage, even while racing. It is found in the surrender to shipboard routine, submission to the tyranny of four hours on and four off, and accommodation to the fuzzy-headed feeling brought on by hard work, clamorous interruptions of sleep, and much food. The peace is made more delicious by the knowledge of its likely transience. At any moment, conditions may radically change. Much-coveted dry clothes, once wet, will never dry till landfall. And with a rising sea, sleep becomes difficult, yielding only to the forceful soporific of true exhaustion. When the sea changes, food quickly loses its appeal, and a hard knot replaces the appetite. The knot is seldom fear, for the amateur sailor is only slightly familiar with his own mortality, as when, gazing into the swells during a night watch, he realizes that to fall overboard is probably to drown. It is, instead, the forecast of discomfort for an indeterminate period—of being tired, and cold, and wet, and sick, the specific miseries of sailboat crews in heavy weather.

It seemed unlikely, to the 2,000 men on the 303 boats that ran toward Ireland that Monday afternoon, that the fine conditions could hold. But what this sporting armada could not know, as their spinnakers pulled in a dying breeze, was how quickly, and to what degree, their idyll would be smashed.

Turner spotted Fastnet Rock at about 5:30. It was raining lightly, but in the grayness the craggy outcropping ahead grew steadily, its lighthouse rising out of the stone like a beckoning finger. An electric tension swept the yacht as the big spinnaker was hauled down, and sea boots thundered on the deck as all hands swarmed to their places for the 180-degree rounding maneuver. The wind seemed to be increasing, but it was decided that a reef would be unnecessary for the return trip across the Irish Sea. Turner brought *Tenacious* extremely close to Fastnet, so the crags hove high overhead, and the currents seized the yacht and snapped it by.

Steve Ward, at his position at the extreme bow, looked up admiringly. He had sailed the Fastnet Race twice before, and both times the rock itself had been sheathed in fog and rain, invisible but for green signal rockets its lighthouse keepers fired periodically into the mist. This time, you could at least see the bloody thing—and very well, for Turner, as usual, had cut the corner.

The rock was turned at 6:30 P.M., with *Tenacious* fifth around in fleet. As she headed back toward England, the breeze increased, as if to speed her on her way. Peter Bowker, the navigator, was in his cabin, headphones on. For just as *Tenacious* rounded the rock, the British Broadcasting Corporation was putting out its evening weather forecast. Bowker listened with interest.

What he heard was weather for "Finistere, Sole, Fastnet. Southwesterly gales Force 8, increasing severe gale Force 9, imminent."

Bowker seemed surprised by what he had heard—but in typical Bowker fashion, it was the surprise of a picnicker discovering ants in the basket. "My goodness," he reported. "I guess we're going to have a lot of breeze."

"Better eat fast, team," Turner told the next watch, as they lay waiting in the main cabin. "We're going to want all hands up to shorten sail." Already the yacht was heeled far over, and Jane Potts had to struggle to carve and serve two fat, juice-streaming beef roasts she had devoted her afternoon to cooking. But the swimming plates, piled high with potatoes and red meat, had for many already lost their appeal. While the afterguard looked at the illustrations of destroyers struggling through the Beaufort pictures, Jobson's watch dressed hurriedly. They could easily form their own mental images of wind Force 9, imminent.

Turner stood at the wheel for the watch change at 8:00. The new wind came with the darkness, first as a dirty line on the southwestern horizon, then as a palpable, roaring force. The air temperature was 50 degrees, and a gray rain had begun, stinging needlelike any face that turned to gaze at the windward sky. One by one, fresh crew members emerged from the companionway hatch, making their way to relieve men stationed about the deck. It was difficult to hear anything in the rising breeze, but once at his post, each man was drawn to look astern, at the helmsman's position. There stood Turner, beads of water spinning from his hair, shouting indecipherable challenges against the infant storm. His howls were grasped by the wind as quickly as they were uttered, and cast back into the splashing wake.

Jobson, as watch captain, edged closer, bracing himself to slip quickly behind the wheel as the helm was exchanged. His ski cap was pulled far down over his ears, his eyes almost closed as he squinted into the rain. Turner stepped back and away, Jobson seized the wheel, and the transfer was made.

Before he disappeared down below, Turner looked back once at his watch captain, gesturing violently. "Your hood!" he yelled.

Jobson touched his foul-weather hood, and the warm woolen hat that was his sailing trademark and protection against the cold rain and wind.

"Take your hood off!" Turner screamed. "You got to be able to hear the wind!"

For the next four hours, as the yacht fought on under triple-reefed mainsail and a small jib, Jobson stood bareheaded in the increasing storm. The wind grew stronger, so that every hour the needle on his anemometer touched higher on the dial. With the wind, the sea rose too, as the long fetch of the Atlantic responded to the sudden force across its surface, piling higher and higher under its influence. The crew huddled along the windward rail, clipped on with safety harnesses, waiting to see what would happen next. The windspeed indicator needle was periodically banging against its peg. The peg, which marked the extreme reading on the dial, was located just above the number 60. Sixty knots. Seventy-two miles an hour.

Turner came on deck at midnight. At 11:30 Bowker had received an updated forecast from the BBC, and this forecast reported Force 10 winds. Jobson's watch stumbled below, numb and exhausted.

Turner was surprised at the scene that met his eyes as he took over the wheel. It was obvious to him that the storm was already at Force

10, and much too much sail was still up. The waves had built enormously, and now towered 25 feet high as they raced toward the speeding yacht. As he stood, braced against the wind, a wave crested directly in the path of the boat, and as her bow rammed into the spray a 2-foot-high wall of water cascaded over the deck, blasting the huddled crewmen to the limits of their safety harness lines. Then the yacht fell heavily into the deep hole on the other side of the wave.

Turner wanted the mainsail doused completely, but for that to be done meant five men would have to unclip their protecting harnesses and move about the deck through the waterfalls of green ocean. Yet *Tenacious,* although 61 feet long, was dangerously close to being overpowered. He gave the order, shouting it twice to be heard. His crew, which a week before had seemed, in Turner's eyes, a collection of uncertain talents, sprang to the flogging sail. Slowly, buffeted by breaking seas and blasted off their feet by 70-mile-an-hour gusts, they wrestled the main down, tied it securely to the boom, and returned to their positions along the deck.

Even under Number 4 jib alone, *Tenacious* was still making 9 knots through the exploding sea, and the force of her passage—in opposition to the howling of the storm—shocked the boat to her keelbolts. What Turner saw as he desperately spun the wheel was little comfort. The starlight that penetrated the racing clouds overhead illuminated the glistening forms of six men, clinging to the edge of the boat, positioned there, as in any other race, for the leveling influence of their human ballast. Occasionally Turner could see their faces, wan and streaming in the spray. He was able to avoid the most vicious waves by frantic spinning of the helm, but others of the watery mountains struck the yacht with the force of an avalanche. The men over whom these seas burst disappeared momentarily from sight.

Turner was looking down the mouth of what seemed to be a cyclone lying on its side. The wind struck *Tenacious's* hull from the direction of his right hand, rose up over it in a curve clearly defined in streaming spray, then plunged down to leeward again. His view was that of a surfer caught in the curl of the wave he was attempting to ride. The curl was very clearly defined, since the mad sea was filled with bits of phosphorescence, curving green streaks of light. These same tiny jellyfish streamed also from the edges of the iron-taut jib, the only remaining sail, like tracer bullets in films of nighttime battles in the Coral Sea. Occasionally other projectiles filled the air as well, as men groped up from the sweaty, clanging blackness belowdecks to have their seasickness carried away by the gale.

The wildness of the scene permitted neither conversation nor reflection. The men on the rail sat immobile, heads down and deafened, their eyes bleeding salt water, hands cupped over their mouths as they attempted to create a mask of air in the choking spume all about. Even at such moments, Turner could feel the surge of the old exhilaration. If he could keep going, he could break the course record again. His boat was undamaged and his crew strong. But the moment did not last.

"Boat ahead!"

The cry came dimly back to him from the rail, repeated in his ear by Jim Mattingly, the watch captain by his side.

"Boat ahead!"

In the great, breaking seas, Turner had little directional control of *Tenacious,* no matter how hard he spun the wheel. Roaring through the seas like a train, she bounced from wavehead to wavehead, slewing as much as 30 degrees upwind, then 30 degrees down despite his best efforts. Now he could see them too: tiny specks of light, blinking red and green dead ahead. How far ahead, he did not know. The specks could only be one thing: the running lights of the smaller boats. *Tenacious* had been hours ahead of them upon rounding Fastnet Rock. Now, homeward bound, she would have to sail directly into the teeth of the scattered, storm-lashed fleet.

Turner knew something else, too. These smaller boats would be out of control. That was confirmed as the red specks of light turned green, then red again, for if the fleet ahead had been able to hold a course, only one color running light would show. Yet he could not stop *Tenacious*—the big yacht could only be ridden through this storm like a horse given free rein on a precipitous cliffside. He knew what would happen if his sharp-bowed vessel struck a smaller competitor. The other yacht would be cut in half instantly, and her crew, probably belowdecks, would have little chance of survival.

"Boat dead ahead! Dead ahead!" came more cries from the rail, as

Tenacious's bow lifted on a wave, on target to ram. Then, in the salt-washed blindness, another wave would knock her downcourse, and the dim lights would swirl by. Again and again this happened. The high-pitched warnings floating back, the desperate attempts to alter course. He never could see the other yachts themselves, only the lights, sad and dim, coursing by in helpless profusion. It was very cold, and the sea had penetrated Turner's foul-weather gear through the sleeve ends and neck opening so that in less than an hour at the helm he was completely soaked. He gave the wheel to Mattingly. The watch captain's face was gray and drawn. As Turner turned to go belowdecks for a conference with his navigator, he found a body blocking his way. It was sprawled across the bridge deck, in surrender to seasickness. Turner looked at the face, which seemed older than he had ever seen it, yet still uniquely familiar.

"You OK, boy?" he shouted in the crewman's face.

"Yes sir," said his sixteen-year-old son, Robert Edward Turner IV. It was 2:00 A.M., August 14, and the storm was at its height.

From the 1979 Fastnet Race Inquiry held by the Royal Yachting Association and the Royal Ocean Racing Club. Report by Sir Hugh Forbes, Sir Maurice Lang and Lieutenant Colonel James Myatt. Printed by T. H. Brickell & Son Ltd., The Blackmore Press, Shaftesbury, Dorset.

Section 4G: Fatalities.

The Council of the RYA, the Committee of the RORC and all those concerned with the 1979 Fastnet Race regret most deeply the tragic loss of life that occurred. Fifteen men from yachts participating in the race died. The clinical cause of death, for those whose bodies have been recovered, has been established as drowning, exposure, or exposure and drowning. The circumstances in which these deaths occurred were as follows:

a. Three were lost after the capsize and disintegration of their liferaft.

The yacht first got into difficulty at about 1:00 A.M. on 14 August while motoring to stand by another yacht which was already in trouble. She experienced two severe knockdowns, in the course of which she was dismasted and lost her rudder.

After righting from the second knockdown the skipper was

found to be over the side but still attached by his safety harness. Two of the crew pulled the skipper back on board, while the remainder set about launching the liferaft. The decision to abandon the yacht appears to have been taken instinctively. During the second knockdown the yacht shipped a considerable amount of water and her crew described her as half full. They felt that, without mast or rudder, she was at the mercy of the waves and it was only a matter of time until she was rolled over and sank. In fact the yacht was later recovered and her salvors say that when they found her she had about 2 feet of water in the cabin.

The abandonment to the liferaft was accomplished successfully. The yacht *Morningtown* sighted the liferaft and after several attempts succeeded in laying alongside it. *Morningtown's* crew had great difficulty in holding on to the raft and they were unable to gain access to the canopy opening. While the raft was alongside, *Morningtown's* steering wires jumped the quadrant and by the time this defect had been repaired she had lost contact with the raft.

Shortly after the brief contact with *Morningtown* the raft was capsized and the two buoyancy chambers were torn apart. The crew remained in the lower half of the raft but there was only one attachment point, to which one man was able to clip his safety harness. An hour later two of the survivors were washed out of the raft and it was impossible for the others to rescue them.

Three hours later, at about 6:30 A.M., the lower half of the raft was again capsized and all but one of the survivors found themselves clinging to the lanyards of the upper buoyancy chamber, which had become completely separated from the lower. One man died while still clinging to the lanyards before a helicopter arrived about 9:45 A.M. The helicopter lifted off two survivors but the remaining three were heavily entangled and unable to extricate themselves. By this time the HNLMS *Overijssel* had arrived at the scene and she rescued the remaining survivors.

Belowdecks on *Tenacious* the sounds of the storm were muffled. The wind could barely be heard. It was the sound of seas crashing on deck that caused the thunderous, reverberating roar. It was dark, and the off watch tried to sleep, every man jammed isometrically in some bunk or corner like a fiddler crab backed far into its shell. But the bunks behaved like diabolical instruments of astronaut training, heaving suddenly upward so that gravity tripled and the flesh sagged, then falling like elevators to leave their occupants weightless. *Tenacious* usually took the waves in stride, bullying her way through them. But now she seemed to stop almost dead from time to time, like a battering ram bouncing off a castle door. From the tiny toilet room, gagging sounds issued periodically, and a sickening smell hung in the air. The forward hatch was pinned tightly closed, and there was no other ventilation at all.

Bowker and Turner, back in the owner's stateroom, were learning for the first time of the desperate trouble within the Fastnet fleet. In the radio static, Bowker could hear distress calls criss-crossing each other in the airways, and the relayed reports of searching Royal Navy helicopters. But *Tenacious,* speeding on through the arena of these life-and-death battles, was unable to help. She could not see or otherwise locate the stricken vessels. The word over the radio was: if you can keep going, keep going; stay off the radio unless you are in distress or relaying an SOS.

Turner knew what it must be like on the smaller boats. He remembered his first transatlantic race, when his own six-man crew had suffered from the cold, and the water had run out, and how small that 38-footer had seemed. *Tenacious,* in contrast, was a giant. She was heavily built, and her design made few concessions to the new emphasis on light weight in offshore racers.

"You can be glad you're on my boat tonight, and not somebody else's," he told Bowker. Bowker, who had worked at the navigation table of hundreds of sailboats during his yachting career, nodded in agreement.

b. Three were lost while attempting to climb the pilot ladder of a coaster from their capsized liferaft.

. . . The yacht was caught by a massive breaking wave and rolled quickly through 360 degrees. The three men in the cockpit were all washed overboard. Two remained attached by their lifelines but the third man was washed away, either his harness or the point of attachment having parted.

The survivors then took to the liferaft. The yacht has subsequently been recovered and at the time of recovery there was extensive damage to the bulkhead at the forward end of the cockpit. It would therefore appear reasonable for the crew to have assumed that if she capsized again she might sink very quickly. Flares were lit and a coaster approached. At that point the raft capsized. As help was at hand no attempt was made to right the raft and the men clung to it while the coaster, rolling heavily, put a pilot ladder over the side. The coaster had to make several passes at the raft before lying alongside it. Two young crew members managed to grasp the ladder and climb up it, but two other men were unable to climb it and fell back into the sea, one of them being pulled back by his harness, which was still attached to the raft. The fifth man lost his hold on the liferaft and fell under the stern of the coaster.

With *Tenacious's* mad career through the blackness of the Irish Sea a new danger loomed nearer—that graveyard of ships, the Scilly Isles, awash off the southwesternmost tip of England. Turner could feel the jagged shoreline somewhere ahead, and he had a clear picture of what it must look like at this moment, breaking seas splashing high and fatal currents strongly pulling. In the darkness, with the horizon a heaving indeterminate line, Bowker had no hope of taking star sights with his sextant. Sophisticated navigation aids such as Loran were similarly useless—banned from the Fastnet Race as unfair technological advantage. All Bowker had to work with was an erratic compass course and the chance to locate the Scillies on his radio direction finder. For hours, the navigator searched the airwaves, trying to locate the radio beacon that could confirm their position, but it was no good. There was too much interference from the storm.

Turner was extremely impatient. The fleet around him was in disarray, but he was still racing. If an accurate bearing could not be obtained, he would have to order a course that would give the Scillies a wide berth to assure a safe passage. That would cost valuable time. He did not want to lose any time. He did not want to give the storm anything it could not take by force.

Conditions in the cockpit were abominable, and it was not yet light. But Bowker, the oldest of the nineteen on board, emerged there suddenly nonetheless, clutching his radio direction finder to his chest. Turner watched with amazement as he made his way toward the back of the yacht, inch by inch through the spray. A radio direction finder receives a repeated signal in Morse, followed by a continuous sound not unlike the dial tone of a telephone. The operator swings the instrument back and forth, seeking the point at which the tone disappears. When he locates the null, as the zone of silence is called, the instrument will be pointed directly toward the beacon— in this case the Scillies.

But still Bowker could not get a satisfactory null. The slamming of the boat all but wrenched the RDF from his hands, and the plunging mast, with its array of wire supporting shrouds, obscured the weak electronic signal. Bowker had not taken the time to put on a safety harness. Indeed, he had not even buttoned the coat of his foul-weather gear, which flapped loudly now across his back. But the signal through the earphones was tantalizingly close to a reading—he could hear the tone swinging this way and that, he had only to pin it down.

The navigator stood up, pointing his RDF ahead toward the unseen Scilly Isles. At that moment a large sea struck the bow and Bowker flew sideways like a projectile, crashing past the steering wheel and into the stern railing to fetch up inches from the boiling wake. The RDF had gone overboard, and Bowker nearly with it. The steering wheel itself was twisted several inches out of line by the force of his impact. As the navigator was helped below, Turner glanced back at the wave which had nearly swallowed him up. It receded into the distance at high speed, vicious and plunging, toward the next boat somewhere in its path.

Turner calculated the odds in favor of rescue had the Englishman not been caught by the rail—if at this moment, instead of rubbing his bruises in the cabin, he lay bobbing in the frigid sea behind. The odds in favor of his rescue, Turner reckoned, were zero.

And what would happen if *Tenacious* had to make such an attempt? Turner knew that his yacht's safety lay in her ability to carry on, to maintain steerageway through the peaks and yawning cliffsides of the exploding sea. A yacht that stopped, even for a moment, became a sitting duck. That was when a breaker found its mark. That was when the boat rolled upside down, the incalculable forces stripped away mast and sails, and the hull was left to await the death blow, utterly vulnerable. Turner hated the notion of vulnerability. He hated it even more than the storm itself.

c. One was lost when the liferaft in which he was stowing emergency gear capsized and broke adrift.

The sequence of events leading to this fatality started when the yacht tried to go to the assistance of another. While trying to maneuver through the heavy seas she was capsized and her rudder broke.

. . . The crew decided that they should prepare to abandon the yacht and launched the liferaft. They secured it alongside on a short painter and one man boarded it to stow emergency gear which was passed to him by the others. While he was doing so the raft was capsized, its painter snapped and both raft and crewman were washed away. Nothing could be done to recover the lost man as the yacht was already disabled.

At 3:55 A.M. Jobson stood in the door to Turner's cabin. The skipper had some instructions.

"It's still as bad as it gets up there," he said. "But remember one thing: everything depends on your steering. We're doing OK, but these next four hours are going to be long ones, and I don't want any screwups. Men are dying out there, we heard it on the radio. But we've sailed through the fleet now, and we're still going fast."

So Jobson led his men on deck, back into the maelstrom. The crew he replaced there seemed completely used up by the events of the night; one by one they disappeared down the small hatchway, spinning below like uneaten peas down the drain of a kitchen sink.

The new watch groped into position, crawling from handhold to handhold, and waited for the dawn.

The morning watch from 4:00 to 8:00 A.M. is usually a pleasant one on boats, if for no other reason than the yielding of mysterious night to forthright day. But on this August morning, first light on the Irish Sea presented a vista that chilled the bones more certainly than the coldest dousing wave. The wind still howled, its 70-mile-an-hour gusts striking the yacht like fists, and salt spray still filled eyes, nose, ears and mouth like the atmosphere of some malignant alien planet.

But now a panorama existed too, and its reality matched and exceeded even the nightmarish imaginings of darkness.

Tenacious seemed to be hurtling at breakneck speed through a mountain range in the throes of a cataclysmic earthquake. Towering peaks rose all about, white-topped as Mount Rainier, and yet they moved. Not moved, but raced! Under Force 10 conditions, the average speed of the crest was 30 to 40 knots, and the waves were as tall as three-story buildings. Some seemed to be larger still, and as the boat's low decks were hurled skyward atop a 30-foot swell, the crew had a 10-mile sweep in which to search with their watering eyes. Somewhere out there, they knew, were the rogues. It was statistically inevitable, but no comfort at all, that in any body of water where the average wave height was 30 feet, then once in every three-hour period at least one 60-foot wave would appear. They were the ship-killers, the monsters to be avoided at all costs. They were what Jobson, as he spun the ship's wheel forcefully, looked most intently for on the rushing horizon.

On the windward rail, clinging there like barnacles on a tide-washed rock, the foredeck team had no duty other than to survive. And wait for the one small sail to blow out. Each had seen sails explode many times in their racing careers—overstressed Dacron, carried beyond endurance in a calculated risk toward some sunny finish line, split suddenly down a seam or burst into tatters. Then they had merely cleaned up the mess and hoisted a new sail in its place. That would not be so easy this morning. It would not be easy at all.

So they sat hunched over, watching and waiting for the sudden ripping sound and the call to action. They waited, with nothing to do but wonder how many hours and minutes remained until the end of their four-hour watch.

They waited, conscious of a strange peace that existed there on the windward rail, where sensations of pride and strength fit curiously well with coincident nausea, chill and exhaustion. Each man sat alone, incommunicado in the deafening wind, protected against the solid sea only by his waterproof suit, feeling the lifeline press against his back. The force of the storm cleansed the mind of all inconsequential notions. No mundanities of the business world rose to nag at the consciousness, no recollection of sins of omission or commission. Even sexuality ceased to exist: the men on either side pressed close, the warmth of their shoulders penetrating through the thick layers of sodden wool, in a familiarity impossible elsewhere. By any vantage once removed, the sights and sounds which enveloped them were of a furious hell, unrelenting testament to the vulnerability of the human organism.

And yet, clinging there, these men could feel invulnerable. They were taking the worst that had ever been dished out to them, and to win they had merely to survive. To survive, they had only to continue, for the moment at least, to cling as they were. The simplicity of the equation was amazing. They could not lose.

About 7:00 A.M. one of them fought his way below, and when he emerged again soon thereafter—a soldier quickly returning to his buddies at the front—it was with something clutched in his hand. The object made its way from man to man along the weather rail, through the cascades of spray. Each, as he took it in turn with prune-wrinkly fingers, looked at the merchandise with dull surprise. It was a package of chewing gum. Take one, pass it on. The blast of sugar in the mouth, dispelling the salt taste that seemed permanently established there, brought superb contentment.

The sun poked through a scud cloud then, and for a moment the crazy ocean glistened incongruously. A huge wave roared by ahead, missing the bow by 100 yards, but leaving in its wake a three-foot-deep mantle of pure white foam that perfectly replicated a ski slope newly covered in deep powder.

Down that slope, transient in its smoothness, *Tenacious* swooped with exhilarating speed.

d. Two were lost after being trapped in the cockpit of an inverted yacht.

The exact sequence of events is difficult to ascertain. During the early hours of 14 August the yacht was heavily knocked down several times and then ran off under bare poles with warps streamed. The entire crew remained in the cockpit for most of the night but the skipper went below to send a distress call. While he was doing so he was hit on the head by an item of loose gear, believed to have been a tin of food. He was concussed and therefore lapsed into unconsciousness from time to time.

The yacht was rolled through 180 degrees and remained upside down for a period of time estimated by various members of the crew to be between two and five minutes. Two of the crew were thrown clear but remained attached by their safety harnesses. A third crewman extricated the skipper by cutting his safety harness, but after bringing him to the surface he lost his grasp on him and the skipper was washed out of reach. One of the three crewmen in the water climbed onto the upturned hull, and the craft then righted herself, dismasted.

The three conscious survivors were able to climb back on board. They found that two crew members who had been trapped in the cockpit throughout the capsize were lying motionless in the bottom of the cockpit and assumed they were dead. They launched the liferaft and abandoned the yacht. They were unable to do anything about recovering the skipper and they were subsequently rescued by helicopter.

One of the unconscious casualties came to some time later, in the water alongside the hull. (It seems that the yacht may have capsized again while he was unconscious.) He was able to climb back on board and with the aid of a winch he pulled his semiconscious companion into the boat. His companion was still alive and responded to resuscitation but died about three-quarters of an hour later. The one remaining survivor spent some twelve hours bailing the disabled yacht and keeping a lookout for rescue before being lifted off by a helicopter.

Morning stretched out interminably aboard *Tenacious.* Jobson, coming off watch, collapsed shivering on the edge of his bunk. "It's not fun anymore," he murmured. "I want it to stop." His arms, numb from the strain of fighting the helm, hung at his sides like broken branches on a tree. Although the seas were now larger than ever, their wave lengths had increased and they seemed to crest less often. The yacht began to slide up and down their faces with increasing steadiness.

On deck, Turner scowled with annoyance as the Scilly Isles passed far abeam. He would have preferred to cut close, and he knew that the conservative course set the night before had cost at least an hour in extra distance sailed. The wind seemed to be dropping some, though violent gusts still struck every several minutes. But at least the course was downwind now, and he decided to order another foresail set. Soon the two white sails were filled side by side, and *Tenacious* raced even faster toward Plymouth.

Shortly after noon he emerged again from his cabin and glanced quickly at the ocean behind.

"Storm's over," he announced with finality, taking the deck watch by surprise. "Get the mainsail back up." Within an hour a small spinnaker was also flying. The crew had hardly recovered from this sequence when Jane Potts appeared from below, bearing a tray of juicy beef sandwiches she had somehow prepared in the dripping mess below.

"What? Leftovers?" somebody cracked. It was the first attempt at humor made since the gale had begun sixteen hours before. Shortly the sun came out, and the breeze died to a pleasant 20 knots. Eddystone Light, the last notable mark before the finish line, loomed ahead, and several men broke into song:

"Me father was the keeper of the Eddystone Light,
And he slept with a mermaid one fine night.
From this union there came three,
A porpoise and a porgy and the other was me . . ."

As other voices joined in the old shanty, Turner spoke up.

"Hey, knock it off," he commanded. "We ain't won yet, and already you guys are singing songs and lighting up cigars."

When *Tenacious* slipped over the line at 10:30 P.M.; memories of the storm were already fading on board. There was much work to do before bed, and the men turned to it, comparing notes among themselves as they packed sails and coiled the thousands of feet of lines and sheets. Those who only hours before had lain helpless in the grip of seasickness were now fully recovered, and taking their ribbing in good humor. The crew was aware that some boats had got into bad trouble during the storm, but the BBC had not been specific, and reports were probably exaggerated. Apparently there had been drownings, and even one such fatality would surely cast a pall over the Fastnet Race of 1979. But *Tenacious* had suffered no significant damage, and her crew was unharmed except for a few bruises, most of them the property of Peter Bowker. All in all, things were not bad. And the real stories would only be learned from the friends on other boats, gleaned with many beers in the pubs of Plymouth.

One had only to look back at the cockpit for assurance that everything was fine. There was Turner at the wheel, as usual, talking a mile a minute about life, women and boat racing. He had his engineer's cap on again, even though it was dark. He was kidding Bowker with relish.

"Bowker, I ought to make you steer this boat up to the dock. Look at this steering wheel, Bowker, it's bent like a pretzel. Who do you think you are, Bowker, the Flying Nun? You should've seen yourself during the storm. You're lucky you ain't swimming with the little fishies right now."

Bowker grinned his wan grin. His gray hair, caked with salt, lay on his head like the marble curls of a statue of Julius Caesar.

"But Bowker, think of it! If we've won this race, which I think is entirely possible on account of we kept going fast all the time, you'll be a hero. You'll all be heroes, men," the skipper pronounced, gesturing grandly with his arm.

It seemed a good sign, as *Tenacious* tied up at the quay under a bright moon, that there were very few other boats already in.

e. Six were lost after being washed overboard from yachts.

... A crew member was washed overboard and lost from a yacht which capsized 180 degrees while close reaching under storm jib.

... The skipper was lost from a yacht which capsized while running under bare poles, streaming warps, and traveling at about 5-6 knots. The skipper had been washed away leaving the clip, safety line and webbing belt of his harness still attached to the yacht.

... Three men were washed overboard from a yacht when she was severely knocked down while reaching under storm jib, traveling at about 7 knots. One man remained attached to his harness, but the other two were lost.

... A crew member was washed overboard when the yacht was picked up by a rogue wave and rolled about 140 degrees. At the time the yacht was broad reaching under storm jib, with four warps in use, doing 8-10 knots. The whole harness was left on board and had come undone. As the engine was saturated it took some time to return to the man in the water. At the first attempt they missed him by 10 yards. At the second attempt another crewman tied himself to a long line and jumped into the water to try and pick up the man overboard, but missed him by only a few yards. Several more attempts were made to pick up the man in the water without success, until it became clear there was no sign of life, and that further maneuvering was placing the yacht and her crew in danger.

Fatalities summary: Paragraph 4.45

In every case there were a number of contributory factors which are described elsewhere in this report. The common link between all 15 deaths was the violence of the sea, an unremitting danger to all who sail.

It dawned on Turner only slowly, as his telephone in the Holiday Inn at Plymouth rang off the hook, that he had just been a part of the worst disaster in yachting history. Reporters tracked him everywhere, pressing for what he had seen—for firsthand accounts of his narrow brush with death. The town was in chaos, and rescue ships and helicopters continued to be launched toward the racecourse, where scores of boats were reported still missing.

He arrived back at the quay the next day, clean-shaven and natty, but with a dogged look. There was no joy in Plymouth at all, it was a town in the embrace of tragedy. On the wharves, where more and more bright-colored yachts now lay drying out, women with shawls over their heads interrogated passersby with hopeless questions. "Were you in the race? Did you see the yacht ——— out there? They have not been reported, and my husband is aboard. . . ." These women—there were at least two of them—did not seem to expect an answer; they moved quickly on, touching another shoulder, searching for a familiar face in the crowd of visitors to the dock.

"Boy," Turner complained to several of his crew, who were spreading out clothes to dry on the deck of *Tenacious* despite an intermittent drizzle. "This wasn't a race, it was tragedy. There're people crying all over the place. I was down at the Royal Western Yacht

Club and a guy looked at me and said, 'You'd be singing a different tune if you'd been on a smaller boat.' I felt like punching him in the nose, but I just walked away. Newspapers are spread out on the tables there, and they have headlines that say 'Fastnet of Death,' and 'Caldron of Death.'

"It's even worse at home. Do you realize they all think we're dead back there? They had us listed as missing yesterday. The whole world's gone crazy over this thing."

Much of the craziness, in fact, centered on Turner. Harassed, demanded at every turn to admit his fear during the gale and thank God, or at least his lucky stars, for a narrow escape, he was having none of it. "That ain't the ultimate storm," he said, astounding the English journalists. When this seemed to make them angry, he drove another theory home.

"The trouble with the boats sailing today is that they're designed to cheat some stupid racing rule. They're not built strong enough, they're not fit to go up against the sea. The reason we got through all right was that I've got a big, strong boat. And I made sure I had one before I entered the race."

These remarks did not sit well at that moment in Plymouth. The response of the moment was rather expected to be in the British tradition, as exemplified by former Prime Minister Heath, who termed the experience "the worst I have ever had," and gave ample thanks to the rescue efforts of Her Majesty's Coast Guards and the Royal Navy. Gratitude, humility, prayer, thanksgiving and sorrow for fellow sailors lost at sea characterized nearly every other response from competitors.

Furthermore, Turner appeared to have won the race. Though handicaps were still being computed on Wednesday, it seemed that his fifth-place finish—the first yacht over the line was the 79-foot *Condor of Bermuda*—would carry the day. All the more reason for a low profile.

But when *The New York Times* got to Turner at his hotel room and asked him how things had been, he was characteristically flamboyant.

"It was rough, r-u-f-f," he cracked. "We never slowed once. In fact, they forgot to put the checkered flag out for us and we just kept coming in full speed." He concluded his interview by remarking, "Like any experience, whenever you come through it you feel better. We're not talking about the other people who died, but to be able to face it all and come through it is exhilarating. Sailing in rough weather is what the sport is all about."

Meanwhile, in the press room at Plymouth's cavernous Duke of Cornwall Hotel, computer printouts were being fed into the hands of more than a hundred reporters. The printouts offered a horrifying overview of the havoc. Of the 303 boats that had started the race, only ninety crossed the finish line. Twenty-five yachts were abandoned, five of which eventually sank. More than 160 individual sailors required rescue, most of them plucked from the sea by helicopters. The race death toll was fifteen. Four more men had died when a trimaran, pacing the fleet, had been capsized by the same storm.

The reporters, lined up in banks before phones into which each seemed to be shouting his account in a separate language, tried their best to satisfy the demands of their editors. Mumm's champagne flowed freely, but the scene was in no way jolly.

At every press conference, Alan Green, secretary of the Royal Ocean Racing Club, defended the race against emotional charges of mismanagement and bad judgment. He, in turn, blasted back at the press—singling out American and Australian newspapers—for shoddy, sensationalized reporting. The British tabloids, however, had set a pace in that regard that few foreign papers could follow. In Germany, one newspaper went so far as to devote its front page to a large death cross, headlining the single word: "Regatta."

Turner held a provisional victory dinner anyhow, gathering his crew around him in a seaside restaurant for a private evening of boister. While hundreds of calls and telegrams flooded Atlanta, and the families of each crewman sifted through conflicting reports about the safety of husbands or sons, the wine flowed and the laughter became almost as raucous as had the storm. Toasts were raised "to being alive and having won!" By 11:00 P.M. Turner was groggy. He had no acceptable credit card and very little English money. The waitresses were annoyed. He pulled out thirty or forty hundred-dollar bills and began passing them in every direction. His crew, combining several of their own credit cards, wound up paying its own tab—and seeing the skipper home.

Back aboard *Tenacious,* where many of the crew remained in residence on still-wet bunks, madness gave way to further madness. By midnight, word had reached everyone aboard of a new posting in the window where the computer-printed race results were hung. *Tenacious* was no longer in the number-one position. A boat half her size had just crossed the finish line—nearly two days after Turner's crossing—and this yacht had been declared overall winner. The boat was named *Illusion,* and she was a total unknown.

Steve Ward and Bud Sullivan, two veteran crewmen who had led the team that furled the heavy mainsail as the storm rose to its climax, looked at each other disconsolately.

"I sure don't want to be the one to tell Ted," Sullivan said.

"Me either," answered Ward.

At 9:00 A.M. Greg Shires was out of breath. He had been running all over Plymouth, looking for Turner. Each time he found a *Tenacious* crewman moping along a street, or gazing into space wondering how to get home, he tackled him like a linebacker. Shires seemed delirious and in need of immediate medical attention. His eyes rolled around in their sockets like pinballs in a machine that had scored jackpot.

"It's true, it's true," he screamed, rolling in the street, a stupefied watch mate in his grasp. "That little boat that beat us because she finished so early? She hadn't gone around Fastnet Rock! She was just coming into Plymouth for shelter! They've revised the standings again! We still won it!" Shires wanted to be the one who brought Turner the good news. He hurtled off, still searching.

At 9:30 A.M., a seabag in hand, Turner arrived at his boat. The tide was out, so he looked down a full 8 feet from the concrete wharf to the upturned faces below.

"Well, that's it," he said flatly. "Teddy and I are catching the 11:30 train back to London." Turner looked pretty good, at least for a man who had just had victory pulled out from under him like a rug in a magic show. He had a hangover from his ill-fated provisional victory dinner the night before, but he had his *Courageous* sweater on straight and his upper lip was extremely stiff. He had just given another series of interviews back at his hotel, and in each one he had had to correct the interviewer: "No, actually, we didn't win it. We only came in second. Some little boat called *Illusion* apparently beat us."

"Uh, Ted, have you, uh, seen Greg Shires this morning?" one of the upturned faces asked him.

"No, I haven't seen Shires. So what?"

"Oh. You mean you haven't heard anything?"

"What's to hear?" Turner said, irritated. "Don't tell me there's some kind of problem."

"Yeah, a computer problem, you could call it."

By now a crowd had gathered, drawn by Turner's booming voice and his unmistakable white sweater. Some of them had cameras, and began snapping pictures.

"What is it, dammit?" Turner said.

"Well, it's an error they just corrected in the computer. See, *Illusion* didn't really officially finish the race. So she doesn't count. We won. They gave it back to us."

Turner looked down in disbelief. "Are you serious?"

"Yeah."

"Are you serious?"

"Dead serious."

"Are you serious? Don't tell me that. Look, don't put me on like that."

"No."

"You're serious?"

Laughter from the crowd.

"Yeah, we're serious."

"You're serious—and I was just on ABC's *Good Morning America* and I said we came in second."

Laughter.

"We won, we really won!" Jane Potts called up at him.

Turner could only sputter at first. He turned completely around. Then he breathed a huge sigh. Like an accomplished actor, he turned from the boat below to the larger audience behind him on the dock. "Folks," he said in a rush, "it's not worth committing suicide. If I'd had a pistol this morning when I heard we'd lost, I would've pulled the trigger. Son of a gun, I was in my room and I nearly cried. Somebody give me a cigar."

Somebody did, and Turner lit up, his dockside audience rapt. "I'll tell you what else I did. I came up with a great line, and it's going to be on British television tonight. They said, 'How can we avoid tragedies like this in the future?' And I said, 'You ought to be thankful there are storms like that, or you'd all be speaking Spanish. 'Cause it was a storm like that that sank the Spanish armada.' "

To the scattered, somewhat uncertain applause, he replied in verse:

"Hew down to the bridge, Sir Consul,
With all the speed ye may;
I, with but two more to help me
Will hold the foe in play.
In yon straight path a thousand
May well be stopped by three.
Now who will stand on either hand,
And keep the bridge with me?"

"Aw," Turner continued, breaking away from "Horatius at the Bridge" and back into speech without losing stride, "it's hard to be real happy today because so many people have gone up to that great yacht race in the sky. But at least they won't have to worry about setting the storm trysail anymore. In a way, I'll be happy when my turn comes, too."

He spoke this last with the American flag draped over one shoulder, a photographer having insisted he pick up and wave the yacht ensign on *Tenacious*'s stern. "OK, that's enough, isn't it?" he said, the performance over. "Would you leave me alone now?"

On Friday night, the members of the *Tenacious* crew who remained in England attended the crowded memorial service for the Fastnet dead at St. Andrew's Church, Plymouth. Edward Heath was there, and the Lord Mayor served as chief mourner. The Bishop of Plymouth read a brief passage from Psalm 137, beginning: "They that go down to the sea in ships and occupy their business in great waters . . ."

The service followed a muted prize-giving elsewhere, so that a number of those in solemn attendance clutched silver trophies of

Cowes Week under their arms. Turner had won more than anyone else, and it took Teddy's help to guard and carry the sterling.

The crew gathered for drinks thereafter, since the skipper was departing on the midnight train for London and Atlanta. Turner tried to cheer the quiet group by telling tales of the other 350 yachting trophies he had won, but when it was Peter Bowker's turn to contribute, Bowker said:

"I knew a fellow once who had a lot of trophies. They were all over his house, and his wife couldn't stand to polish them. So he took them to a silversmith and had all the trophies melted down into a single large cube, and the words 'Trophies, 1956–1971,' inscribed on top."

"Come on, Bowker," Turner said, circles of fatigue showing under his eyes. "It's over. There's nothing we can do about it now."

9 The Biggest News of All

THE DRUM ROLL from the four combined military bands filled the air of Atlanta, and by satellite the air of many other cities too, as Cable News Network flickered to life at 6:05 P.M. that June 1. Turner stood on the reviewing stand with his hand over his heart, gazing over the reflecting pool at the snapping flags. The drum roll went on for what seemed like a long time, and in two large yellow-and-white-striped circus tents nearby, a half-dozen projection-screen television monitors kept visual accompaniment.

The series of images that cut across their screens began with Ted Turner, who had just completed his introductory speech and the homespun dedicatory poem. Now the cameras played over the tall trees that surrounded the 21 acres of the new Turner Communications estate, refocused on expectant faces in the crowd, touched on the white-colonnaded building itself, and finally, as the drum roll continued, fixed on the six brand-new earth receiving stations rising out of the raw clay. Nearer and nearer the cameras zoomed, until the soft-curved hardware of the space age filled the screens.

The image of parabolic dishes slid suddenly to the right, leaving in its place a newfangled television studio presided over by an anchor team of two. Superimposed under their desk was a graphic: "The News Channel," it said. The graphic rolled over and disappeared, replaced by a new electronic legend: "Cable News Network."

The man spoke first.

"Good evening, I'm David Walker," he said.

"And I'm Lois Hart," his companion added. "Now here's the news."

The news was that Vernon Jordan, director of the National Urban

League, had been shot in Fort Wayne, Indiana, and that police had new leads in the case.

With the flick of a switch, the scene changed to Fort Wayne, and live coverage of a vigil in progress for Jordan. The strains of the old civil-rights anthem "We Shall Overcome" poured forth as supporters of Jordan swayed shoulder to shoulder in an impromptu choir.

Then it was back to Atlanta again, where Hart and Walker reported that Reggie Jackson, the Yankee slugger, had been shot at on a New York street earlier that day after a dispute over a parking space.

Next to Mount St. Helens in Washington State, live, for a look at more volcanic ash piling up on streets and the desecration by nature of her own landscapes.

Cable News Network's first advertisement followed, drawing titters from the audience of 300 guests who by now had drifted from the reviewing-stand area into the tents, and watched fascinated, cocktails in hand. The first commercial was for Maalox Plus—the solution, E. G. Marshall solemnly advised, for nervous-stomach disorders. The second commercial was to be for Nestea, but it was quickly interrupted in the CNN control rooms, and the scene returned to Fort Wayne, where President Carter had arrived to discuss the matter of the Jordan shooting. Then live to the Middle East, via satellite. Then live to Key West, for a report on a new wave of Cuban refugees by boat across the Gulf Stream.

The News Channel was alive, all right. Nervous and fast-moving and unpredictable. Its ability to switch locations and news topics with speed and candor was nowhere more apparent than in the Key West story—where CNN's own correspondent, unaware he was on the air, was seen literally picking his nose.

Turner circulated in the crowd in the tent. His guests patted him on the back.

"I'm so happy I could die," he kept saying. "Nobody believed we could do it. But there it is."

As Turner wandered through the stream of congratulations he seemed distracted, as if he were looking for something. "I got to find a crow," he said. "Where can I get a crow? It should be a nice, large, dead crow, so I can put it in a box with a knife and fork, and serve it to a certain guy in Washington who said I'd never get on the air."

Meanwhile, in the lower reaches of the former country club, teams of reporters and editors and cameramen and videotape specialists and producers and directors and weathermen and electricians flowed back and forth and around the sets and equipment of the minutes-old television news network. They had been told so many times that what they were attempting to do was potentially an epochal break-through in communications that each had tired mightily of listening and talking about it. They were tired of the dry runs, of the theoretical problems, and of the anticipation. Now, after months of waiting and preparation, they were finally on the air. Somewhere out there, from Honolulu to Miami Beach, an initial audience of two million was being offered continuous, twenty-four-hour-a-day video news. They had set in motion an apparatus of perpetual motion that was designed to continue, as Lois Hart had announced, "from now on, and forever." Turner, in fact, had ordered a tape of "Nearer My God to Thee" prepared. "In the event the end of the world comes," he explained, "we'll play that and then sign off."

Reese Schonfeld, the president and chief architect of CNN, stood in a corner of the brand-new newsroom. Schonfeld had been inter-viewed within an inch of his life during the past few months, and now he stood bent over, leaning against his desk. It was 6:30 P.M. and the News Channel had been on the air for half an hour.

"Now I can say it," Schonfeld said, grimacing. "Now I can say that I've got the damnedest hernia you ever heard of. I've had it for three weeks, and I couldn't tell anyone, because it's the stupidest thing. I've got to go to the hospital and have the operation. I'm not going on with this any longer."

There came shouting from the master control room, where scores of tiny television monitors revealed the content of many of the ninety pictures simultaneously available from North America's fleet of orbiting satellites.

"This is live! This is live! I've got the Pope live!" a director was hollering.

Schonfeld appeared at his side. "Well, let's take it."

"Get our guy over there on the phone," yelled Ted Kavanaugh, the operations director.

"I got the Pope! Goddammit, I've got the Pope here," hollered the director. "Can't we cue our guy?"

Meanwhile, a clear image from Jerusalem popped up on another screen.

"We'll take this live," called one of the control room team.

"Cue him, come on!" said Kavanaugh.

Five thousand miles away, where the Israeli cabinet and Prime Minister Menachem Begin were having a parting of the ways, Jay Bushinsky, a *Chicago Sun Times* correspondent now also working for CNN, began to talk:

"It's 12:34 A.M. here in Jerusalem," he said, "and we've been following the fast-moving Israeli President throughout the day for this live satellite transmission to Cable News Network. . . ."

Schonfeld, delighted, limped away toward the office sector of the building, past the temporary makeup room where a new wave of announcers were being daubed with cosmetics from a desktop collection of vials, shaking his head. Despite his hernia, the hyperactive president was making good time, although as usual it was in several directions at once.

"Boy," he said, "we'll probably never be able to do all this stuff at once again. Cutting all over the world from story to story is what it's all about, but it's also the way the networks manage to spend $100 million a year on their news operations. Our budget is a quarter of that."

Through the brightly lit newsroom came Ted Turner, trailing his son Rhett. He passed the interview set, with its living-room chairs and eighty-seat spectator gallery; he passed the buzzing Atlanta Control console; he skirted the revolving set, with its weather map, and its three camera locations, and its tall-windowed view of the earth stations silently in place outside, and the hundreds of tiny monitors that flicked electronic life through the large studio, and the scores of flushed employees dashing this way and that.

He looked vaguely lost, like a new father who had taken a wrong turn in the hospital and found himself in the delivery room, surrounded by congratulatory doctors and nurses.

"Ted," Schonfeld chortled happily, straightening up. "How did you like the way we cut away from our first commercial to go to Carter. It couldn't have been better if God had written it."

"Yeah," said Turner. "That'll show them we'll never bow down to the advertisers. You can always run the ads later. Who cares about ads anyhow—it's a news operation."

This reaction, delivered by the chairman in his bullhorn voice, brought smiles from the nearby staff. But Turner had other things on his mind.

"Hey, Reese," he said almost sheepishly. "Is there anyplace I can watch the Braves game? They're on the Superstation now, and they're beating the Dodgers 9 to 5."

So as the debut of Cable News Network continued, as reporters and TV critics and curious subscribers elsewhere studied and analyzed the first airing of a venture designed to usher in a new era of communications, Ted Turner was led into the office of Sam Zelman, his executive producer, and placed in front of a somewhat beat-up standard-model television set.

Zelman's office was not wired for cable, and Turner's Superstation —clear as a bell in Honolulu—appeared on the screen there as a fuzzy blur, the UHF images of his last-place baseball team rolling and flickering.

As CNN plunged on with its first newscast only one door away, Turner sat transfixed, caught in the slow cadences of the ninth inning on a diamond far, far away.

"Two outs, which puts the Braves one out away from splitting the series with the LA Dodgers," the announcer intoned. "Uh oh! There's a hit!"

Turner leaped forward in his chair. "Now we got trouble—runners at the corners," he groaned.

The count was 2 and 1 when the Dodgers' batter swung, knocking a slow grounder *toward* first base. The Braves' Chris Chamblis grabbed it for the final out.

Braves 9, Dodgers 5.

"Awright. . . ." Turner said. "Now I'd better watch the News Channel awhile. I better see if it's as good as I've been saying it is all these months. Did you hear? They're putting me on the cover of

Newsweek. Yeah, but you can never be sure until it actually comes out."

Twice before, Turner had been considered as the subject of a news-magazine cover, and twice he had been bumped at the last minute by another story. But when the June 9, 1980, issue of *Newsweek* appeared, there he was: painted as a wolfishly smiling entrepreneur, with sailboats and baseball and basketball players surrounding him like planets around a sun, under the headline "Sports King Takes on TV."

Turner savored the *Newsweek* cover as a great trophy, and he savored the memory of obstacles thrown in his way, and most of all he savored the image of a large crow, and a knife, and a fork. Surely now the doubters would have to change their tune.

As the decade of the 1970s went out, it seemed to be issuing a new Ted Turner in. The evidence was contradictory, and the metamorphosis far from complete, but something was clearly going on. Tom Snyder, as host of NBC's late-night *Tomorrow* interview program, had been one of the first to notice:

SNYDER: But Ted, the news on Channel 17 is on at four o'clock in the morning. When other stations are running news, you're running the kinds of programs people would rather watch. You were quoted as saying that.

TURNER: Yeah. We tried to do something different. You know, counterprogramming.

SNYDER: But, but—so you're not against television news after all?

TURNER: Well, I wouldn't be starting a twenty-four-hour news service if I was, would I?

SNYDER: But then, don't you think you've kind of changed your tune on news? Because you used to make fun of it. You used to put it down.

The fact was that by 1980, Ted Turner had changed his tune a great deal. He was no longer the underweight, underrated twenty-four-year-old who had had to fight to take back his father's billboards. He was now a millionaire, a professional sports magnate, the newly crowned winner of the most eventful yacht race in history, and the self-proclaimed point man of a revolution in television.

He had become well known—but as what? As a baseball owner who did handsprings on the field? He had quietly toned down those antics years before. As a wunderkind of superstation technology, bringing *I Love Lucy* to the masses? But now he had added Jacob Bronowski's ambitious *The Ascent of Man* to prime time on Channel 17, and a six-hour-long series on energy and oil. Besides—the wunderkind was forty-one years old.

Of all his public images, the one Turner felt most comfortable with was that of folk hero. The sportswriters might use the phrase jestingly, but Turner did not. It was an identity that appealed to his sense of antiquity, suggesting companionship with the Greek and Roman leaders he had first met in the enforced study halls of military school. And as important, it set him apart from the contemporary bigwigs he delighted in having as adversaries. To the Roman Laws of War, he had added his own personal mythology, one which he shared with Walt Disney's Daniel Boone: "If You Know You're Right, Go Ahead and Do It." He was acutely aware of the faults of his archaic mentors —Julius Caesar's ambition, Alexander's fatal tantrums—and discounted them as he did the faults of his father. Turner's heroes strove not to be perfect, but to be remembered, and that was the sense in which he too sought immortality. When he joked that he must buy a horse, else never be the subject of equestrian statuary, his friends did not laugh, but nodded. In Caesar's time, he would say, you could buy a bust of your favorite leader on the street. Where were the busts of Turner?

In fact he had them—for today's celebrations of individuals are broadcast through the airways or committed to newspaper and magazine, and he was everywhere so celebrated. There were frequent speaking invitations ($3,000 to address the advertising clients of *Sports Illustrated)*, and product endorsement opportunities ($12,500 to smoke a Tiparillo on board his yacht; $40,000 for a Cutty Sark ad campaign).

As the 1980s began, Turner found no trouble whatsoever in gathering an audience for whatever he had to say, and he noted that whenever he rose to speak the laughter came right on cue. Everywhere, people expected—almost demanded—the Ted Turner Show.

They wanted to see fireworks. They wanted to hear him call the three networks the Mafia; to hear him lambast the Commissioner of Baseball ("Mr. Turner, what would be the effect on organized baseball if Bowie Kuhn were alive today?"); to hear about his battles for the America's Cup, and about the Fastnet storm.

But Turner's down-home accent had worn off some in recent years, and unlike his audiences he was less and less amused. His comedy act, like most, had been based all along on an inner seriousness, a perception of the world that found things funny only because they were so obviously fouled up.

He had read George Orwell's *1984* and Aldous Huxley's *Brave New World,* and visions of the snuffing out of individual accomplishment and ambition preyed on his mind. He seemed to see Bigness as the enemy of the people, and he saw it in a literal image: David and Goliath. He was chairman of a corporation himself, but he did not trust corporations. Corporations obeyed their own laws, he often said: flourish, and destroy the competition. But Turner did not want to destroy his competition, he wanted to defeat it. He wanted the game, and the argument, to continue.

It had come almost as a revelation to Turner that the game of continued argument, of perpetual debate, of clashing, well-armored opinion, already existed and had a name: its name was News.

With his own news, he could take everybody on. And with a little luck, he might not only go down in history as a journalism pioneer, but make a couple of hundred million dollars, too.

There was one slight wrinkle in this quilted plan: Ted Turner knew almost nothing about journalism.

"Yeah," he would explain, "but then I didn't know anything about radio when I bought my radio stations, and I didn't know anything about television when I bought my TV stations. I've got a real fast learning curve. I always rely on being able to learn stuff. Experts are the easiest thing there are to hire."

The first expert Turner hired was Schonfeld, a graduate of Dartmouth and Columbia Law School who had spent his career in "alternative" television news. Schonfeld was running the Independent Television News Association, an organization which supplied news programming for more than twenty TV stations, when Turner dangled the bait and reeled Schonfeld in like a fish.

"Actually," Schonfeld says, "Ted had wanted to start Cable News Network a year before he did. He wanted the cable operators to help pay for it, but they wouldn't go along. Then in the summer of 1979 he came back to me and said, 'Reese, I'm going to do it *myself.* And you're going to run it.'

Back in Atlanta, however, there was hardly any sign of the grand venture. The only new face so far in evidence was that of CNN vice president Burt Reinhardt, a Humphrey Bogart–like figure whose background was Paramount Pictures and UPI Television News. Reinhardt dined with Turner at the Capital City Club, a downtown facility which counted Bert Lance among its members, and got a firsthand view of his new boss's learning curve. The topic was sports coverage.

"I'm going to have to learn a lot about the news business," Turner was saying, "but it doesn't make any difference because I already know what I want. I want us to have terrific coverage of the Olympics, so start planning now for 1984."

Reinhardt hardly knew Turner, and he swallowed hard.

"Well, Ted, that could be tough," he said. "ABC bought the rights already."

"What?" Turner said. "You can't buy the rights to the Olympics. The Olympics belong to everybody."

It was explained that the sale of TV rights for such events was a long-standing fact of life.

"Yeah, well, how much do you have to pay? I mean, let's get our people out there bidding. The Olympics is big news."

It was explained that the stakes had somewhat increased since 1972, when ABC ponied up $13.5 million for the Munich games. For the ill-fated Moscow summer games of 1980, NBC had bid $83 million. And Roone Arledge was saying that ABC had committed a total of $225 million for Los Angeles in 1984—$100 million for the rights and $125 million for facilities and production equipment.

The entire first-year budget of CNN was $24 million.

"That ain't fair," Turner said.

There were other lessons, too. When he was interviewed by reporters, and they came in droves to write about the first all-news television channel, he shot straight from the hip.

When a reporter asked what would stop Turner from "managing" the news on CNN, he would reply. "Nothing, dummy. Of course I'm going to manage the news. I own the thing, don't I?"

The answer usually left reporters aghast. Turner was going to slant things his way? He was going to cover only events of his choice, and so bend the minds of the people? He was going to present a one-sided picture of the world? He was going to *manage the news?*

"No, you idiot!" Turner exploded at one such response. "It's the opposite of that. That's what the networks do. They don't tell you Chrysler's going under, because they don't want to lose the car ads. They don't investigate DC-10 engines falling off because they don't want to lose the airline ads. But we're not dependent on advertising, because half our income is the 15 cents a viewer pays each month to watch us. Don't any of you news guys understand the way Cable News Network works?"

It fell to Schonfeld to explain that Turner did not use or understand the same code words that professional journalists did. Actually, Schonfeld would say, CNN was harder to manipulate than regular TV news. "The reason is that the networks have an absolute deadline every afternoon. Somebody forced to make a public statement can wait until the deadline is at hand, speak his piece, and flee. He knows it will be reported on the evening news more or less as he said it because there was no time to check it out. But we're not on for just a half hour. Our reporters can come right back on the air forty-five minutes later, correcting and amplifying. On CNN, the news will keep on unfolding all night, and you'll be watching our reporters at work."

There were other false steps. Addressing the Washington Press Club later that fall, Turner, in a rambling discourse on the faults of the networks and of society, expounded on his hope that Cable News Network would carry cheerful news, as well as depressing news.

But the next day the wires ran a story saying Turner had issued a call for "happy news." Happy News, a term coined by *Variety* to describe the ratings-hungry gigglings of hair-sprayed TV news teams, was not a term of approbation. It was also not exactly what

Turner meant. But he had begun to learn the terms, at least—and how seriously reporters took themselves and their work.

Curiously, the press seemed to like him. He was certainly not a phony—no phony would say the things he did. He seemed to be hard on everyone equally. He lambasted advertising in the same breath as news coverage, which gave him a certain zany balance. When asked if he would personally control Cable News Network, he would bristle and say, "Sure, if I want to. I'm paying for it, why shouldn't I?" And then, citing his record with Channel 17, he would add that only once in ten years of ownership had he played his editorial trump—and that was a warning about the wasting of our oil resources and increasing dependence on the Middle East.

Schonfeld, in the months preceding CNN's much-publicized debut, spent most of his time hiring people. It was a little like shopping in a meat market, except that the meat talked, and was represented by an agent. He found himself dealing at length, if in vain, with such diverse personalities as Geraldo Rivera, the super-personalized second-generation New Journalist, and David Frost, the super-depersonalized transatlantic interviewing machine. Phil Donahue, whom Schonfeld admired most of all, he could not have. Donahue had performed the most impressive negotiating stunt possible—he made the cover of *Time* magazine during the course of their talks. In Washington, he picked up George Watson, the ABC bureau chief. Watson was being promoted to New York to free up his slot for Watergate star Carl Bernstein, but Watson preferred to remain in Washington—with CNN. Schonfeld did go to New York, however, searching for a black anchorman, and opened negotiations with John Johnson at Channel 7, the ABC affiliate there. Johnson wanted to go to Atlanta, but had a five-year contract with the network. So he sued, claiming racial discrimination, "in that ABC view plaintiff as a special 'asset' or 'property' because of his race." But when the smoke cleared, Johnson stayed with ABC.

Wherever Schonfeld went, however, TV personalities seemed dissatisfied with their current lot. When Cable News Network's man appeared, they sometimes behaved like chorus girls who had heard that Flo Ziegfeld was in the audience.

At one point Schonfeld found himself barely awake in a suite of the Hay Adams Hotel in Washington that was still littered with the crusty remains of a job candidates' cocktail party the night before. He was already into his first interview of the day when the phone rang at 8:30 A.M. It was Turner, with a list of commands, questions and ruminations. In a half hour, Schonfeld was due at the CNN Washington bureau, in mid-refurbishing, to help Daniel Schorr select his personal office. He would have to hurry to get to New York by midafternoon. It occurred to Schonfeld that his schedule would work only if he did not take time to visit the bathroom.

"You know," he said, rushing out of the hotel to his next stop, "I'll be glad when we get on the air."

While Schonfeld was hiring people, Schorr was talking to people—mostly about Turner, and about his role with Cable News Network. While Turner was just discovering news, Schorr had been covering it all his life. He had been the CBS bureau chief in Moscow when Turner was walking punishment tours at military school. Schorr had a reputation as more than a pretty face in television news. His twenty-three-year association with CBS had ended abruptly. How could Schorr and Turner possibly work together?

"Ted and I are just about as different as night and day," Schorr said one day in his house in Washington, somewhat wearied by his role as a spokesman and ornament of a news operation yet to cover the news. "I didn't know him at all before he hired me, but I must say that I sense a kind of destiny in what he's up to. Bill Paley, when he founded CBS News, had made a great deal of money in entertainment, and his path just happened to intersect with that of a man named Edward R. Murrow.

"Turner is in much the same position. He's a young tycoon who's looking around for a way to account for his sins, and he just happens to have a powerful new technology to work with. I think Ted's motivation is to pay back past slights, pay back the networks for what he imagines they've done, pay back the newspapers. He wants to vindicate himself.

"From my point of view, it's perfect. The problem with network news is that the news departments are small parts of large entertainment organizations, constantly fighting for time on the air. When Fred Friendly resigned as president of CBS News it was because he was turned down when he asked to interrupt the regular programs with live coverage of the Senate Foreign Relations Committee on Vietnam. He was told it would simply cost too much. Friendly says he gave them the choice between *War and Peace* and the third rerun of *I Love Lucy,* and they chose *Lucy.*

"That won't happen to us. Cable News Network isn't part of anything else. It's all news."

While Schorr was out talking, and Schonfeld was out hiring, the newly named television personalities scooped up in CNN's net were drifting into Atlanta like army recruits into boot camp. Many were print journalists who held a certain disdain for television news, thinking it must be a snap. This impression usually vanished after their first stammering discourse into a studio camera, and their gulping appraisal of their own videotape ("God, is that me?").

Some, the chips on their shoulders gone, were sent into the clutches of a young media consultant named Eric Huguelet, a specialist in dealing with raw material. Huguelet arrived at the hotel suite of one such TV newcomer at 9:00 A.M., carrying a portable videotape camera, a lighting kit and a monitor.

"I should warn you that you'll be tired when this is over," he said, setting up his gear. "Now sit down, make yourself comfortable, and read your script into the camera. Now let's take a look at the tape. See, you're skiing your voice. When you *talk* into the *cam*era you're *try*ing to add *emp*hasis to your *story* but it's *ran*dom *emp*hasis and you *sound* like *this.* You have to decide what words you want to hit. You can't emphasize them all. It doesn't work. Also, you don't have to shout. And your voice—is it normally that high? It's usually nervousness that makes the pitch go up. And that's how people can tell you're nervous. Let's try it again.

"Maybe a little better. But you're thinking about yourself. You should be thinking about your audience. You're being guarded. We also want energy and vitality, and we'll attack those through speed. I'll snap my fingers whenever your pace slows.

"Are you losing interest? Speed it up, speed it up! Energy! Vitality! OK, let's look at the tape. What do you think? I agree with you. Let's try it again. Do you realize you're licking your lips every paragraph? This time let's have some body language. Imagine you're having a conversation with a friend. You're telling him something you're really interested in. You're trying to convince him.

"That was all right, but watch the random head movement. It's ill defined. It's distracting. Also, you're still skiing your voice. No, I don't need any lunch. You want some lunch? We've only been at it three hours, not even half finished. Good, we'll keep right on. This time try to look more interested.

"Well, you could use your hands once in a while, couldn't you? People do, in conversation. You should be leaning forward against the desk, holding the weight of your torso on your elbows. If you bear the weight on your hands, you won't be able to gesture with them. Give us a little body language. And by the way, you're still skiing your voice.

"There was some improvement in that tape. Let's do it again. This time try for some variety of inflection. Don't make the spaces between all the words the same. Relax, your voice keeps rising. What did you think of that tape? I agree with you.

"Try it again, faster.

"Try it again, slower.

"Don't ask me what to do. Whatever is good has to come from you. We're finding out what's good in your delivery, in your personality, and we're developing it. And as we recognize what isn't good, we eliminate it. But don't try to be Dan Rather. Be the best of what you are.

"Let's try it again. Getting hoarse, huh? A professional could talk all day long and still be fresh. You're tired because you're straining. It's natural. Let's call it a day. Come back in two years and see me again—then you'll have picked up some bad habits, and they'll be very hard to get rid of.

"Good luck. And remember to practice. You've only got a thirteen-week contract."

It was just before Christmas of 1979 that Turner's grand plan began to take on the first shape of reality. As often before, he had worked so hard to convince other people that Cable News Network could work that somewhere along the line he had also succeeded in convincing himself.

His feet were up on the desk in his cluttered office at the Superstation on West Peachtree Street, and a half-dozen of his TV executives were arrayed in front of him, facing a videotape machine. Dee Woods brought each man a cup of coffee as their leader chortled happily.

"I want you guys to see this promo tape again," he said. "Back last June, when we announced that Cable News Network would be on the air in a year, lots of people had their doubts. But when you see this tape, you know it's coming true. I've seen it about twelve times, and it still gives me a thrill."

The screen flickered to life, revealing a panoramic view of fog-shrouded Atlanta from a helicopter hovering at 3,000 feet, and as the sound track swelled an announcer intoned:

"Turner Broadcasting System, the nation's pioneering trendsetter, which has already changed the course of TV history, is on the threshold of again revolutionizing the American television industry. With Ted Turner at the helm, TBS launches on June 1, 1980, the Cable News Network, the most ambitious news program ever produced. CNN—the twenty-four-hour commitment to in-depth national and international live journalism. News when it's news, not history."

Cut to Daniel Schorr: ". . . As senior Washington correspondent of CNN I shall preside over a staff that will bring to America a longer and deeper look at the news of the day than America has ever seen before . . ."

Cut to Ted Turner, strolling on the grounds of the former country club destined to be the new seat of the TBS empire: ". . . What we want to do is provide both sides of the issues, and then let people make up their minds as to what to believe. . . ."

Cut to brief, enthusiastic statements by the first wave of personalities signed on: Evans and Novak, Ralph Nader, Phyllis Schlafly, Bella Abzug, Dr. Neil Solomon, Joyce Brothers, William E. Simon . . .

Cut to Turner, amid the rubble of heavy construction: "It's going to be the greatest achievement in the history of journalism, more important than your newspaper. . . ."

Cut to announcer: "The future begins June 1, and CNN will make it happen. Produced in the most advanced studios, with more than fifty on-air personalities and bureaus across the nation and in international capitals. The $100 million commitment has been made—the Turner Broadcasting System has made it."

"Pretty strong," Turner said forcefully. "That'll show the other guys we mean business."

The other guys, as usual, were very important. At that moment they were *Time, Post–Newsweek,* and *The New York Times*—any one would do. Each was reported to be girding for a major role in cable television news, and it was clear that the team that got there first would have the advantage.

Competition, to Turner, was proof that he was on the right track. For months he watched *Post–Newsweek* like a hawk, pushing his people harder and harder, warning that Katharine Graham, the publisher who had broken Watergate, was breathing down their necks.

It was almost a disappointment when *Post–Newsweek,* the last of the saber-rattlers, dropped out of the race. A prime advocate of the challenge there had been corporate president Joel Chaseman, who had already proved the electrical power of news by leading New York's WINS radio to a highly successful all-news format in the mid-1960s. But Chaseman's high profile had crumbled in September, and he announced that a bid to exploit his company's formidable bench of reporters on TV had been adjudged untimely. The word was that Mrs. Graham had put the kibosh on any such video adventure, however glamorous, for the time being.

To Turner, this withdrawal was as disappointing as if the Braves had taken the field and found the opposing team had elected not to play. He fretted for months. Then, in the April issue of *Panorama* magazine, an interview with J. Christopher Burns appeared. Burns, vice president for planning of *The Washington Post,* had this to say about CNN's chances for survival, and why *Post–Newsweek* was holding back for the moment:

"We formed some conclusions about the realities of the marketplace," Burns was quoted. "The reason Ted Turner decided to go ahead with it in the form that he's doing may be that he doesn't understand the problem. He's not paying attention. The cable industry doubts that Ted Turner knows his ass from a hole in the ground about news. If he had looked at it carefully, he would have changed his offering. But, in time, his going ahead will help those of us who can do it better. That may turn out to be expensive for him."

When the *Panorama* interviewer asked how the *Post* would have "changed the offering," Burns replied: "I'm not going to help Turner. It's to our benefit to be selfish about it."

These remarks by J. Christopher Burns brought Turner to life like a spring tonic. When the going got rough, as it shortly would, he would refer to them with sarcasm and delighted scorn. Burns's name became almost a mantra to him during the next months, a challenge thrown down, a slap, a wonderful, audacious dare. (It was to Burns, when CNN finally went on the air, that Turner most wanted to send the dead crow, and the fork. It took a phalanx of fast-talking friends to talk him out of it.)

In the meantime, Turner tried to hire Walter Cronkite.

> Dear Walter:
> It has been some time since you were sailing with us in Newport, 1977.
> I feel that when you learn the way we plan to deliver the news twenty-four hours a day on Cable News Network you will want to join us. I think we should at least talk. Maybe you could come to my South Carolina plantation for a weekend. . . .

Cronkite was said to have replied that he would sail with Turner anytime.

Events were moving quickly, but even Turner did not know in what direction.

"Nobody thinks we can do it," Turner confided in the semiprivacy of his office one day. "Everybody who walks through this door tells me we'll never get on the air by June 1, in less than a year. I tell them—tough. We've got to. And they don't even know the problems. I based our entire start-up funds on the sale of my Charlotte TV station to Westinghouse—that's my $20 million ante right there. But the sale hasn't even gone through yet, because there's a group down there that's contesting the license. I've got Bunky Helfrich working full-time redoing the new headquarters here, and that depends on a $10 million bond issue that the City of Atlanta hasn't even approved yet. We haven't figured out a way to bring satellite pictures back to Atlanta, which is where all our news has to come before it can go back out. Terry McGuirk is trying to sell this new service to cable systems while all this is going on—without anything to show them except the promo tape. He's just blowing smoke, a huge amount of smoke. And we're hiring people right and left. Schonfeld already signed on about fifty, and we'll have a staff of three hundred before we actually click on. If any of this stuff goes bad on me, I'll be up the creek. It's going to be goodbye, Ted Turner, it was nice to know you.

"The one smart thing I did was to get that satellite when I did," Turner said. "See, when I got the Superstation transponder I got another one too, because I could see something like Cable News coming along. Now if you want a satellite you have to stand in line. They're totally full up and booked solid."

Indeed, satellite-fed cable television had become so popular that RCA had scheduled a new rocket launching for December 6, 1979. The new Satcom III bird was to replace Satcom I in orbit, and open up new channels exclusively for the cable television industry. One of them was to be for CNN.

Satcom III blasted off right on schedule from Cape Canaveral—and was never heard from again.

Once up in the sky, the ill-mannered satellite simply disappeared. RCA to this day does not know what happened to it. Maybe it just kept on going on a joyride to a universe far, far away. Maybe it rolled over on its back and died, to remain geosynchronously entombed, 22,300 miles up, forever. Or maybe it disintegrated.

Turner was in Disneyland when he received the news. For company, he had 5,500 other cable television conventioneers. Word of Satcom III's disappearance reached them all by network news. There was very little amusement in the amusement park that night.

"Disaster," said Terry McGuirk. "That was the bleakest period in CNN history, and it got worse a few months later, when RCA decided to assign us to another satellite. It was another satellite, all right. The trouble was, the cable companies who were supposed to be signing up for Cable News couldn't receive signals from it—unless they installed a whole new earth receiving dish."

Turner was in Nassau, racing *Tenacious,* when McGuirk got him on the phone with the news that things were coming unraveled, fast.

"I'd just got off the boat," Turner says. "We'd raced over there from Miami, and we'd only been in for an hour. As soon as I heard I grabbed Janie and we got the next plane home, and started to put together a plan.

"We had two big problems. One was that RCA didn't want to give us the right satellite. And the other was that the deal in Charlotte wasn't going through. There went everything right down the drain, unless we could do something."

What Turner did first was to pay a visit to RCA.

"The meeting was really tense," says McGuirk. "It looked like we were out, but Ted was on the warpath. He told the RCA guys that if they didn't fulfill their contract to get him on the right satellite in time for June 1, he was going to break RCA into a lot of little pieces. It wouldn't be a huge conglomerate anymore, he said, it would just be little pieces. When Ted gets that mad, he gets tremendously theatrical and very effective. He said to the guys we were dealing with that there was no use in his talking to them. They were making such a mistake, these executives, that they would be gone—fired—within ninety days. He said he didn't want to deal with executives who weren't going to be around much longer. When he demanded to see the president of RCA, and they said he was in a meeting, Ted got even more worked up. They could see how serious he was, and how strongly he felt."

RCA's problem was that there were several cable television enterprises scheduled to use the vanished satellite, and they could not all be accommodated on the old Satcom I—where the Superstation's transponder was located, and where Turner insisted Cable News Network had to be, too. Kick somebody else off, and put me on, he said. I'm the one putting up $30 million.

RCA said it would see what it could do. Turner filed suit against RCA for $30 million. In the meantime, a coalition of ten minority interest groups in Charlotte, North Carolina, had seized upon the sale of station WRET there as a time to wring hiring and other concessions from the new owners. If the sale of WRET didn't go through, Turner would be short $20 million in venture capital for CNN.

By April, both matters—much to Turner's chagrin—had been thrown in the lap of the Federal Communications Commission. And no one knew how the FCC would decide.

April 8 was a gray day in Washington, humid and oppressive. Turner lunched at Tiberios, an expensive restaurant on K Street, with a bevy of lawyers. He was exhausted and furious, and he looked worse at that moment, his suit jacket rumpled and Braves tie askew, than he ever had during the Fastnet race.

One of the lawyers was William Henry, a former chairman of the FCC. Turner didn't mince words.

"This is about it," Turner said. "The whole deal is crumbling, and when it goes, it'll take everything I've got with it. I'm just about flat broke. We haven't got a transponder and we haven't got the Charlotte money. The banks are calling in their notes on me, and the insurance company already has. I've got 300 people on the Cable News payroll, and no money coming in to pay them. I just had to borrow $20 million to tide me over. The interest rate is 25 percent. Twenty-five percent of $20 million is $5 million a year, and there's twelve months in a year, and that's $400,000 a month in interest alone. I can't pay it."

The lawyers at the table said little. They shifted about in their seats, keeping their faces devoid of expression. From another table, a memento arrived to be signed, but Turner brusquely told the waiter: "No autographs. Forget it."

Turner looked up at Bill Henry.

"What if we go directly to Congress?" he said. "How do you do that? I'm not letting Cable News Network die. Do we need a bill introduced or something?"

"Maybe you don't want to do it that way," said Henry. "You couldn't do it in this time frame anyway. Not by June 1."

"Well, let's go right to the chairman of the commission," Turner said.

"Then the staff sees you're going over their head," Henry said gently.

It was not a pleasant luncheon. When it was over, Turner and Henry went off for an afternoon of lobbying. The next day Turner flew to Cincinnati for the opening of the baseball season, and to Chicago to stave off his bank's loan foreclosure.

Shortly thereafter he grabbed his friend Henry Aaron, who directed the Braves farm teams and had broken Babe Ruth's home run record in a Braves uniform, and presented himself in Charlotte. "We met with the Charlotte Coalition down there in a lawyer's office," Turner says. "Hank Aaron and me. We talked over their problems one to one. They agreed to stop opposing the sale of the station, and we made some concessions. We made a lot of concessions. In fact, that little trip cost me close to half a million dollars. But at least it got the sale going again."

Less than a month before CNN was scheduled to make its debut, the Federal Communications Commission, acting on short notice, approved the sale of WRET in Charlotte to Westinghouse, and also gave CNN a six-month-long temporary transponder on Satcom I. It had been hairy, but the hurdles were down.

There was even a financial benefit in the end, which seemed to amuse Turner. He was supposed to start payments in November of $100,000 a month for the new Satcom III satellite. After that disappeared, the battle to obtain space on Satcom I ran through May. "It was six months of panic—but as a matter of fact, for all the trouble, it saved us $600,000, because they didn't start charging us until May."

By May, Cable News Network had become not one reality, but two. The skein of financing and salesmanship was one reality; and the twenty-four-hour-a-day news itself, and its dramatic new building and hardware, was the other.

When Turner said his venture was intended to be the "greatest achievement in the history of journalism," he was talking, in his hyperbolic way, about providing an account of the world day and night, with plenty of time to air both sides of any argument.

The News Channel, of course, was also designed to make money. Its first source of revenue would be the 20 cents per subscriber each cable system would pay monthly for the service—or 15 cents, if the system already offered the Superstation. Turner asked that the cable operators not pass that subscriber charge on to their customers, because CNN was intended to be a basic cable service, not a "pay tier" such as Home Box Office.

He told cable operators that they would surely get many new viewers by offering twenty-four-hour-a-day news; but he also offered the cable companies two minutes of advertising to sell out of CNN's twelve-minute hourly total.

It was by the sale of such local advertisements, he pointed out, that network television affiliates made hefty profits. Now cable operators had the opportunity to make money from the Turner network in the same way. It was as much a challenge as an offer, for few cable systems are presently set up to solicit, produce and insert their own ads. But Turner demanded more ambition. "You all ought to buy yourselves a plantation," he advised members of the New England Cable Television Association. "I've got one, and they're great!"

As if to set an example for the new, sunny future of cable, Turner Communications itself began to take on a new, more glamorous look. When Edward Turner had first arrived in Atlanta, he had dispatched Dick McGinnis to find a suitable antebellum mansion in which to house his business. Ed Turner never found it, but Ted Turner did.

In the summer of 1980, Cable News Network, and the Superstation too, left the seedy building under the tower on West Peachtree Street for a new home three blocks away: a gracious property just north of Georgia Tech that had been the home of an Atlanta institution called the Progressive Club.

The new HQ, as the building came to be known, looked precisely like the country club it once was. Its entrance was a U-shaped drive which passed a reflecting pool and led to an impressive portico, inside of which was a lobby set off in Corinthian columns. Green lawns spread out all about, and there were tennis courts on the grounds. Turner had ordered the courts plowed under, but McGuirk and architect Helfrich, crazed by the prospect of lunch-hour round robins, had bilaterally conspired to save them.

The most telling revelation of the new HQ was the office of Ted Turner himself. He had never complained, and seemed in fact to take a curious pride in his near-shabby accommodations on Peachtree street. At the new building, however, the steel fire door and the yellowed venetian blinds were gone, replaced by executive splendor.

On the second floor, in the right wing, the chairman's quarters had become a three-room suite. The first was a small chamber. This chamber led to Dee Woods. *Miss Woods.* Those whom she admitted would then pass into the largest room of all, dominated at one end by a fireplace, and containing a private washroom and a wet bar for the entertaining of business visitors. There were specially built cases to display Turner's personal museum of yachting trophies. The view was east, and it looked out over both the gleaming new earth stations and, three-quarters of a mile away, the obsolete UHF broadcasting tower of old Channel 17. You could also see the tennis courts—and who was playing. Helfrich, however, planned a "visual barrier" of some sort, in order to spare the chairman that distraction. One had only to walk into the three-room suite to understand that Robert Edward Turner III was no longer fooling around.

It was the ground floor of the new HQ that had been set aside as the television studio of the future. Only a few months before, the area had looked like and exuded the smell and charm of an abandoned subway tunnel. Layers of ancient paint peeled from the masonry walls, and water stood an inch deep in oily pools. Now it had been transformed into an electronic control center straight from a science-fiction film. During the month of May, the nonstop television show that played there daily was called "The Dry Runs."

CNN had no fewer than fifteen anchor-desk personnel based in Atlanta, and they came and went in shifts around the clock. As they slipped in and out of their places in the four multipurpose sets, batteries of directors and producers moved synchronously behind them, writing scripts and headlines, editing tape, and deciding which of the scores of satellite pictures to air at any time. In Washington, New York, Los Angeles, Dallas, San Francisco, London and Rome, CNN bureaus waited to feed in their material—live, if possible, from interesting news sites.

"The Dry Runs" were a surrealistic blend of excitement and disaster. In one simulated production of *Take Two,* a two-hour noontime talk and news show, co-anchors Chris Curle and Don Farmer found themselves on camera while electricians drilled holes in their set with power drills. They introduced a gossip columnist in the Washington bureau, who appeared by satellite without audio. A television critic then appeared and delivered his five-minute monologue into the wrong camera. The red "on air" lights weren't hooked up, the Tele-prompters didn't work, and even the bathrooms were unfinished. When that day's dry run was over, Farmer looked into the camera and said: "That's it for now. Tune in tomorrow, when our guests will be Judge Crater, Francisco Franco, and the entire Rockettes chorus line from Radio City."

"Well, I think we proved something today," Farmer confided to Curle back in their dual office.

"What?" said Curle to her co-anchor and husband.

"That it can't be done," said Farmer.

But at 6:00 P.M. on June 1, 1980, it was.

Tom Shales, *The Washington Post*'s orotund and persnickety TV critic, called CNN's long-awaited debut "a news smorgasbord of no particular distinction except for an utter lack of organization." But nobody expected perfection that first night, and even Shales conclud-ed his report on a glowing note: "It was obvious from the premiere, for all the rough edges, that CNN means business and that it is anything but the plaything of a playboy. A new day dawned at dusk."

Turner was beside himself with enthusiasm. It was as if for him not only a new day but also a new identity had risen on the horizon.

Cable News Network lost no time in developing an identity of its own. Even before June 1, network viewers watching Presidential press conferences had seen Daniel Schorr appear on their screen with CNN identification. But when the News Channel clicked on, its subscribers were struck immediately by the number of new faces it presented day and night, and with the helter-skelter, as-it-happens tone of their reports. The ritualistic, star-borne reportage of *The CBS Evening News* with Walter Cronkite had yielded—for CNN's charter subscribers, at least—to a nonstop parade of events brought live from all over the world, day and night, by waves of eager newcomers.

Especially at first, there were frequent technological problems. Sat-ellite pictures would appear without sound, or sound without pic-tures, and a familiar refrain from the Atlanta anchor desk was "We're

having a little difficulty bringing that story to you at this time
... we'll come back to it as soon as we can." CNN capitalized on these
flubs by presenting them as proof of the immediacy of the newsgath-
ering process. "Process" was one of Schonfeld's favorite words. The
implication was that viewers who left the News Channel on had a
window to the world through which all knowledge could be seen.

That Faustian notion presented CNN as a monitor of the Global
Village described by communications theorist Marshall McLuhan.
Television, McLuhan argued, had never achieved its true potential
because its programmers did not understand their own medium.
Whereas contemporary radio saw itself as a subliminal voice-in-the-
background, television still aped the old-fashioned "linear" format of
books, movies and traditional music. Each program was arranged
carefully so as to have a beginning, middle and ending, and in that
respect, *I Love Lucy, Jaws,* Beethoven's Fifth Symphony and *The CBS
Evening News* were the same. Each *ended.* Lucy and Ricky made up; the
shark was destroyed; Beethoven resolved to the C-major chord; and
Walter Cronkite intoned, "And that's the way it is . . ."

CNN, because it never went off the air, and could have no beginning, middle or end, was therefore a different kind of television.
Viewers were not offered a plot to follow, or a carefully arranged
sequence of news stories designed to stop the world in its tracks for
examination at 7:00 P.M. Instead, it offered itself as an eye on an
unfolding world.

It was immediately apparent that CNN worked best when the
world chose to unfold in an interesting way; as when, in Damascus,
Arkansas, a Titan II missile exploded in its silo and hurled a bit of
debris several hundred yards across the landscape. Whether the piece
of debris was a nuclear warhead or not was not known for almost two
days.

CNN's James Allen Miklasewski was among the first reporters on
the scene, and stayed with the story as it unfolded slowly over the
weekend of September 21, 1980. The situation was inconvenient for
daily newspapers and network correspondents precisely because it
was developing so slowly. They had deadlines, and when their deadlines came, they could only report that the story had refused to budge
further. The Air Force was not saying whether the missile had been

armed with a nuclear warhead or not. Workmen labored at the damaged silo, but newsmen were not admitted to the base. It was an informational impasse.

Not for Miklasewski however. He was in his element. He was feeding raw data—describing what he could see with his own eyes, and interviewing anyone he could find—in the middle of an event of unknown proportions. Standing at a roadside, he could be overheard chatting with a Damascus County official who was still steaming from an encounter with the military forces. In a colorful regional dialect, the official complained to CNN viewers that he didn't know whether there was a warhead involved or not—but that nobody was going to use his county road to truck anything out until he found out.

When Miklasewski's view of the missile site proved inadequate, he got his cameraman into a truck equipped with a cherrypicker crane, and soon the television vantage point was 50 feet higher. Even small movements at the site then took on dramatic overtones.

"You see that tarpaulin?" the reporter asked, as the CNN camera picked up what appeared to be a visual barrier set up by the Air Force. "We don't know what that's hiding, but we'll stay with it. Now it appears the military has moved a truck in to block our view. What they are blocking may be the 10-megaton nuclear warhead that was apparently blown 200 yards from the missile silo.

"Now some military personnel are pointing to our cherrypicker," Miklasewski went on, like a football sportscaster when the scene has shifted from the players on the field to the players on the bench. "By the way, these pictures are being brought to you by CNN cameraman Ron Dean, who is perched in the cherrypicker 50 feet above the ground. That was the only way we could bring you these live pictures of the apparent removal of what is said to be a nuclear . . ."

The live pictures, in fact, were very shaky, since the mobile crane was unsteady and the scene was being viewed through a powerful telephoto lens. Even that contributed to the visual drama, however. And when nothing else was happening, Miklasewski still made hay by reporting on the "process."

". . . Here we are in Damascus, 650 miles from Atlanta, and here's how our story is getting to you. The signal rises from our mobile unit that you see here. It goes up 22,500 miles to the satellite, then returns down to Atlanta, is fed to our studios, and then is sent back out by satellite again to you. And that is how we come to you, live, from Arkansas. The truck and its crew drove sixteen hours to get here, by the way. . . ."

Even when CNN cut back to its regular weekend news coverage, Damascus was not forgotten. The cherrypicker picture merely shrank down to postage-stamp size on a corner of the television screen, keeping silent video vigil until the Air Force revealed that there had been a nuclear warhead after all, that it had not been damaged in the explosion, and that it had been safely trucked away.

CNN could cover an event like that in a way the networks could not. And when a news event was designed specifically for network coverage—like the Carter–Reagan debate—CNN tried another tack: counterprogramming.

The debate, as far as Schonfeld was concerned, had everything it needed except one thing: Candidate John Anderson, who had been shut out. But not by Cable News Network.

So while Jimmy Carter and Ronald Reagan stood before the network cameras in Cleveland, John Anderson found himself in Constitution Hall in Washington, D.C., as a guest of CNN. The idea was that after Carter and Reagan had had their say, Anderson would also reply to the same question. Thus CNN viewers would be treated to a three-way debate.

It was an innovative idea, and it involved some fancy technological footwork, because while Anderson responded on CNN, his adversaries would go right on talking to each other in Cleveland. Anderson—and a Constitution Hall audience of 2,000—would have to catch up with the debate on videotape before the third candidate could respond. Because of Anderson's participation, the CNN debate would also lag further and further behind the Cleveland debate, although presumably no one would notice.

Outside the hall in Washington, in a control truck rented from the local public television station, four CNN producers, four tape operators and a director waited in an atmosphere of growing tension. None of them had tried this stunt before, and each was acutely aware that there had been no time for a rehearsal. They were also acutely aware that mighty ABC, as the pool network televising the 1976 debate between President Gerald Ford and Candidate Carter, had embarrassed itself by losing audio for a full twenty-six minutes. But if anything went wrong in Washington, at least Atlanta would be standing by as a fail-safe backup.

The debate in Cleveland began. In the truck, the tape machines began to roll. When the first exchange between Carter and Reagan was completed, Anderson spoke his piece—while the CNN truck recorded the debate in Cleveland that continued on without him.

Then, inexplicably, two of the CNN tape machines malfunctioned. "We've lost it!" the director shouted into his telephone. "Two machines are down. Atlanta! You've got to take over!"

But the tape operators in Atlanta, confused by the sudden switches from tape time to real time, were equally helpless.

"We can't help you!" came the reply. "We're lost too! We don't know where you are!"

Candidate Anderson, on stage in front of his audience, was also lost. He could only watch as Carter and Reagan went on without him. And while CNN grappled with the snafu.

"The first half hour was a complete disaster," one Cable News staffer admitted later. "But we eventually got back on track and finished up OK. The annoying thing was that it would probably have worked out fine, if Atlanta had handled the whole production from the start. And if they'd started rehearsing a couple of days in advance."

The three-way debate was eventually declared a success because it proved two things: that Anderson had a sense of humor, and that CNN, the "outsider" news channel, could itself make the news. Anderson's remarks, and the method by which CNN had permitted him to make them, were widely reported the next day. The technical difficulties were seldom mentioned.

For Schonfeld and his bureaus, however, there was hardly time to look back. As everyone at Cable News had discovered, twenty-four hours was a long work day. CNN, in fact, was being run much the way Ted Turner ran his ocean-racing crews: a few hours on duty, a few hours of sleep, and then back on duty again. There was not much time for sightseeing along the way, because although the News Channel looked like a network on screen, it was not at all staffed like one. The total number of its employees, including Atlanta and the domestic and foreign bureaus, was just over 300. Each of the Big Three networks employed more people than that in Washington, D.C., alone.

That was one of the reasons why Schonfeld, in his hiring expeditions, had sought out "young and hungry" applicants—people who would be willing to work long hours at relatively low pay for a chance to learn the ropes and perhaps hack themselves an entry path into the competitive jungle of television.

After six months with CNN, Wendy Walker and Elissa Free, associate producers in the Washington bureau, were still hungry, all right. But it was mostly the result of having skipped so many meals since signing on with Ted Turner, the Christopher Columbus of television news. Free had been a secretary and researcher for the CBS program *Face the Nation;* Walker, secretary to the director of news operations at ABC in Washington.

"At ABC, it was a big deal just to be allowed to do anything outside your regular duties," Walker explained. "I used to go in on my day off just to log a show like *Meet the Press.* All that means is that you write down what was said and when it was said. I hoped I could learn something, but you could only watch. You couldn't touch anything. They didn't need you."

After a few months at CNN, Walker, at twenty-seven, was named an associate producer.

"All of a sudden I was going out on locations with news crews, I was editing pieces, I was writing scripts, I was doing everything except running the cameras—not that they didn't ask me to. It was entirely different."

Walker also pitched story ideas. One was for an interview with J. Carter Brown, the head of the National Gallery of Art. "I said that I'd be glad to write the questions down for any reporter they assigned. They said, 'No, you'll have to be the reporter. There's nobody else available.' I was scared. But I combed my hair, and I went out and did it, and it came out pretty well."

Free, twenty-five, noticed other differences, too. "When I was at CBS, *Face the Nation* had two producers, a researcher and a secretary," she said. "That half-hour show was all the producers had to think about, and they didn't have to start thinking until Thursday. They had long lunches. Even the secretaries had master's degrees, because that was how you started out. You waited three or four years, and if you played your cards right, maybe you got to be an associate producer. Maybe not."

At CNN, by their own estimation, Walker and Free carried a workload that would have required fifteen people at ABC, CBS or NBC. With six months' experience each, they were jointly in charge of the following programs:

—*Newsmaker Sunday,* an hour-long interview show in which a prominent figure in the news was interviewed by Daniel Schorr and two other journalists.

—*Newsmaker Saturday,* a similar program for which the host was managing editor Stuart Loory.

—*Press Box,* a thirty-minute program in which three journalists discussed the week's events with Loory.

They also produced the daily commentaries of nine CNN contributors, among them Senator Barry Goldwater, Ralph Nader, and the syndicated columnists Evans and Novak. These and other responsibilities kept them in the studio from 8:30 A.M. until midnight several times each week. Every other week they got two days off in a row.

Their pay for this regimen was roughly $15,000 a year—considerably more than that of Bob Waterson, a twenty-seven-year-old former ski instructor who sometimes put in as much as thirty hours a week assisting them.

"I'm an intern," Waterson explained. "I don't get any salary at all. I'm just doing it for the experience."

It was 8:00 at night, and in the newsroom, Jeff Smith, twenty-seven, a CNN director, was setting up a camera for a taping that would keep him there until midnight. There were a half-dozen night staffers scattered about, several of whom began to sing at the top of their lungs, joined in an impromptu chorus line that kicked up its heels to the title melody of "There's No Business Like Show Business":

"There's no network like our network
Like no network we know.

Everything we do is innovative,
Covering the news where'er it's found.
If we cannot find it we create it
Or try to fake it . . . the show goes on.

There's no people like our people, though work
Keeps us down low . . .
Where else could you find someone like Teddy K
Or Reese, both screaming their lungs away.
We just try to carry on from day to day,
And so . . .
On with the show."

"Now you know why we call this place Chaos News Network,"
said Smith, deadpan.

In its first year of operation, Cable News Network lost more than
$2 million a month, causing Turner's financial obituary to be pub-
lished again and again. There were recurring reports that he had run
out of money, and from time to time, in fact, CNN employees received paychecks drawn against the petty cash account. Interest rates
were high, and the climate for new enterprises harsh. It was said that
Turner's idea for twenty-four-hour television news was a good idea
whose time had not yet come. That he was paving the road to the
future with his own carcass. That the financial drain of CNN would
wipe him out once and for all, casting his 350 new employees to the
winds and causing the entire interlocking structure of the Superstation, the billboards, the Braves and the Hawks to tumble down like
a house of cards.

For the first quarter of 1981, Turner Broadcasting System, Inc.
reported a net loss of $6.5 million. Curiously, however, its stock was
selling at an all-time high. Perhaps this was because, despite the crisis
atmosphere, CNN was delivering what it had promised. With fewer
than two million subscribers at sign-on, the News Channel by its first
anniversary was in 6.5 million homes—precisely as projected. It had
begun with only seventeen charter subscribers, and a year later had
117—more, in fact, than anticipated by its founder. As a twenty-

four-hour television news network, it was of course unequaled, since it was the only one. But it scored its share of beats. When Pope John Paul II was shot in Rome, CNN was the first television news to report it in America (beating CBS by two minutes) and was first with videotape of the scene, too.

The News Channel tried to be as unpredictable as its founder, but that competition was tough: as CNN hit the one-year mark, Ted Turner announced that he was quitting ocean racing. Chins fell at yacht clubs around the world.

"Why'd I quit?" he said. "Because with everything else that was going on I didn't have the time to organize it and really do it right. And I was kind of tired of it, too. Besides, there's a lot of cheating going on in ocean racing right now. Yeah—*cheating.* But that's not my problem anymore."

After the America's Cup of 1980 he had sold *Courageous,* and now he divested himself of his beloved *Tenacious,* too. "I sold her to Warren Brown, the same guy who bought *American Eagle* from me, for five hundred Big Ones, which was twice what I paid for the boat five years before. Pretty good, huh? Naw, I wasn't emotionally upset. Well, maybe a little bit, because *Tenacious* is the best boat that ever was, and she took us through the Fastnet storm. But you've got to move on."

Several weeks after quitting ocean racing, Turner was back racing on the ocean. This time, however, at the tiller of his 18-foot catamaran, crewed by his son, Rhett.

"Hey," he exclaimed, "you should've seen us. We sailed right out through the surf at Myrtle Beach. It was blowing about twenty knots and my trapeze harness broke and we turned over and my son got wiped away from the boat and it was a half an hour before I could get him back. But that's why you wear lifejackets. It was great."

Can America's best-known yachtsman be content racing an off-the-shelf 18-footer, wearing a bathing suit with only his son as crew?

"I don't know—I'm going to try it for a while, though."

His withdrawal from grand prix sailing left a two-month annual hole in Turner's schedule, which he immediately filled with other challenges.

In May, he and Schonfeld sued the three networks, the President of the United States, and his White House staff, claiming that they conspired to violate the antitrust laws of the United States. CNN, Turner claimed, was not being accorded status equal to ABC, CBS and NBC in the coverage of White House events and presidential trips.

Almost simultaneously, he called for a Congressional investigation into whether the networks, and the movie industry, too, weren't "having a detrimental effect on the morals, attitudes and habits of the people of the country." This brought him several times to Washington, where he lobbied Senators and Congressmen in their offices, and held press conferences complete with videotape evidence of violence in such films as *Apocalypse Now.* Turner said he didn't know what the result of a Congressional investigation might be, but he hoped it would result in "the glorification of the good guys instead of the bad guys."

CNN mirrored his aggressive style in many ways. When the Cooney–Norton prizefight was shown on Home Box Office, it also wound up on CNN. This made ABC very angry, because ABC had a contract to air the fight on *Wide World of Sports* more than a week later. Schonfeld replied that CNN's sports department had a long-standing agreement with Home Box Office that permitted use of up to one minute of any sporting event. Schonfeld said it wasn't his fault that Cooney had knocked Norton out in fifty-four seconds.

The White House, and its press corps, also learned that CNN was dancing to a slightly different drummer. At the noon briefing on April 24, 1981, Assistant Press Secretary Larry Speakes announced to the Washington press corps that President Reagan would be lifting the Soviet grain embargo that day—but the story must be kept under wraps until 4:00 P.M. What Speakes did not realize was that CNN was covering his briefing. Live.

Turner was pressing forward on as many fronts as he could find, and declaring himself at war. "It's a war of survival, a war against the establishment, against the bigwigs. I'm either going to go broke, or I'm going to revolutionize television. We can't stop now."

With CNN his continual topic, attention by the summer of 1981 had slipped away from the Superstation, which had been his battle cry a few years before. As it happened, the Superstation had become a resounding success. Turner estimated that it would generate a cash flow of $20 million for 1981, and be in seventeen million American homes, "just about enough to cover the losses from Cable News Network," he said. The Superstation, like Turner himself, had changed dramatically in the past two years. Whereas it once played the news at 3:00 A.M., it now presented a nightly hour of international and national news taken from its sister, CNN. And moreso than the News Channel, it reflected the specific ideas of Ted Turner.

The most successful of the Superstation's new programs was one called *Nice People,* an interview show precisely described by its title. Turner had ordered up the program to show "good news," and he quickly followed with a spin-off called *Smart People,* later called *The Winners.* The spin-off celebrated such persons as Jim Bouton, the former pitcher, writer and sometime actor.

"Bouton got this idea for bubble gum, which he calls Big League Chew," Turner said. "All it is is regular bubble gum shredded up and put into a sort of chewing tobacco pouch for kids. Bouton thought it up, so he gets two percent royalty, which is worth about a million bucks a year forever. Pretty smart for just a dumb baseball player, huh? That's the kind of people *The Winners* is about."

Turner also directed the Superstation to produce a one-hour homage to the Boy Scouts of America, a documentary about the environment, and a multi-part investigation of sex and violence on television, which fully aired the views of Rev. Jerry Falwell's Moral Majority.

In the meanwhile, however, the Superstation also developed a weekly program that was the antithesis of the Moral Majority. It was called *Tush,* and starred former gag newscaster Bill Tush and an ensemble of talented improvisational actors.

Tush, produced by R. T. Williams along the lines of *Saturday Night Live,* was consistently funny and scathingly satirical. Written and produced entirely in Atlanta, its skits and surreal comedy routines relentlessly poltrooned southern accents and lifestyles, Superstation advertisers and other targets of opportunity. It laid waste television evangelists spared not the Reverend Jerry Falwell and even went so far as to hilariously parodize Ted Turner's own Cable News Network.

But the coexistence of the overt boosterism of *Nice People* and the giddy irreverence of *Tush* were proof of the diversity Turner had promised. More diversity at times, than Turner himself had bargained for. "I don't think Ted is really crazy about everything we do on *Tush*," R. T. Williams commented. "But he does let us do it."

By the summer of 1981, Turner felt he was over the hump with CNN. He still owned 87 percent of the stock of Turner Broadcasting System, and he now thought he could keep CNN afloat even without selling his billboard company. "We might see a little black ink as early as November," he said. "That is, if Schonfeld doesn't come up with some riot in Europe that costs millions of dollars to cover. Even so, we'll be looking real good in 1982."

Turner was forty-three, and had survived another storm. He had the first two basic service networks on cable television, the awakening communications giant that was scheduled to be in half the homes in America in just nine years. When cable got there, Turner would be there, too.

He was not, however, planning to sit around and wait. He set no specific goal for himself—he believed that the goal of "millionaire," once attained, had ended his father's life. He sought also to avoid the fate of his boyhood hero, Alexander the Great, who wept because there were no worlds left to conquer. Turner, with worlds enough and time, has another intention and message.

"What I've got to do now is to broaden myself," Turner mused one recent afternoon at his plantation. "And I've got a plan. I'm going to hook up a two-way send-and-receive station here, so I won't have to run around so much talking to people. Instead of spending half my life on airplanes, I want to put on my wizard's cap and think. I want to confer with the best and the smartest people there are, and with the send-and-receive station I can do that right here, without burning any fuel. There'll be a little shack down a dirt path from the house, and I can stroll over there and tune in anybody I want. That's the great thing about the satellite—it lets people talk to one another directly. Hey, I'll be like the guru on the mountaintop," Turner chortled. "It'll be guru-to-guru communication.

"But I'm also going to make my own kind of pilgrimage, around the world. There's so much I don't know, but I'm going to find it out.

I'm going to visit every country that will let me in, in Europe and Asia and Africa, wherever they have a lot of problems. I'm going to meet with the leaders and I'm gonna find out what they're thinking. Reading only gives you so much, but if you actually go there you can figure it out. Boy, are those foreign kings and presidents going to be surprised to see me. It'll be interesting as hell for both of us."

The notion of an international diplomatic mission of entrepreneurship and investigation seemed to please and amuse Turner. He ruminated about the fact-finding mission of Muhammad Ali, whom he admires. When Ali was sent by President Carter to chat with African leaders, the champion boxer made headlines with his observations that in some cases, the complaints about America had merit. Turner saw himself in the same role, although without the diplomatic passport.

"Hell, I can't start being diplomatic now," he said. "Maybe I'll tone things down a bit, but don't expect too much. Believe me, it's better to be yourself. That's what being a citizen of this country is all about, and if that sounds simplistic, think about it. Sometimes things are simple. Sometimes problems can be solved just by doing what comes naturally.

"Listen," Turner said finally, ending what had been an evening-long discourse on man's fate and the burden of individuals in determining their own future. "The world hasn't changed that much over the centuries. Men are still men, and they still die like the deer, one way or another. We've got a whole lot of deer here at the plantation —if you take a flashlight out on the lawn right now you'll see a dozen of them. I want the herd to get big, and fat, and for the deer to be happy. But that's not what's happening. I looked into it—why are so many deer dying? The experts said, 'Well, your deer have no natural enemies here. You're going to have to shoot more and more deer, in order that individuals become large and healthy. If you don't, the whole herd will be weakened.'

"But I don't really like shooting deer. I do it, but it's not that great a sport. So I came up with the answer—get a cougar. The cougar could live on the land, and keep the deer population down naturally. What this plantation definitely needs is a cougar. Of course, I couldn't do it. They said, 'Gee, a cougar? What if it escapes? You can't have cougars running around Georgia. You'd have to fence the whole plantation in, and it wouldn't be practical.' No, it wouldn't. We have progressed past cougars, and we have to learn how to broaden our outlooks and our methods of dealing with our problems. But remember, the cougar's instinct is right, and a civilization can't survive if it ignores its own instincts. It'll die, just like the deer."

Turner paused then, slipping into a reverie for ten seconds, and Turner in a ten-second reverie is an amazing sight.

"Sometimes I amaze myself thinking about stuff like that," he said, breaking into a sheepish grin. "But tell me the truth," he added quickly. "Wouldn't you really rather be Ted Turner?"

As usual, Turner neglected to wait for a reply.

"You're right," he said. "It's a lot of fun, but it ain't as easy as it looks."

Index